W9-AYG-740

A Longman Cultural Edition

THE CASTLE OF OTRANTO

by Horace Walpole

and

THE MAN OF FEELING

by Henry Mackenzie

Edited by

Laura Mandell

Miami University of Ohio

PEARSON
Longman

New York   Boston   San Francisco
London   Toronto   Sydney   Tokyo   Singapore   Madrid
Mexico City   Munich   Paris   Cape Town   Hong Kong   Montreal

Editor-in-Chief: Joseph P. Terry
Development Editor: Christine Halsey
Executive Marketing Manager: Ann Stypuloski
Production Coordinator: Scarlett Lindsay
Project Coordination, Text Design, and Electronic Page Makeup: Grapevine
   Publishing Services, Inc.
Cover Designer/Manager: John Callahan
Senior Manufacturing Buyer: Dennis Para
Printer and Binder: R.R. Donnelley & Sons Company/Harrisonburg
Cover Printer: Coral Graphics Services, Inc.

Cover Image: Courtesy of The Lewis Walpole Library, Yale University

Library of Congress Cataloging-in-Publication Data

Walpole, Horace, 1717–1797.
  The castle of Otranto / by Horace Walpole. And, The man of feeling / by
  Henry Mackenzie ; edited by Laura Mandell.
      p. cm. — (Longman cultural edition)
  Includes bibliographical references.
  ISBN 0-321-39892-0
      I. Mandell, Laura. II. Mackenzie, Henry, 1745–1831. Man of feeling.
III. Title. IV. Title: Man of feeling.

  PR3757.W2C3 2006
  823'.6—dc22
                                                              2006025220

Copyright © 2007 by Pearson Education, Inc.

All rights reserved. No part of this publication may be reproduced, stored in a
retrieval system, or transmitted, in any form or by any means, electronic, mechanical, photocopying, recording, or otherwise, without the prior written permission of
the publisher. Printed in the United States.

Please visit our Web site at www.ablongman.com

ISBN: 0-321-39892-0

1 2 3 4 5 6 7 8 9 10—DOH—09 08 07 06

Contents

List of Illustrations

Cover: South view of the Castle of Otranto, ca 1785. The Acro-ceraunian Mountains of Epirus in the distance—copied from a drawing made in March 1785 by W. Reveley (1760–1799). Courtesy of The Lewis Walpole Library, Yale University.

About Longman Cultural Editions

Reading always seems to vibrate with the transformation of the day—now, yesterday, and centuries ago, when the presses first put printed language into wide circulation. Correspondingly, literary culture has always been a matter of change: of new practices confronting established traditions; of texts transforming under the pressure of new techniques of reading and new perspectives of understanding; of canons shifting and expanding; of informing traditions getting reviewed and renewed, recast and reformed by emerging cultural interests and concerns; of culture, too, as a variable "text"—a reading. Inspired by the innovative *Longman Anthology of British Literature*, Longman Cultural Editions respond creatively to the changes, past and recent, by presenting key texts in contexts that illuminate the lively intersections of literature, tradition, and culture. A principal work is made more interesting by materials that place it in relation to its past, present, and future, enabling us to see how it may be reworking traditional debates and practices, how it appears amid the conversations and controversies of its own historical moment, how it gains new significances in subsequent eras of reading and reaction. Readers new to the work will discover attractive paths for exploration, while those more experienced will encounter fresh perspectives and provocative juxtapositions.

Longman Cultural Editions serve not only several kinds of readers but also (appropriately) their several contexts, from various courses of study to independent adventure. Handsomely produced and affordably priced, our volumes offer appealing companions to *The Longman Anthology of British Literature*, in some cases enriching and expanding units originally developed for the *Anthology*, and in other cases presenting this wealth for the first time. The logic and composition of the contexts vary across the series. The constants are the complete text of an important literary work, reliably edited, headed by an inviting introduction, and supplemented by helpful annotation; a table of dates to track its composition, publication, and public reception in relation to biographical, cultural, and historical events; and a guide for further inquiry and study. With these common measures and uncommon assets, Longman Cultural Editions encourage your literary pleasures with resources for lively reflection and adventurous inquiry.

SUSAN J. WOLFSON
General Editor
Professor of English
Princeton University

About This Edition

Horace Walpole's *The Castle of Otranto* and Henry Mackenzie's *The Man of Feeling* are landmark events in the history of the novel. In different but related modes, these are the first novels to feature passion—not only in language but also in their very forms, which focus on the welter of feelings in their characters. The passions do involve sexual desire but extend much more widely to general human compassion. This development was important in an age of commercial determinations of value, rational science, and philosophical skepticism. The emphasis on passionate feeling took the pulse of a social system in which the hereditary aristocratic class was no longer, and not necessarily, the model of ideal behavior. The (always) rising middle classes were particularly receptive to a new, more liberally inclusive "aristocracy of feeling" and the attendant critique of the old aristocracy. Gothic fiction delights in delineating aristocratic and monastic corruption with conscious horror (and secret transport), and it liberates the sentimental value of feudal chivalry as a model for bourgeois virtue. In the new sentimental fiction—for example, Samuel Richardson's epic *Clarissa*—the virtuous heroine opposes, unto death, the aristocratic villain-rapist Lovelace, exposing the corruption hidden beneath his notions of "honor." Mackenzie's more compact novel reflects this esteem of honor over class: Miss Walton prefers the virtuous Harley to the "honorable" Sir Harry Benson. Harley's attitudes and actions are contrasted to the behavior of corrupt aristocrats and the parasitical "sharpers" from whom the aristocrats are barely distinguishable. The new values generated by these two signal publications—the gothic novel and the novel of sentiment—paved the way for a host of literary and cultural developments: the psychological novel (and its interior world, its streams of consciousness) and a popular culture of gothic thrills and sentimental weepers, everywhere in evidence (often together) in movies, soap operas, bestselling fiction, and even video games.

The Context units in this volume are designed to help you appreciate the immediate culture in which these novels were written and published, read, reviewed, imitated, and parodied. Often called "the first gothic novel," *The Castle of Otranto* drew upon and popularized a new aesthetic sensibility, a kind of gothic sublime based on terror, against which realists (empiricists and writers alike) contend. As you'll see, it wasn't just the gothic novel that seemed perilous. There were perils in the sentimental mode, too. These had to do with "a certain drunkenness of imagination," as Mackenzie describes the inspiration he was "indulging" when he wrote *The Man of Feeling* (qtd. in Thompson 109). Even so, both gothic and sentimental enthusiasms report the spirit of the age. The unnamed referent of the Castle of Otranto was Walpole's neogothic castle on his estate, Strawberry Hill—a star in "gothic revival" architecture and the antiquarian researches that were flourishing by mid-century.

On another front, both *The Castle of Otranto* and *The Man of Feeling*, for all their differences of temper and mode, manage to reflect changing standards of female conduct. The longstanding strictures requiring a daughter's obedience to a father's determination of her marriage were being challenged by the authority of her own heart: Love was becoming the best, the only reason to marry. The new culture of feeling rippled widely and even took hold of philosophy, particularly (if seemingly paradoxically) the Scottish commonsense school. Like the novels' arguments for virtue regardless of class, the new philosophy advanced sentiment as the principle to bind a benevolent and civilized social body. These developments, like any innovation, were not without controversy. Both the gothic vogue and the cult of sentimentality provoked rebuke and satire, and the cultural monitors (especially the periodical reviews) made their misgivings clear in either ignoring or condescending to both *The Castle of Otranto* and *The Man of Feeling*. But the novels were reviewer-proof, becoming bestsellers and also, by the force of their popularity, earning status as "canonical" in the first major collections of British novels published in the nineteenth century (by Anna Letitia Barbauld and by Walter Scott).

Dated 1765 on the title page, the first edition of *The Castle of Otranto* was issued in 500 copies by bookseller Thomas Lownds on December 24, 1764, a Christmas-eve offering for the new year. A second edition, with a new preface signed by the real author, "H. W.," was issued in April 1765 by Lownds and William Bathoe, in another print run of 500. A French translation of 1767 was the first to put Horace Walpole's full name on the title page. Ever since the third English edition of 1766, it has been customary to print both prefaces. My text is based on *The Works of Horatio Walpole, Earl of Orford*, 5 vols., edited (unsigned) by Mary Berry (London: G. G. and J. Robinson, and J. Edwards, 1798; 2.1–90), reflecting corrections overseen by Walpole before his death in 1797. A 1791 Parma edition was the first to present pictures of the castle of Otranto as it actually exists in Italy, based on drawings by Willey Reveley that he made while visiting Italy and subsequently sent to Walpole in 1786 (cover). Reveley's pictures also appear in Berry's 1798 edition of *The Castle of Otranto*. Because the Italian castle of Otranto is much more Romanesque than gothic in architectural style, and because Walpole admittedly modeled the castle of *The Castle of Otranto* on his own little castle, Strawberry Hill (see p. 227), I have decided to use primarily pictures of the latter rather than Reveley's drawings.

In my text of *The Castle of Otranto*, I follow Walpole's practice of using brackets to report actions simultaneous with the dialogue. I also follow Walpole in marking such dialogue with dashes, rather than modern quotation marks. Mackenzie does not distinguish discourse markers such as "he said" or "she said" from the body of the speech (for example, "I like him, she said, and so will you"). I retain this practice and all original punctuation and spelling, except my conversion of words ending in "ew" to modern "ow" (for example, "shew" to "show"), to facilitate reading aloud.

First published in April 1771, all copies of *The Man of Feeling* in both Edinburgh and London were sold out by June. The second edition, issued in August 1771 and corrected by Mackenzie, is the one used in this volume. It was first translated into French in 1775 with the title *L'homme et la femme sensibles*, shifting the title to "The Man and Woman of Feeling," to reflect Harley's relations with Miss Walton. From 1777 on, in England, *The Man of Feeling* was typically published in editions bound with Mackenzie's second and third novels, *Man of the World* (1773) and *Julia de Roubigné* (1777). Unless otherwise credited, all annotations and translations in this Longman edition are mine; Judith de Luce helped with Latin translations. Full bibliographical information on sources cited in headnotes and footnotes appears in the "Further Reading" section.

I would like to thank Alan Richardson for encouraging me originally to undertake an edition of Walpole's *The Castle of Otranto*, and Susan Wolfson for her inspiration, patience, and generosity, especially the unsurpassable energy with which she oversaw production of this volume. I am grateful to Miami University for the pictures from Mary Berry's edition of "A Description of Strawberry Hill." I would like to thank the Newberry Library for helping me track down Scott's preface to the Bentley and Colburn *Select Novels*. I would also like to thank Frank Jordan for his vast knowledge of Walter Scott (and almost equally vast collection of Scott's works), Judith de Luce for providing classical knowledge, Alison Hurley for references as well as good advice, and my children Joey and Julia for being who they are.

LAURA MANDELL
Miami University of Ohio

Introduction

Two mid-eighteenth-century novels signal a departure from the dominant mode of social realism represented by the novels of Henry Fielding and Daniel Defoe, whether in satire or in a focus on the everyday life of common people. Horace Walpole's *The Castle of Otranto* was the first "gothic novel," and Henry Mackenzie's celebrated novel of sentiment, *The Man of Feeling*, became a vanguard in the cult of sensibility. Though seemingly of different worlds, both modes share a focus on emotion—emotion as the means for knowing, judging, and ultimately understanding the world. This focus was especially compelling in the eighteenth century, when the relation between people and the knowable world was undergoing a sea change. Unmoored by science and philosophy from the assurances of religion that the world is not only meaningful but also knowable to a benevolent God who guides human action, and disinherited of innate moral ideas by John Locke's notion of the mind as a *tabula rasa*, people began to wonder how perceptions are affected by the passions. How are passions to be manipulated by others? Could a social utopia be realized by the cultivation of feeling? Could novels advance this project?

The popularity of *The Castle of Otranto* and *The Man of Feeling* suggests a positive answer. Both sold out immediately, with multiple reprintings and several new editions necessary in the first year. Their popularity stands in stark contrast to the cool reception of the formal reviews. Here is Mackenzie's report to his beloved cousin Betty Rose, in June 1771, about *The Man of Feeling*:

> The reception which the public indulgence has given has exceeded my expectations: the copies allotted to Edinburgh were

all sold in about a week's time, and when a fresh demand was made upon London, it was found that the whole impression had already been exhausted—Not so has it fared with the Reviewers. [. . .] They have treated it very roughly.[1]

The public prevailed over the reviewers. By the first quarter of the next century, both novels were included as essential reading in two major, multivolume collections of British novels, compiled respectively by Anna Letitia Barbauld and Walter Scott. The influence was as undeniable as the popularity. Gothic themes and sentimental modes have been as vital to Romantic poetry as to the development of the realistic and highbrow novel. The report about Romanticism may seem unsurprising, but what about highbrow realism? "Realism" actually needs both the gothic and the sentimental as its self-constituting antitheses, making its claim by advertising itself as "not gothic" or "anti-sentimental."

The literary value of both the gothic and the sentimental modes was a question from the start. *The Castle of Otranto* and *The Man of Feeling* seemed to many critics to degrade the genre that was managing to gain respectability in the hands of Defoe and Fielding, and in later assessments scarcely seemed to rank with the esteemed novels of psychological realism to be refined by the likes of Jane Austen, Charles Dickens, and George Eliot. But would the Brontës' success have been possible without both Walpole and Mackenzie? It is in their novels that the rhetorical forms anticipating psychological realism are worked out.[2] At first glance, it seems ludicrous that texts with such one-dimensional characters could have psychological depth. And yet they do.

The seeming surfaces often involve unexpected dimensions. As one critic has remarked, *The Castle of Otranto* offers the first sustained instance of "psycho-narration—the direct transposition into third-person narrative of the immediate thought processes of the characters."[3] Villain Manfred is acutely attentive to the young characters' actions: It *does* look as if Isabella and Theodore were having

---

[1]Qtd. in Thompson 112. Walpole writes a similar letter about *The Castle of Otranto* (see p. 267).

[2]For relevant critical discussion, see Sedgwick (1981), Hogle (2002), and Brown (2005).

[3]Brown 31.

an illicit affair. They aren't, and yet Walpole conveys a sense of Isabella's repressed desires, which he allows Manfred to intuit. In this way, his novel's very title is emblematic: a psyche fortified like a castle against self-knowledge, yet unconsciously threaded with subterranean passages accessible in very unexpected ways. While Walpole's frequently campy tone seems incongruous with this psychological resonance, this attitude does not suppress it from our perception.

So, too, the sentimental novel seems to stage one-dimensional characters: purely good, sentimental souls, and sophisticated, worldly rogues who trample on their feelings. These types are partly the effect of sentiment itself; everywhere dashes and exclamation points punctuate a sudden rising or stifling of emotion. Harley's feeling-laden tears and his solitary actions and thoughts are translated by the narrator, a friend who once lived in the neighborhood of the "editor" who has rescued fragments of Harley's writing. By using these various reporters and narrators, Mackenzie is able to certify Harley's purity (he is not performing for the approbation of anyone) and to use the more worldly characters to convey a critique of the society in which he lives.[4] This narrative procedure looks forward to the novel of psychological realism. Like Harley's narrator-friend, Jane Austen's narrators are omniscient, and her irony functions like the critical commentary provided by Mackenzie's narrator and the editor.

Yet for all the anticipations of developments to come, *The Castle of Otranto* and *The Man of Feeling* are very much of their times, especially in their preoccupation with the passions of horror and its near kin, sentimental sympathy—both vibrant elements in that signature of the eighteenth century, "The Cult of Sensibility."

Sensibility

Gothic novelists liked to claim ancestry from the literary genre known as "Romance"—not love stories, but tales of exotic adventure and heroic exploits, where men were knights and ladies were damsels fair, and often in distress.[5] The "ghosts" of gothic novels

---

[4]See Starr 186.

[5]While Clara Reeve's essays develop this notion (see p. 218), modern critic J. Paul Hunter argues that the self-constituting lineage is debatable, even fraudulent.

are there to distill epic events that cause epic emotions. In *The Castle of Otranto*, a Lord is poisoned by his valet, who forges a will bequeathing him the title; a daughter is stabbed to death by her father in a tragedy of mistaken identity. While sentimental novels drop the epic events, they capitalize on the pretended ancestry of Romance by keeping the emotions. Harley's "sentiments are occasionally expressed and the features of his mind developed," Mackenzie writes to a friend in 1770, "as the incidents draw them forth."[6] The incidents themselves are almost negligible, neither epic nor intriguing. "You would find the hero's story," Mackenzie explains to his cousin, "simple to excess":

> I would have [*Man of Feeling* be] as different from the entanglement of a novel as can be. [. . .] Heroes amidst the blaze of war, or the glare of courts, have been in every one's hands; I have sought one unattended by those adventitious circumstances; I have found him in a simple farm-house; yet, I flatter myself, he is not the less a hero.[7]

This last hero, Edwards, does go to war, but the signal "incident" is his preventing the beating of an "old Indian" man, at his own expense (the ruffians beat him instead): Edwards is compelling for virtuous self-abnegation, not militaristic prowess. This heroizing of ordinary individuals is hailed by another novelist of sentiment, Laurence Sterne, in a famous passage from *A Sentimental Journey*:

> Dear Sensibility! source inexhausted of all that's precious in our joys, or costly in our sorrows! [. . .] Here I trace thee [. . .]—that I feel some generous joys and generous cares beyond myself— all comes from thee, great—great SENSORIUM[8] of the world! which vibrates, if a hair of our heads but falls upon the ground, in the remotest desert of thy creation.[9]

---

[6]Qtd. in Thompson 112. In the early 18th c. "sentiment" meant "pithy statement" (an adage), but the word was evolving to mean (as it does today) "pure feeling."

[7]Qtd. in Thompson 112.

[8]The center of feeling in the brain.

[9]*A Sentimental Journey Through France and Europe, by Mr. Yorick*, 2 vols. (London: T. Becket and P. A. De Hondt, 1768), 2.182–83.

We hear echoed in this language Christ's idea of God for whom "the very hairs of your head are all numbered," and who is provident even of the fall of a sparrow (Matthew 10.29–30). Sensibility literature makes epic the pain of every human being.

In *The Man of Feeling*, Harley is as deeply moved by a smirk or a leer as are the onlookers of Frederic's pathetic near-death at the hands of his daughter's defender in *The Castle of Otranto*. Walpole puts his characters on a stage of emotional torment, punctuated by soliloquy-like brooding. Mackenzie places passion on the stage of simple events. No longer limiting passion to the world of epic or tragic theater, these two novels test the possibility that ordinary events may be of epic importance and consequence. But this innovation was not without its critics.

One concern was that the credit of ordinary feeling could give impressionable minds false ideas about social possibility—an issue especially for reformers of female culture, who regarded both the gothic and the sentimental novel not just as junk literature but also as a dangerous influence:[10] "had she thought while she read" (Mary Wollstonecraft says about a character who has "read all the sentimental novels"), "her mind would have been contaminated."[11] Another concern was that such fiction reduced feeling to a cheaply purchased aesthetic spectacle. One could weep over fictional characters while remaining unconcerned about the real suffering in the world. Here, for example, is Wollstonecraft worrying about sensibility at the end of the eighteenth century:

> Where is the dignity, the infallibility of sensibility, in the fair ladies, whom, if the voice of rumour is to be credited, the captive negroes curse in all the agony of bodily pain, for the unheard of tortures they invent? It is probable that some of them, after the sight of a flagellation, compose their ruffled spirits and exercise their tender feelings by the perusal of the last imported novel.—How true these tears are to nature, I leave you to determine.[12]

---

[10]See Samuel Johnson (p. 215) and Clara Reeve (p. 218).

[11]*Mary, a Fiction* (London, 1788), rpt. *Mary and Maria, by Mary Wollstonecraft*, ed. Janet Todd (New York: Penguin, 1992), 6.

[12]*Vindication of the Rights of Men* (2nd ed., London: J. Johnson, 1790), 111.

Here the reader's tears are part of her reading pleasure, with no necessary connection to any true ("natural") desire to eradicate suffering. Similarly, Samuel Taylor Coleridge wishes to "distinguish benevolence from mere sensibility—Benevolence impels to action, and is accompanied by self-denial."[13] Wollstonecraft and Coleridge are concerned about the implicit immunity to the actual miseries of our fellow creatures (African slaves, for instance) fostered by the novel of sensibility. A version of this concern appears in critiques of the gothic novel as well, which also discriminates feeling by class.

The Gothic Novel

In *The Castle of Otranto*, Walpole tends to dignify the emotions of his principal characters, of the aristocratic class, and play the fears of lower characters for laughs. Ann Yearsley, the "milkwoman poet," takes him to task exactly for this (see p. 268). And yet there is another way to assess the function of these credulous characters: It is through their reactions to supernatural events that the novel brings a mocking perspective to its own supernaturalism. This self-mockery is as much an element of the gothic tradition as anything else.

In the second, signed edition of *The Castle of Otranto*, Walpole adopts an epithet for his "new species of romance" from one of the first reviews (p. 266), calling it "A GOTHIC STORY." We usually think of the gothic as a world of ghosts, haunted ruins, supernatural doings; but in the eighteenth century, "gothic" indicated a confabulation of incongruous aesthetic elements. This is why "gothic" originally meant (none too kindly) "barbarous," with special reference to the mixtures of grotesque gargoyles with sublime arches, spires, and vaulting ceilings in the architecture of the medieval gothic cathedral.[14] Neoclassical poet and critic John Dryden had similar complaints about the way native English literature ignored classical rules of decorum, most evident in that mixed genre "tragi-comedy." Walpole, who defended the mixture in plays such as Shakespeare's *Hamlet*, used "gothic" to signal a tale where intense, tragic passions interplay with comic repartee between masters and servants. Adopting the phrase "A GOTHIC STORY" from the reviewer who took the

[13]*The Watchman* 4.25 (25 March 1796); rpt. in *The Collected Works of Samuel Taylor Coleridge*, ed. Lewis Patton (Princeton: Princeton Univ. Press, 1970), 2.140.
[14]See John Carter, p. 225.

bait that *The Castle of Otranto* was an authentic translation of a very old printed book (so the "editor" of the first edition claimed), Walpole spun "gothic" into a jokey term for fake medievalism. There is something campy about his highly styled, anti-realist gothicism—a campiness discernible in the faux signature to the first edition. Editors have sensed that "Onuphrio Muralto" has something to do with Walpole's name. I think it is part of the joke: One can see in the name an anagram for *Hori* (nickname for Horace) and *upon*; *Mur alto* in Italian means "Wall high." "Horace upon a Wall (pole-)high." Has Walpole climbed out on a limb by bringing supernatural events into a tale in straightforward style?

To some literary critics today, gothic seems more a matter of aesthetics than a specific genre of fiction. To others, following the lead of eighteenth-century commentators, gothic is "poetic romance," as distinct from novelistic realism.[15] To still others, gothic is "the oscillation between the 'real' and the 'supernatural'" that is Walpole's signature.[16] It is a "generic hybrid" that "achieves a genuine transformation," developing the dramatic soliloquy "into third-person narrative of the immediate thought-processes of the characters," a "theater of the mind" in the form of a novel.[17] It is in this interiority that the gothic novel finds common ground with the novel of sensibility.[18] While a realist such as Fielding has little of this interiority, for the novelist of sentimental fiction the world of external events is secondary to psychological development. No wonder Mackenzie took Hamlet as the prototype of his Man of Feeling: The "extreme sensibility of mind" exerts an "indescribable charm."[19]

The Castle of Otranto and *The Man of Feeling* bring the modern theater of consciousness into the novel, the "new" genre that was taking shape in the eighteenth century, in modes that continue to excite us in the twenty-first.

[15]See the discussions by Gamer, Miles, and Williams. For the 18th-c. view, see Clara Reeve, who argues that novel and romance are two distinct genres, the gothic novel mixing the two (p. 218).

[16]Jerrold Hogle, *The Undergrounds of* The Phantom of the Opera (New York: Palgrave, 2002), 28.

[17]Brown (2005), 28–34.

[18]Peter de Voogd, "Sentimental Horrors: Feeling in the Gothic Novel," in Tinkler-Villani and Davidson, 75–88.

[19]For the comments on *Hamlet*, see Thompson 207, and Mackenzie in *Mirror* No. 99 (*Works* 4.375, 378).

Table of Dates

1750	Walpole declares, "I am going to build a little gothic castle at Strawberry Hill" (Twickenham, England) and starts planning with architect Richard Bentley; construction from 1753 to 1776.
1751	Tobias Smollett, *Peregrine Pickle.*
1752	Charlotte Lennox, *The Female Quixote.*
1757	Edmund Burke, *A Philosophical Enquiry into the Origin of Our Ideas of the Sublime and the Beautiful.*
1759	Adam Smith, *A Theory of Moral Sentiments.*
1759–67	Laurence Sterne, *Tristram Shandy* (serialized).
1760	George III becomes king.
1761	Jean-Jacques Rousseau, *La Nouvelle Heloise.*
1762–71	Walpole, *Anecdotes of Painting in England*, coauthored with George Vertue.
1764	*The Castle of Otranto* ("1765") by "Onuphrio Muralto."
1765	Second edition of *The Castle of Otranto*, by "H.W." Walpole goes to Paris, cultivating a friendship with Mme. Du Deffand. Mackenzie goes to London. Thomas Percy, *Reliques of Ancient English Poetry.*
1767	Walpole resigns his seat in Parliament.
1768	Walpole, *The Mysterious Mother, a Tragedy*; Sterne, *A Sentimental Journey.* Sterne dies.
1771	Mackenzie, *The Man of Feeling*; second edition three months later. Smollett, *Humphrey Clinker.*
1772	Mansfield Decision declares slaves free in England.
1773	Mackenzie, *The Man of the World.*
1774	Goethe's international sensation, *The Sorrows of Young Werther.*
1775	War with American Colonies begins.
1776	U.S. Declaration of Independence.
1777	Mackenzie, *Julia de Roubigné*; Clara Reeve, *The Champion of Virtue* (first edition of *The Old English Baron*), proclaimed "offspring" of Walpole's *Otranto.*
1779–80	Mackenzie edits (and largely writes) *The Mirror.*

1781   Sick and dying slaves are hurled off the slave ship Zong into shark-infested waters, as if spoiled cargo. Henry Fuseli's gothic painting, *The Nightmare*.

1784   Walpole, *Description of the Villa of Horace Walpole at Strawberry Hill*; Charlotte Smith's extravaganza of performative feeling, *Elegiac Sonnets*.

1785   William Cowper, *The Task*.

1785–87   Mackenzie edits (and largely writes) *The Lounger*.

1788   George III's mental illness occasions the Regency Crisis; Mary Wollstonecraft, *Mary*, a novel interrogating the connection between virtue and sensibility.

1789   French Revolution; William Blake, *Songs of Innocence*.

1790   Edmund Burke's reactionary *Reflections on the Revolution in France*, replete with gothic writing about the horrors; Wollstonecraft, *Vindication of the Rights of Men* (first edition published anonymously).

1791   Walpole becomes fourth Earl of Orford upon the death of his nephew; Tom Paine, *The Rights of Man*; 100,000 slaves revolt in the West Indies, led by Toussaint-L'Ouverture ("The Black Napoleon").

1792   Mary Wollstonecraft, *Vindication of the Rights of Woman*.

1793   France and Britain declare war.

1793–94   The Reign of Terror in France, a gothic horror led by Robespierre, an avid reader of Rousseau, in which thousands are executed without trial, including ultimately Robespierre himself.

1794   Ann Radcliffe, *The Mysteries of Udolpho*.

1797   Walpole dies; Radcliffe, *The Italian*.

1798   Mary Berry publishes Walpole's *Works*; William Wordsworth and Samuel Taylor Coleridge, *Lyrical Ballads*; Charles Brockden Brown (American), *Wieland*.

1799   John Pinkerton, *Walpoliana*, anecdotes about and conversations with Horace Walpole; Brown, *Ormond*, *Edgar Huntly*.

1804   Napoleon crowns himself "Emperor."

1805   Admiral Horatio Nelson defeats the French and Spanish fleets at the Battle of Trafalgar and dies a martyr. Wordsworth finishes a thirteen-book version *The Prelude* (an autobiographical epic with several episodes of feeling and sentiment, and several memories, from childhood to the French Revolution, cast as gothic terrors).

1808   Mackenzie, *Works*.

1810   Anna Letitia Barbauld's *The British Novelists* includes *The Castle of Otranto* and *The Man of Feeling*.

1811   Ballantyne publishes *The Castle of Otranto* with a preface by Walter Scott. The Prince of Wales becomes Regent as George III is declared insane.

1814   Scott dedicates his first historical romance *Waverley* to Mackenzie, "our Scottish Addison."

1815   Napoleon finally defeated at the Battle of Waterloo.

1818   Mary Shelley, *Frankenstein*, published anonymously.

1820   Scott, *Ivanhoe* (also anonymous, though Scott was guessed). The Regent becomes George IV on the death of his father.

1822–23 *Ballantyne's Novelists Library* includes *The Castle of Otranto*, *The Man of Feeling*, and *Man of the World*, with Scott's Prefatory Memoirs to Mackenzie and Walpole.

1831   Mackenzie dies. Shelley's *Frankenstein* published with new gothic-tuned Introduction.

1832   Scott dies.

1834   Bentley and Colburn's *Standard Novels* series presents *Otranto* introduced by a generous excerpt of Scott's Prefatory Memoir to Walpole.

The Castle of Otranto

by Horace Walpole

THE

CASTLE OF OTRANTO

A

STORY.

Translated by

WILLIAM MARSHAL, Gent.

From the Original ITALIAN of

ONUPHRIO MURALTO,

CANON of the Church of St. NICHOLAS

at OTRANTO.

LONDON:

Printed for THO. LOWNDS in Fleet-Street.

MDCCLXV.

Preface

To the First Edition.[1]

The following work was found in the library of an ancient catholic family in the north of England. It was printed at Naples, in the black letter,[2] in the year 1529. How much sooner it was written does not appear. The principal incidents are such as were believed in the darkest ages of christianity; but the language and conduct have nothing that savours of barbarism.[3] The style is the purest Italian. If the story was written near the time when it is supposed to have happened, it must have been between 1095, the æra of the first Crusade, and 1243, the date of the last, or not long afterwards. There is no other circumstance in the work that can lead us to guess at the period in which the scene is laid: the names of the actors are evidently fictitious, and probably disguised on purpose: yet the Spanish names of the domestics seem to indicate that this work was not composed until the establishment of the Arragonian Kings in Naples had made Spanish appellations familiar in that country. The beauty of the diction, and the zeal of the author [moderated, however, by singular judgment] concur to make me think that the date of the composition was little antecedent to that of the impression.[4] Letters were then in their most flourishing state in Italy, and contributed to dispel the empire of superstition, at that time so forcibly attacked by the reformers. It is not unlikely that an artful priest might endeavour to turn their own arms on the innovators; and might avail himself of his abilities as an author to confirm the populace in their ancient errors and superstitions. If this was his view, he has certainly acted with signal address.[5] Such a work as the following would enslave a hundred vulgar[6] minds beyond half the books of controversy that have been written from the days of Luther to the present hour.[7]

---

[1]By the alleged translator.

[2]Used in early printed texts, this medieval calligraphy is quintessentially gothic.

[3]Of the dark ages, the era of the tale; "conduct" refers to narrative procedure or method.

[4]Printing.

[5]Skill.

[6]Uneducated.

[7]The controversy is the Protestant Reformation instigated by Martin Luther (1483–1546). From the protestant perspective, Catholicism was "superstition," maintaining its ecclesiastical authority by playing on the fears of the uneducated.

This solution of the author's motives is however offered as a mere conjecture. Whatever his views were, or whatever effects the execution of them might have, his work can only be laid before the public at present as a matter of entertainment. Even as such, some apology for it is necessary. Miracles, visions, necromancy, dreams, and other preternatural events, are exploded now even from romances.[8] That was not the case when our author wrote; much less when the story itself is supposed to have happened. Belief in every kind of prodigy was so established in those dark ages, that an author would not be faithful to the *manners* of the times who should omit all mention of them. He is not bound to believe them himself, but he must represent his actors as believing them.

If this *air* of the *miraculous* is excused, the reader will find nothing else unworthy of his perusal. Allow the possibility of the facts, and all the actors comport themselves as persons would do in their situation. There is no bombast, no similes, flowers,[9] digressions, or unnecessary descriptions. Every thing tends directly to the catastrophe.[10] Never is the reader's attention relaxed. The rules of the drama[11] are almost observed throughout the conduct of the piece. The characters are well drawn, and still better maintained. Terror, the author's principal engine,[12] prevents the story from ever languishing; and it is so often contrasted by pity, that the mind is kept up in a constant vicissitude of interesting passions.

Some persons may perhaps think the characters of the domestics too little serious for the general cast of the story; but besides their opposition to the principal personages, the art of the author is very observable in his conduct of the subalterns.[13] They discover[14] many passages essential to the story, which could not be well brought to light but by their *naïveté* and simplicity: in particular,

---

[8]Tales of adventure, chivalry, and love, popular from medieval times to Walpole's day, even though the specific events were no longer credited.

[9]Poetic flourishes.

[10]A plot's climax and resolution.

[11]The unities of action, time, and place, set by Aristotle's *Poetics*, and adhered to by neoclassical aesthetics.

[12]Means of interest; for this new aesthetic principle, see Edmund Burke's *Sublime and the Beautiful* (1757), p. 209.

[13]Subordinate characters.

[14]Uncover; reveal.

the womanish terror and foibles of Bianca, in the last chapter, conduce essentially towards advancing the catastrophe.

It is natural for a translator to be prejudiced in favour of his adopted work. More impartial readers may not be so much struck with the beauties of this piece as I was. Yet I am not blind to my author's defects. I could wish he had grounded his plan on a more useful moral than this; that *the sins of fathers are visited on their children to the third and fourth generation.*[15] I doubt whether in his time, any more than at present, ambition curbed its appetite of dominion from the dread of so remote a punishment. And yet this moral is weakened by that less direct insinuation, that even such anathema[16] may be diverted by devotion to saint Nicholas. Here the interest of the monk plainly gets the better of the judgment of the author.[17] However, with all its faults, I have no doubt but the English reader will be pleased with a sight of this performance. The piety that reigns throughout, the lessons of virtue that are inculcated, and the rigid purity of the sentiments, exempt this work from the censure to which romances are but too liable. Should it meet with the success I hope for, I may be encouraged to reprint the original Italian, though it will tend to depreciate my own labour. Our language falls far short of the charms of the Italian, both for variety and harmony. The latter is peculiarly excellent for simple narrative. It is difficult in English *to relate* without falling too low or rising too high; a fault obviously occasioned by the little care taken to speak pure language in common conversation. Every Italian or Frenchman of any rank piques himself on speaking his own tongue correctly and with choice. I cannot flatter myself with having done justice to my author in this respect: his style is as elegant as his conduct of the passions is masterly. It is a pity that he did not apply his talents to what they were evidently proper for, the theatre.

[15]Exod. 20.5, 34.7; Num. 14.18; Deut. 5.9: "for I, the Lord your God, am a jealous god. I punish the children for the sins of the fathers to the third and fourth generations of those who hate me."

[16]Excommunication and damnation.

[17]The monk means to show how praying to St. Nicholas, the Pope who instituted papal infallibility, magically mitigates the bad effects of divine justice. In Walpole's day, a good author would prefer realism to supernatural intervention. In the first edition, Walpole blames his imaginative leaps on monkish superstition; in the Preface to the second, he justifies it (see p. 8, n. 4).

I will detain the reader no longer, but to make one short remark. Though the machinery[18] is invention, and the names of the actors imaginary, I cannot but believe that the ground-work of the story is founded on truth. The scene is undoubtedly laid in some real castle.[19] The author seems frequently, without design, to describe particular parts. *The chamber*, says he, *on the right hand; the door on the left hand; the distance from the chapel to Conrad's apartment*: these and other passages are strong presumptions that the author had some certain building in his eye. Curious persons, who have leisure to employ in such researches, may possibly discover in the Italian writers the foundation on which our author has built. If a catastrophe, at all resembling that which he describes, is believed to have given rise to this work, it will contribute to interest the reader, and will make *The Castle of Otranto* a still more moving story.

---

[18]Supernatural occurrences.

[19]A tease. A 1791 Parma edition included images of the Castle of Otranto in Italy, drawn by Willey Reveley and sent to Walpole in 1786 (cover). Mary Berry's 1798 edition included them, too. The actual castle is more Romanesque than Gothic. A more gothic-style villa was the one Walpole built on his estate, Strawberry Hill, which became a tourist attraction over the course of the 18th c. See p. 226.

Preface

To the Second Edition.

The favourable manner in which this little piece has been received by the public, calls upon the author to explain the grounds on which he composed it. But before he opens those motives, it is fit that he should ask pardon of his readers for having offered his work to them under the borrowed personage of a translator. As diffidence of his own abilities, and the novelty of the attempt, were the sole inducements to assume that disguise, he flatters himself he shall appear excusable. He resigned his performance to the impartial judgment of the public; determined to let it perish in obscurity, if disapproved; nor meaning to avow such a trifle, unless better judges should pronounce that he might own it without a blush.

It was an attempt to blend the two kinds of romance, the ancient and the modern.[1] In the former, all was imagination and improbability: in the latter, nature is always intended to be, and sometimes has been, copied with success.[2] Invention has not been wanting; but the great resources of fancy have been dammed up, by a strict adherence to common life. But if in the latter species Nature has cramped imagination, she did but take her revenge, having been totally excluded from old romances. The actions, sentiments, conversations, of the heroes and heroines of ancient days were as unnatural as the machines[3] employed to put them in motion.

The author of the following pages thought it possible to reconcile the two kinds. Desirous of leaving the powers of fancy at liberty to expatiate through the boundless realms of invention, and thence of creating more interesting situations, he wished to conduct the mortal agents in his drama according to the rules of probability; in short, to make them think, speak, and act, as it might be

---

[1] In *Rambler* No. 4 (31 March 1750), critic Samuel Johnson exhorted the "modern" 18th-c. romancers to write realistic fiction; in her essay *The Progress of Romance* (1785), Clara Reeve called "modern romance" "the novel" (as we do now). See pp. 215 and 218.

[2] Aristotle's *Poetics* advocates writing about "probable impossibilities" rather than "improbable possibilities" (24.10; Butcher translation).

[3] Plot devices.

supposed mere men and women would do in extraordinary positions.[4] He had observed, that in all inspired writings, the personages under the dispensation of miracles, and witnesses to the most stupendous phænomena, never lose sight of their human character: whereas in the productions of romantic story, an improbable event never fails to be attended by an absurd dialogue. The actors seem to lose their senses the moment the laws of nature have lost their tone. As the public have applauded the attempt, the author must not say he was entirely unequal to the task he had undertaken: yet if the new route he has struck out shall have paved a road for men of brighter talents, he shall own with pleasure and modesty, that he was sensible the plan was capable of receiving greater embellishments than his imagination or conduct of the passion could bestow on it.

With regard to the deportment of the domestics, on which I have touched in the former preface, I will beg leave to add a few words. The simplicity of their behaviour, almost tending to excite smiles, which at first seems not consonant to the serious cast of the work, appeared to me not only not improper, but was marked designedly in that manner. My rule was nature. However grave, important, or even melancholy, the sensations of princes and heroes may be, they do not stamp the same affections on their domestics: at least the latter do not, or should not be made to express their passions in the same dignified tone. In my humble opinion, the contrast between the sublime of the one and the *naïveté* of the other, sets the pathetic of the former in a stronger light. The very impatience which a reader feels while delayed by the coarse pleasantries of vulgar actors from arriving at the knowledge of the important catastrophe he expects, perhaps heightens, certainly proves, that he has been artfully interested in the depending event. But I had higher authority than my own opinion for this conduct. That great master of nature, Shakespeare, was the model I copied. Let me ask if his tragedies of *Hamlet* and *Julius Cæsar*[5] would not lose a considerable share of their spirit and wonderful beauties, if the humour of the grave-diggers, the fooleries of Polonius, and the clumsy jests of

---

[4]Walpole's willingness to depart from the realism of common life anticipates Coleridge's interest in the "dramatic truth" of emotions in "supernatural" situations that are experienced as "real." See his paragraph in *Biographia Literaria*, p. 222.

[5]Titles are not italicized in the 1798 edition.

the Roman citizens were omitted, or vested in heroics?[6] Is not the eloquence of Antony, the nobler and affectedly-unaffected oration of Brutus, artificially exalted by the rude outbursts of nature from the mouths of their auditors? These touches remind one of the Grecian sculptor, who, to convey the idea of a Colossus within the dimensions of a seal, inserted a little boy measuring his thumb.

No, says Voltaire, in his edition of Corneille, this mixture of buffoonery and solemnity is intolerable.—Voltaire is a genius[7]— but not of Shakespeare's magnitude. Without recurring to disputable authority, I appeal from Voltaire to himself. I shall not avail myself of his former encomiums on our mighty poet; though the French critic has twice translated the same speech in *Hamlet*, some years ago in admiration, latterly in derision; and I am sorry to find that his judgment grows weaker, when it ought to be farther matured.[8] But I shall make use of his own words, delivered on the general topic of the theatre, when he was neither thinking to recommend or decry Shakespeare's practice; consequently at a moment when Voltaire was impartial. In the preface to his *Enfant prodigue*,[9] that exquisite piece of which I declare my admiration,

[6]While French neoclassical dramatists such as Corneille and Racine would never mix genres, Dryden's *Of Dramatick Poesie* (1668) defends Shakespeare's practice.

[7]The following remark is foreign to the present question, yet excusable in an Englishman, who is willing to think that the severe criticisms of so masterly a writer as Voltaire on our immortal countryman, may have been the effusions of wit and precipitation, rather than the result of judgment and attention. May not the critic's skill in the force and powers of our language have been as incorrect and incompetent as his knowledge of our history? Of the latter his own pen has dropped glaring evidence. In his preface to Thomas Corneille's Earl of Essex, Monsieur de Voltaire allows that the truth of history has been grossly perverted in that piece. In excuse he pleads, that when Corneille wrote, the noblesse of France were much unread in English story; but now, says the commentator, that they study it, such misrepresentation would not be suffered—Yet forgetting that the period of ignorance is lapsed, and that it is not very necessary to instruct the knowing, he undertakes from the overflowing of his own reading to give the nobility of his own country a detail of Queen Elizabeth's favourites—of whom, says he, Robert Dudley was the first, and the earl of Leicester the second.—Could one have believed that it could be necessary to inform Monsieur de Voltaire himself, that Robert Dudley and the earl of Leicester were the same person? [Walpole's note]

"Voltaire" is the pen-name of Françoise Marie-Arouet (1694–1778), French dramatist and Enlightenment philosopher who exhorted, "Think for yourself!" *Le Comte d'Essex* (1678) was written by Pierre Corneille's brother.

[8]Voltaire translated "To be or not to be" (*Hamlet* 3.1) in *Lettres Philosophiques* or *English Letters* (1734) and in *Appel à toute les nations de L'Europe* (1761).

[9]A play produced in 1736.

and which, should I live twenty years longer, I trust I shall never attempt to ridicule, he has these words, speaking of comedy [but equally applicable to tragedy, if tragedy is, as surely it ought to be, a picture of human life; nor can I conceive why occasional pleasantry ought more to be banished from the tragic scene, than pathetic seriousness from the comic] *On y voit un melange de serieux et de plaisanterie, de comique et de touchant;* souvent meme une seule avanture *produit tous ces contrastes. Rien n'est si commun qu'une maison dans laquelle* un pere gronde, une fille occupée de sa passion pleure; *le fils se moque des deux, et quelques parens prennent part differemment à la scene, etc. Nous n'inferons pas de là que toute comedie doive avoir des scenes de bouffonerie et des scenes attendrissantes: il y a beaucoup de tres bonnes pièces où il ne regne que de la gayeté; d'autres toutes serieuses; d'autres melangées: d'autres où l'attendrissement va jusqu'aux larmes:* il ne faut donner l'exclusion à aucun genre: *et si l'on me demandoit, quel genre est le meilleur, je repondrois, celui qui est le mieux traité.*[10] Surely if a comedy may be *toute serieuse,*[11] tragedy may now and then, soberly, be indulged in a smile. Who shall proscribe it? Shall the critic, who in self-defence declares that *no kind*[12] ought to be excluded from comedy, give laws to Shakespeare?

I am aware that the preface from whence I have quoted these passages does not stand in Monsieur de Voltaire's name, but in that of his editor; yet who doubts that the editor and author were the same person? Or where is the editor who has so happily possessed himself of his author's style and brilliant ease of argument? These passages were indubitably the genuine sentiments of that great writer. In his epistle to Maffei,[13] prefixed to his *Merope,* he

---

[10]From Preface de l'editeur, *Mérope* (1743): *One sees there a mixture of the serious and pleasantries, of the comic and the touching;* often even a single adventure *producing all these contrasts. Nothing is so common as a house in which* a father rages, a daughter occupied with her passion cries; *a son laughs at both, and a few relatives take different sides in the scene, etc. We will not infer from this that all comedy must have scenes of buffoonery along with pathetic scenes: there are many very good plays where gaiety alone reigns; others completely serious; others mixed: others where the pathetic brings us to tears:* we must not exclude any genre: *and if someone were to ask me, which kind is the best, I would respond, that which is best handled.*

[11]Completely serious.

[12]No genre.

[13]A letter to Italian playwright Machese Scipione Maffei (1675–1755) who also wrote a play titled *Merope.*

delivers almost the same opinion, though I doubt with a little irony. I will repeat his words, and then give my reason for quoting them. After translating a passage in Maffei's *Merope*, Monsieur de Voltaire adds, *Tous ces traits sont naïfs: tout y est convenable à ceux que vous introduisez sur la scene*, et aux mœurs que vous leur donnez. *Ces familiarités naturelles eussent été, à ce que je crois, bien reçues dans Athenes; mais Paris et notre parterre veulent une autre espece de simplicité.*[14] I doubt, I say, whether there is not a grain of sneer in this and other passages of that epistle; yet the force of truth is not damaged by being tinged with ridicule. Maffei was to represent a Grecian story: surely the Athenians were as competent judges of Grecian manners, and of the propriety of introducing them, as the parterre[15] of Paris. On the contrary, says Voltaire [and I cannot but admire his reasoning], there were but ten thousand citizens at Athens, and Paris has near eight hundred thousand inhabitants, among whom one may reckon thirty thousand judges of dramatic works.—Indeed!—But, allowing so numerous a tribunal, I believe this is the only instance in which it was ever pretended, that thirty thousand persons, living near two thousand years after the æra in question, were, upon the mere face of the poll, declared better judges than the Grecians themselves of what ought to be the manners of a tragedy written on a Grecian story.

I will not enter into a discussion of the *espece de simplicité*,[16] which the *parterre* of Paris demands, nor of the shackles with which *the thirty thousand judges* have cramped their poetry, the chief merit of which, as I gather from repeated passages in *The New Commentary on Corneille*, consists in vaulting in spite of those fetters; a merit which, if true, would reduce poetry, from the lofty effort of imagination, to a puerile and most contemptible labour—*difficiles nugæ* with a witness![17] I cannot help however mentioning a couplet, which to my English ears, always

---

[14]*All these traits are unsophisticated: all found here are appropriate to those characters whom you introduce on the scene, and in keeping with the manners that you give them. These natural familiarities would have been, according to my beliefs, well received in Athens; but Paris and our audience want another sort of simplicity.*

[15]The ground-level orchestra section, the cheapest seats.

[16]Kind of simplicity.

[17]Pointless difficulties (*difficile nugae*), monitored by "witnesses" to neoclassical dramatic rules. The phrase comes from Martial's *Epigrams* 2.86.9.

sounded as the flattest and most trifling instance of circumstantial propriety; but which Voltaire, who has dealt so severely with nine parts in ten of Corneille's works, has singled out to defend in Racine;

De son appartement cette porte est prochaine,
Et cette autre conduit dans celui de la reine.

In English,
To Cæsar's closet through this door you come,
And t'other leads to the queen's drawing-room.[18]

Unhappy Shakespeare! hadst thou made Rosencraus inform his compeer Guildenstern of the ichnography[19] of the palace of Copenhagen, instead of presenting us with a moral dialogue between the prince of Denmark and the grave-digger, the illuminated pit of Paris would have been instructed *a second time* to adore thy talents.

The result of all I have said, is to shelter my own daring under the canon of the brightest genius this country, at least, has produced. I might have pleaded, that having created a new species of romance, I was at liberty to lay down what rules I thought fit for the conduct of it: but I should be more proud of having imitated, however faintly, weakly, and at a distance, so masterly a pattern, than to enjoy the entire merit of invention, unless I could have marked my work with genius as well as with originality. Such as it is, the public have honoured it sufficiently, whatever rank their suffrages[20] allot to it.

---

[18]Such lines were necessitated by neoclassic strictures against changing scenes within a single act.

[19]Floor plans; Rosencrantz and Guildenstern are two characters in *Hamlet*.

[20]Approval.

SONNET

TO THE RIGHT HONOURABLE
LADY MARY COKE.[21]

The gentle maid, whose hapless tale
These melancholy pages speak;
Say, gracious lady, shall she fail
To draw the tear adown thy cheek?

No; never was thy pitying breast
Insensible to human woes;
Tender, tho' firm, it melts distrest
For weaknesses it never knows.

Oh! guard the marvels I relate
Of fell ambition scourg'd by fate,
  From reason's peevish blame.
Blest with thy smile, my dauntless sail
I dare expand to Fancy's gale,
  For sure thy smiles are Fame.

H. W.

---

[21]Lady Mark Coke, née Campbell (1727–1811), was a lifelong and somewhat contentious friend of Horace Walpole. She and the Campbells were accused by the
Cokes of trying to murder her abusive husband. His natural death in 1753 delivered
her from this six-year marriage into esteem (so Walpole phrased it) as "the
youngest, handsomest, and wittiest widow in England." This sonnet appeared only
in the second edition; "H. W." identified Walpole as the author of the novel.

Chapter I

Manfred, prince of Otranto, had one son and one daughter: the latter, a most beautiful virgin, aged eighteen, was called Matilda. Conrad, the son, was three years younger, a homely youth, sickly, and of no promising disposition; yet he was the darling of his father, who never showed any symptoms of affection to Matilda.[1] Manfred had contracted a marriage for his son with the Marquis of Vicenza's daughter, Isabella; and she had already been delivered by her guardians into the hands of Manfred, that he might celebrate the wedding as soon as Conrad's infirm state of health would permit. Manfred's impatience for this ceremonial was remarked by his family and neighbours. The former, indeed, apprehending the severity of their prince's disposition, did not dare to utter their surmises on this precipitation. Hippolita, his wife, an amiable lady, did sometimes venture to represent the danger of marrying their only son so early, considering his great youth, and greater infirmities; but she never received any other answer than reflections on her own sterility, who had given him but one heir. His tenants and subjects were less cautious in their discourses: they attributed this hasty wedding to the prince's dread of seeing accomplished an ancient prophecy, which was said to have pronounced, *That the castle and lordship of Otranto should pass from the present family, whenever the real owner should be grown too large to inhabit it.* It was difficult to make any sense of this prophecy; and still less easy to conceive what it had to do with the marriage in question. Yet these mysteries, or contradictions, did not make the populace adhere the less to their opinion.

Young Conrad's birth-day was fixed for his espousals. The company was assembled in the chapel of the castle, and every thing ready for beginning the divine office, when Conrad himself was missing. Manfred, impatient of the least delay, and who had not observed his son retire, dispatched one of his attendants to summon the young prince. The servant, who had not stayed long enough to have crossed the court to Conrad's apartment, came running back breathless, in a frantic manner, his eyes staring, and foaming at the month. He said nothing, but pointed to the court.

---

[1]The preference reflects the system of inheritance that would bequeath the title and lands to male heirs only.

North View of Strawberry Hill (King Library, Miami University)

The company were struck with terror and amazement. The princess Hippolita, without knowing what was the matter, but anxious for her son, swooned away. Manfred, less apprehensive than enraged at the procrastination of the nuptials, and at the folly of his domestic, asked imperiously, what was the matter? The fellow made no answer, but continued pointing towards the court-yard; and at last, after repeated questions put to him, cried out, Oh, the helmet! the helmet! In the mean time some of the company had run into the court, from whence was heard a confused noise of shrieks, horror, and surprise. Manfred, who began to be alarmed at not seeing his son, went himself to get information of what occasioned this strange confusion. Matilda remained endeavouring to assist her mother, and Isabella staid for the same purpose, and to avoid showing any impatience for the bridegroom, for whom, in truth, she had conceived little affection.

The first thing that struck Manfred's eyes was a group of his servants endeavouring to raise something that appeared to him a mountain of sable plumes. He gazed without believing his sight. What are ye doing? cried Manfred, wrathfully: Where is my son? A volley of voices replied, Oh, my lord! the prince! the prince! the helmet! the helmet! Shocked with these lamentable sounds, and dreading he knew not what, he advanced hastily—But what a sight for a father's eyes!—He beheld his child dashed to pieces, and almost buried under an enormous helmet, an hundred times more large than any casque[2] ever made for human being, and shaded with a proportionable quantity of black feathers.

The horror of the spectacle, the ignorance of all around how this misfortune had happened, and above all, the tremendous phænomenon before him, took away the prince's speech. Yet his silence lasted longer than even grief could occasion. He fixed his eyes on what he wished in vain to believe a vision;[3] and seemed less attentive to his loss, than buried in meditation on the stupendous object that had occasioned it. He touched, he examined the fatal casque; nor could even the bleeding mangled remains of the young prince divert the eyes of Manfred from the portent before him. All who had known his partial fondness for young Conrad, were as much surprised at their prince's insensibility, as thunderstruck themselves at the miracle of the helmet. They conveyed the disfigured corpse into the hall, without receiving the least direction from Manfred. As little was he attentive to the ladies who remained in the chapel: on the contrary, without mentioning the unhappy princesses his wife and daughter, the first sounds that dropped from Manfred's lips were, Take care of the lady Isabella.

The domestics, without observing the singularity of this direction, were guided by their affection to their mistress, to consider it as peculiarly addressed to her situation, and flew to her assistance. They conveyed her to her chamber more dead than alive, and indifferent to all the strange circumstances she heard, except the death of her son. Matilda, who doted on her mother, smothered her own grief and amazement, and thought of nothing but assisting and comforting her afflicted parent. Isabella, who had been treated by Hippolita like a daughter, and who returned that tenderness with equal duty and affection, was scarce less assiduous about the princess; at the same time endeavouring to partake and lessen the weight of sorrow which she saw Matilda strove to suppress, for

[2]Helmet.
[3]Illusion.

whom she had conceived the warmest sympathy of friendship. Yet her own situation could not help finding its place in her thoughts. She felt no concern for the death of young Conrad, except commiseration; and she was not sorry to be delivered from a marriage which had promised her little felicity, either from her destined bridegroom, or from the severe temper of Manfred, who, though he had distinguished her by great indulgence, had imprinted her mind with terror, from his causeless rigour to such amiable princesses as Hippolita and Matilda.

While the ladies were conveying the wretched mother to her bed, Manfred remained in the court, gazing on the ominous casque, and regardless of the crowd which the strangeness of the event had now assembled around him. The few words he articulated tended solely to inquiries, whether any man knew from whence it could have come? Nobody could give him the least information. However, as it seemed to be the sole object of his curiosity, it soon became so to the rest of the spectators, whose conjectures were as absurd and improbable, as the catastrophe itself was unprecedented. In the midst of their senseless guesses a young peasant, whom rumour had drawn thither from a neighbouring village, observed that the miraculous helmet was exactly like that on the figure in black marble of Alfonso the Good, one of their former princes, in the church of St. Nicholas. Villain! What sayest thou? cried Manfred, starting from his trance in a tempest of rage, and seizing the young man by the collar: How darest thou utter such treason? Thy life shall pay for it. The spectators, who as little comprehended the cause of the prince's fury as all the rest they had seen, were at a loss to unravel this new circumstance. The young peasant himself was still more astonished, not conceiving how he had offended the prince: yet recollecting himself, with a mixture of grace and humility, he disengaged himself from Manfred's gripe,[4] and then, with an obeisance which discovered more jealousy of innocence, than dismay,[5] he asked, with respect, of what he was guilty! Manfred, more enraged at the vigour, however decently exerted, with which the young man had shaken off his hold, than appeased by his submission, ordered his attendants to seize him, and,

---

[4]Grip.

[5]An obedience revealing more care for his own innocence than fear.

if he had not been withheld by his friends whom he had invited to the nuptials, would have poignarded[6] the peasant in their arms.

During this altercation, some of the vulgar spectators[7] had run to the great church, which stood near the castle, and came back open-mouthed, declaring that the helmet was missing from Alfonso's statue. Manfred, at this news, grew perfectly frantic; and, as if he sought a subject on which to vent the tempest within him, he rushed again on the young peasant, crying, Villain! monster! sorcerer! 'tis thou hast slain my son! The mob, who wanted some object within the scope of their capacities on whom they might discharge their bewildered reasonings, caught the words from the mouth of their lord, and re-echoed, Ay, ay, 'tis he, 'tis he: he has stolen the helmet from good Alfonso's tomb, and dashed out the brains of our young prince with it:—never reflecting how enormous the disproportion was between the marble helmet that had been in the church, and that of steel before their eyes; nor how impossible it was for a youth, seemingly not twenty, to wield a piece of armour of so prodigious a weight.

The folly of these ejaculations brought Manfred to himself: yet whether provoked at the peasant having observed the resemblance between the two helmets, and thereby led to the farther discovery of the absence of that in the church; or wishing to bury any fresh rumour under so impertinent a supposition; he gravely pronounced that the young man was certainly a necromancer,[8] and that till the church could take cognizance of the affair, he would have the magician, whom they had thus detected, kept prisoner under the helmet itself, which he ordered his attendants to raise, and place the young man under it; declaring he should be kept there without food, with which his own infernal art might furnish him.

It was in vain for the youth to represent[9] against this preposterous sentence: in vain did Manfred's friends endeavour to divert him from this savage and ill-grounded resolution. The generality[10] were charmed with their lord's decision, which to their apprehensions

---

[6]Stabbed; a poignard is a dagger.
[7]Peasants.
[8]Sorcerer.
[9]Contest.
[10]Public.

carried great appearance of justice, as the magician was to be punished by the very instrument with which he had offended: nor were they struck with the least compunction at[11] the probability of the youth being starved, for they firmly believed that by his diabolic skill he could easily supply himself with nutriment.

Manfred thus saw his commands even cheerfully obeyed; and appointing a guard with strict orders to prevent any food being conveyed to the prisoner, he dismissed his friends and attendants, and retired to his own chamber, after locking the gates of the castle, in which he suffered none but his domestics to remain.

In the mean time, the care and zeal of the young ladies had brought the princess Hippolita to herself, who amidst the transports of her own sorrow frequently demanded news of her lord, would have dismissed her attendants to watch over him, and at last enjoined Matilda to leave her, and visit and comfort her father. Matilda, who wanted[12] no affectionate duty to Manfred, though she trembled at his austerity, obeyed the orders of Hippolita, whom she tenderly recommended to Isabella; and enquiring of the domestics for her father, was informed that he was retired to his chamber, and had commanded that nobody should have admittance to him. Concluding that he was immersed in sorrow for the death of her brother, and fearing to renew his tears by the sight of his sole remaining child, she hesitated whether she should break in upon his affliction; yet solicitude for him, backed by the commands of her mother, encouraged her to venture disobeying the orders he had given; a fault she had never been guilty of before. The gentle timidity of her nature made her pause for some minutes at his door. She heard him traverse his chamber backwards and forwards with disordered steps; a mood which increased her apprehensions. She was however just going to beg admittance, when Manfred suddenly opened the door; and as it was now twilight, concurring with the disorder of his mind, he did not distinguish the person, but asked angrily who it was? Matilda replied trembling, My dearest father, it is I, your daughter. Manfred, stepping back hastily, cried, Begone! I do not want a daughter; and flinging back abruptly, clapped the door against the terrified Matilda.

[11]Guilt about.
[12]Lacked.

She was too well acquainted with her father's impetuosity to venture a second intrusion. When she had a little recovered the shock of so bitter a reception, she wiped away her tears, to prevent the additional stab that the knowledge of it would give to Hippolita, who questioned her in the most anxious terms on the health of Manfred, and how he bore his loss. Matilda assured her he was well, and supported his misfortune with manly fortitude. But will he not let me see him? said Hippolita mournfully: Will he not permit me to blend my tears with his, and shed a mother's sorrows in the bosom of her lord? Or do you deceive me, Matilda? I know how Manfred doted on his son: Is not the stroke too heavy for him? Has he not sunk under it?—You do not answer me—Alas, I dread the worst!—Raise me, my maidens: I will, I will see my lord. Bear me to him instantly; he is dearer to me even than my children. Matilda made signs to Isabella to prevent Hippolita's rising; and both those lovely young women were using their gentle violence to stop and calm the princess, when a servant on the part of Manfred arrived, and told Isabella that his lord demanded to speak with her.

With me! cried Isabella. Go, said Hippolita, relieved by a message from her lord: Manfred cannot support the sight of his own family. He thinks you less disordered than we are, and dreads the shock of my grief. Console him, dear Isabella, and tell him I will smother my own anguish rather than add to his.

It was now evening; the servant who conducted Isabella bore a torch before her. When they came to Manfred, who was walking impatiently about the gallery, he started, and said hastily, Take away that light, and begone. Then shutting the door impetuously, he flung himself upon a bench against the wall, and bade Isabella sit by him. She obeyed trembling. I sent for you, lady, said he,—and then stopped under great appearance of confusion. My lord!—Yes, I sent for you on a matter of great moment, resumed he:—Dry your tears, young lady—you have lost your bridegroom:—yes, cruel fate, and I have lost the hopes of my race![13]—But Conrad was not worthy of your beauty.—How! my lord, said Isabella; sure you do not suspect me of not feeling the concern I ought? My duty and affection would have always—Think no more of him, interrupted

---

[13]Hereditary line.

Gallery, Strawberry Hill (King Library, Miami University)

Manfred; he was a sickly, puny child, and heaven has perhaps taken him away that I might not trust the honours of my house on so frail a foundation. The line of Manfred calls for numerous supports. My foolish fondness for that boy blinded the eyes of my prudence—but it is better as it is. I hope in a few years to have reason to rejoice at the death of Conrad.

Words cannot paint the astonishment of Isabella. At first she apprehended that grief had disordered Manfred's understanding. Her next thought suggested that this strange discourse was designed to ensnare her: she feared that Manfred had perceived her indifference for his son: and in consequence of that idea she replied, Good my lord, do not doubt my tenderness; my heart would have accompanied my hand. Conrad would have engrossed all my care; and wherever fate shall dispose of me, I shall always cherish his memory, and regard your highness and the virtuous Hippolita as my parents. Curse on Hippolita! cried Manfred: forget her from this moment, as I do. In short, lady, you have missed a husband un-deserving of your charms: they shall now be better disposed of. In-stead of a sickly boy, you shall have a husband in the prime of his age, who will know how to value your beauties, and who may ex-pect a numerous offspring. Alas, my lord, said Isabella, my mind is too sadly engrossed by the recent catastrophe in your family to think of another marriage. If ever my father returns, and it shall be his pleasure, I shall obey, as I did when I consented to give my hand to your son:[14] but until his return, permit me to remain under your hospitable roof, and employ the melancholy hours in assuaging yours, Hippolita's, and the fair Matilda's affliction.

I desired you once before, said Manfred angrily, not to name that woman; from this hour she must be a stranger to you, as she must be to me:—in short, Isabella, since I cannot give you my son, I offer you myself.—Heavens! cried Isabella, waking from her delu-sion, what do I hear! You, my lord! You! My father in law! the fa-ther of Conrad! the husband of the virtuous and tender Hip-polita!—I tell you, said Manfred imperiously, Hippolita is no longer my wife; I divorce her from this hour.[15] Too long has she cursed me by her unfruitfulness: my fate depends on having sons,—and this night I trust will give a new date to my hopes. At those words he seized the cold hand of Isabella, who was half-dead with fright and horror. She shrieked, and started from him. Manfred rose to pursue her; when the moon, which was now up, and gleamed in at the opposite casement, presented to his sight the plumes of the fatal helmet, which rose to the height of the win-dows, waving backwards and forwards in a tempestuous manner, and accompanied with a hollow and rustling sound. Isabella, who gathered courage from her situation, and who dreaded nothing so much as Manfred's pursuit of his declaration, cried, Look, my lord! see heaven itself declares against your impious intentions!— Heaven nor hell shall impede my designs, said Manfred, advancing again to seize the princess. At that instant the portrait of his grand-

---

[14]Where land, money, and titles were at stake, a daughter could not exercise her own wishes about marriage but was expected to obey her father's determination. See pp. 239–40.

[15]By 18th-c. standards, Manfred's overture is incestuous; moreover, divorce was forbidden to Catholics (the Pope's refusal to grant Henry VIII an annulment led to the cataclysmic split of the English Church from Rome).

father, which hung over the bench where they had been sitting, uttered a deep sigh, and heaved its breast. Isabella, whose back was turned to the picture, saw not the motion, nor knew whence the sound came, but started and said, Hark, my lord! what sound was that? and at the same time made towards the door. Manfred, distracted between the flight of Isabella, who had now reached the stairs, and his inability to keep his eyes from the picture, which began to move, had however advanced some steps after her, still looking backwards on the portrait, when he saw it quit[16] its pannel, and descend on the floor with a grave and melancholy air. Do I dream? cried Manfred returning, or are the devils themselves in league against me? Speak, infernal spectre! Or, if thou art my grandsire, why dost thou too conspire against thy wretched descendant, who too dearly pays for—Ere he could finish the sentence the vision sighed again, and made a sign to Manfred to follow him. Lead on! cried Manfred; I will follow thee to the gulf of perdition. The spectre marched sedately, but dejected, to the end of the gallery, and turned into a chamber on the right hand. Manfred accompanied him at a little distance, full of anxiety and horror, but resolved. As he would have entered the chamber, the door was clapped-to with violence by an invisible hand. The prince, collecting courage from this delay, would have forcibly burst open the door with his foot, but found that it resisted his utmost efforts. Since hell will not satisfy my curiosity, said Manfred, I will use the human means in my power for preserving my race; Isabella shall not escape me.

That lady, whose resolution had given way to terror the moment she had quitted Manfred, continued her flight to the bottom of the principal staircase. There she stopped, not knowing whither to direct her steps, nor how to escape from the impetuosity of the prince. The gates of the castle she knew were locked, and guards placed in the court. Should she, as her heart prompted her, go and prepare Hippolita for the cruel destiny that awaited her, she did not doubt but Manfred would seek her there, and that his violence would incite him to double the injury he meditated, without leaving room for them to avoid the impetuosity of his passions. Delay might give him time to reflect on the horrid measures he had conceived, or

---

[16]Leave.

STAIRCASE AT STRAWBERRY HILL.

Staircase, Strawberry Hill (King Library, Miami University)

produce some circumstance in her favour, if she could for that night, at least avoid his odious purpose.—Yet where conceal herself! How avoid the pursuit he would infallibly make throughout the castle! As these thoughts passed rapidly through her mind, she recollected a subterraneous passage which led from the vaults of the castle to the church of saint Nicholas. Could she reach the altar before she was overtaken, she knew even Manfred's violence would not dare to profane the sacredness of the place; and she determined, if no other means of deliverance offered, to shut herself up for ever among the holy virgins, whose convent was contiguous to the cathedral. In this resolution, she seized a lamp that burned at the foot of the staircase, and hurried towards the secret passage.

The lower part of the castle was hollowed into several intricate cloisters; and it was not easy for one under so much anxiety to find the door that opened into the cavern.[17] An awful silence reigned throughout those subterraneous regions, except now and then some blasts of wind that shook the doors she had passed, and which grating on the rusty hinges were re-echoed through that long labyrinth of darkness. Every murmur struck her with new terror;— yet more she dreaded to hear the wrathful voice of Manfred urging his domestics to pursue her. She trod as softly as impatience would give her leave,—yet frequently stopped and listened to hear if she was followed. In one of those moments she thought she heard a sigh. She shuddered, and recoiled a few paces. In a moment she thought she heard the step of some person. Her blood curdled; she concluded it was Manfred. Every suggestion that horror could inspire rushed into her mind. She condemned her rash flight, which had thus exposed her to his rage in a place where her cries were not likely to draw anybody to her assistance.—Yet the sound seemed not to come from behind;—if Manfred knew where she was, he must have followed her: she was still in one of the cloisters, and the steps she had heard were too distinct to proceed from the way she had come. Cheered with this reflection, and hoping to find a friend in whoever was not the prince; she was going to advance, when a door that stood a-jar, at some distance to the left, was opened gently; but ere her lamp, which she held up, could discover who opened it, the person retreated precipitately on seeing the light.

Isabella, whom every incident was sufficient to dismay, hesitated whether she should proceed. Her dread of Manfred soon outweighed every other terror. The very circumstance of the person avoiding her, gave her a sort of courage. It could only be, she

---

[17]Underground tunnel to the church.

thought, some domestic belonging to the castle. Her gentleness had never raised her an enemy, and conscious innocence made her hope that, unless sent by the prince's order to seek her, his servants would rather assist than prevent her flight. Fortifying herself with these reflections, and believing by what she could observe that she was near the mouth of the subterraneous cavern, she approached the door that had been opened; but a sudden gust of wind that met her at the door extinguished her lamp, and left her in total darkness.

Words cannot paint the horror of the princess's situation. Alone in so dismal a place, her mind imprinted with all the terrible events of the day, hopeless of escaping, expecting every moment the arrival of Manfred, and far from tranquil on knowing she was within reach of somebody, she knew not whom, who for some cause seemed concealed thereabouts; all these thoughts crowded on her distracted mind, and she was ready to sink under her apprehensions. She addressed herself to every saint in heaven, and inwardly implored their assistance. For a considerable time she remained in an agony of despair. At last, as softly as was possible, she felt for the door, and having found it, entered trembling into the vault from whence she had heard the sigh and steps. It gave her a kind of momentary joy to perceive an imperfect ray of clouded moonshine gleam from the roof of the vault, which seemed to be fallen in, and from whence hung a fragment of earth or building, she could not distinguish which, that appeared to have been crushed inwards. She advanced eagerly towards this chasm, when she discerned a human form standing close against the wall.

She shrieked, believing it the ghost of her betrothed Conrad. The figure advancing, said, in a submissive voice, Be not alarmed, lady; I will not injure you. Isabella, a little encouraged by the words and tone of voice of the stranger, and recollecting that this must be the person who had opened the door, recovered her spirits enough to reply, Sir, whoever you are, take pity on a wretched princess, standing on the brink of destruction: assist me to escape from this fatal castle, or in a few moments I may be made miserable for ever. Alas! said the stranger, what can I do to assist you? I will die in your defence; but I am unacquainted with the castle, and want— Oh! said Isabella, hastily interrupting him; help me but to find a trap-door that must be hereabout, and it is the greatest service you can do me, for I have not a minute to lose. Saying these words, she felt about on the pavement, and directed the stranger to search likewise, for a smooth piece of brass enclosed in one of the stones. That, said she, is the lock, which opens with a spring, of which I know the secret. If we can find that, I may escape—if not, alas, courteous stranger, I fear I shall have involved you in my misfortunes: Manfred will suspect you for the accomplice of my flight, and you will fall a victim to his resentment. I value not my life, said the stranger; and it will be some comfort to lose it in trying to deliver you from his tyranny. Generous youth, said Isabella, how shall I ever requite—As she uttered those words, a ray of moonshine, streaming through a cranny of the ruin above, shone directly on the lock they sought—Oh, transport! said Isabella, here is the trap-door! and taking out the key, she touched the spring, which starting aside, discovered an iron ring. Lift up the door, said the princess. The stranger obeyed; and beneath appeared some stone steps descending into a vault totally dark. We must go down here, said Isabella: follow me; dark and dismal as it is, we cannot miss our way; it leads directly to the church of saint Nicholas—But perhaps, added the princess modestly, you have no reason to leave the castle, nor have I farther occasion for your service; in a few minutes I shall be safe from Manfred's rage—only let me know to whom I am so much obliged. I will never quit you, said the stranger eagerly, till I have placed you in safety—nor think me, princess, more generous than I am: though you are my principal care—The stranger was interrupted by a sudden noise of voices that seemed approaching, and they soon distinguished these words: Talk not to me of necromancers; I tell you she must be in the castle; I will find her in spite of enchantment.—Oh, heavens! cried Isabella, it is the voice of Manfred! Make haste, or we are ruined! and shut the trap-door after you. Saying this, she descended the steps precipitately; and as the stranger hastened to follow her, he let the door slip out of his hands: it fell, and the spring closed over it. He tried in vain to open it, not having observed Isabella's method of touching the spring, nor had he many moments to make an essay.[18] The noise of the falling door had been heard by Manfred, who, directed by the sound, hastened thither, attended by his servants with torches. It must be Isabella, cried Manfred before he entered the vault; she is

---

[18]Attempt.

escaping by the subterraneous passage, but she cannot have got far.—What was the astonishment of the prince when, instead of Isabella, the light of the torches discovered to him the young peasant, whom he thought confined under the fatal helmet! Traitor! said Manfred, how camest thou here? I thought thee in durance[19] above in the court. I am no traitor, replied the young man boldly, nor am I answerable for your thoughts. Presumptuous villain! cried Manfred, dost thou provoke my wrath? Tell me; how hast thou escaped from above? Thou hast corrupted thy guards, and their lives shall answer it. My poverty, said the peasant calmly, will disculpate[20] them: though the ministers of a tyrant's wrath, to thee they are faithful, and but too willing to execute the orders which you unjustly imposed upon them. Art thou so hardy as to dare my vengeance? said the prince—but tortures shall force the truth from thee. Tell me, I will know thy accomplices. There was my accomplice! said the youth smiling, and pointing to the roof. Manfred ordered the torches to be held up, and perceived that one of the cheeks of the enchanted casque had forced its way through the pavement of the court, as his servants had let it fall over the peasant, and had broken through into the vault, leaving a gap through which the peasant had pressed himself some minutes before he was found by Isabella. Was that the way by which thou didst descend? said Manfred. It was, said the youth. But what noise was that, said Manfred, which I heard as I entered the cloister? A door clapped, said the peasant: I heard it as well as you. What door? said Manfred hastily. I am not acquainted with your castle, said the peasant; this is the first time I ever entered it, and this vault the only part of it within which I ever was. But I tell thee, said Manfred [wishing to find out if the youth had discovered the trap-door], it was this way I heard the noise: my servants heard it too.—My lord, interrupted one of them officiously, to be sure it was the trap-door, and he was going to make his escape. Peace, blockhead, said the prince angrily; if he was going to escape, how should he come on this side? I will know from his own mouth what noise it was I heard. Tell me truly; thy life depends on thy veracity. My veracity is dearer to me than my life, said the peasant; nor would I purchase the one by forfeiting

---

[19]Imprisoned.

[20]Exculpate; prove innocent.

the other. Indeed! young philosopher! said Manfred contemptu-
ously: tell me then, what was the noise I heard? Ask me what I can
answer, said he, and put me to death instantly if I tell you a lie.
Manfred, growing impatient at the steady valour and indifference
of the youth, cried, Well then, thou man of truth! answer; was it the
fall of the trap-door that I heard? It was, said the youth. It was!
said the prince; and how didst thou come to know there was a trap-
door here? I saw the plate of brass by a gleam of moonshine,
replied he. But what told thee it was a lock? said Manfred: How
didst thou discover the secret of opening it? Providence, that delivered me from the helmet, was able to direct me to the spring of a
lock, said he. Providence should have gone a little farther, and have
placed thee out of the reach of my resentment, said Manfred: when
Providence had taught thee to open the lock, it abandoned thee for
a fool, who did not know how to make use of its favours. Why didst
thou not pursue the path pointed out for thy escape? Why didst thou
shut the trap-door before thou hadst descended the steps? I might
ask you, my lord, said the peasant, how I, totally unacquainted with
your castle, was to know that those steps led to any outlet? but I
scorn to evade your questions. Wherever those steps lead to, perhaps
I should have explored the way—I could not be in a worse situation
than I was. But the truth is, I let the trap-door fall: your immediate
arrival followed. I had given the alarm—what imported it to me
whether I was seized a minute sooner or a minute later? Thou art a
resolute villain for thy years, said Manfred—yet on reflection I suspect thou dost but trifle with me: thou hast not yet told me how thou
didst open the lock. That I will show you, my lord, said the peasant;
and, taking up a fragment of stone that had fallen from above, he
laid himself on the trap-door, and began to beat on the piece of brass
that covered it; meaning to gain time for the escape of the princess.
This presence of mind, joined to the frankness of the youth, staggered Manfred. He even felt a disposition towards pardoning one
who had been guilty of no crime. Manfred was not one of those savage tyrants who wanton in cruelty unprovoked. The circumstances
of his fortune had given an asperity[21] to his temper, which was naturally humane; and his virtues were always ready to operate, when his
passions did not obscure his reason.

---

[21]Harshness.

While the prince was in this suspense, a confused noise of voices echoed through the distant vaults. As the sound approached, he distinguished the clamours of some of his domestics, whom he had dispersed through the castle in search of Isabella, calling out, Where is my lord? Where is the prince? Here I am, said Manfred, as they came nearer; have you found the princess? The first that arrived, replied, Oh, my lord! I am glad we have found you.—Found me! said Manfred: have you found the princess? We thought we had, my lord, said the fellow, looking terrified—but—But what? cried the prince: has she escaped? Jaquez and I, my lord—Yes, I and Diego, interrupted the second, who came up in still greater consternation—Speak one of you at a time, said Manfred; I ask you, where is the princess? We do not know, said they both together: but we are frightened out of our wits.—So I think, blockheads, said Manfred: what is it has scared you thus?—Oh, my lord! said Jaquez, Diego has seen such a sight! your highness would not believe our eyes.—What new absurdity is this? cried Manfred—Give me a direct answer, or by heaven—Why, my lord, if it please your highness to hear me, said the poor fellow; Diego and I—Yes, I and Jaquez, cried his comrade—Did not I forbid you to speak both at a time? said the prince: You, Jaquez, answer; for the other fool seems more distracted than thou art; what is the matter? My gracious lord, said Jaquez, if it please your highness to hear me; Diego and I, according to your highness's orders, went to search for the young lady; but being comprehensive[22] that we might meet the ghost of my young lord, your highness's son, God rest his soul, as he has not received christian burial—Sot![23] cried Manfred in a rage, is it only a ghost then that thou hast seen? Oh, worse! worse! my lord, cried Diego: I had rather have seen ten whole ghosts.—Grant me patience! said Manfred; these blockheads distract me—Out of my sight, Diego! And thou, Jaquez, tell me in one word, art thou sober? art thou raving? Thou wast wont to[24] have some sense: has the other sot frightened himself and thee too? Speak; what is it he fancies he has seen? Why, my lord, replied Jaquez, trembling, I was going to tell your highness, that since the calamitous misfortune of

---

[22]Apprehensive.

[23]Drunkard.

[24]Usually.

my young lord, God rest his soul! not one of us your highness's faithful servants, indeed we are, my lord, though poor men; I say, not one of us has dared to set a foot about the castle, but two together: so Diego and I, thinking that my young lady might be in the great gallery, went up there to look for her, and tell her your highness wanted something to impart to her.—O blundering fools! cried Manfred: and in the mean time, she has made her escape, because you were afraid of goblins! Why, thou knave! she left me in the gallery; I came from thence myself.—For all that, she may be there still for aught I know, said Jaquez; but the devil shall have me before I seek her there again!—Poor Diego! I do not believe he will ever recover it. Recover what? said Manfred; am I never to learn what it is has terrified these rascals? But I lose my time; follow me, slave! I will see if she is in the gallery.—For heaven's sake, my dear good lord, cried Jaquez, do not go to the gallery! Satan himself I believe is in the chamber next to the gallery.—Manfred, who hitherto had treated the terror of his servants as an idle panic, was struck at this new circumstance. He recollected the apparition of the portrait, and the sudden closing of the door at the end of the gallery—his voice faltered, and he asked with disorder, what is in the great chamber? My lord, said Jaquez, when Diego and I came into the gallery, he went first, for he said he had more courage than I. So when we came into the gallery, we found nobody. We looked under every bench and stool; and still we found nobody.—Were all the pictures in their places? said Manfred. Yes, my lord, answered Jaquez; but we did not think of looking behind them.—Well, well! said Manfred; proceed. When we came to the door of the great chamber, continued Jaquez, we found it shut.—And could not you open it? said Manfred. Oh! yes, my lord; would to heaven we had not! replied he—Nay, it was not I neither, it was Diego: he was grown fool-hardy, and would go on, though I advised him not—If ever I open a door that is shut again—Trifle not, said Manfred, shuddering, but tell me what you saw in the great chamber on opening the door.—I! my lord! said Jaquez, I saw nothing; I was behind Diego;—but I heard the noise.—Jaquez, said Manfred, in a solemn tone of voice; tell me, I adjure[25] thee by the souls of my ancestors, what was it thou sawest; what was it thou heardest? It was

---

[25]Charge.

Diego saw it, my lord, it was not I, replied Jaquez; I only heard the noise. Diego had no sooner opened the door, than he cried out and ran back—I ran back too, and said, Is it the ghost? The ghost! No, no, said Diego, and his hair stood on end—it is a giant, I believe; he is all clad in armour, for I saw his foot and part of his leg, and they are as large as the helmet below in the court. As he said these words, my lord, we heard a violent motion and the rattling of armour, as if the giant was rising; for Diego has told me since, that he believes the giant was lying down, for the foot and leg were stretched at length on the floor. Before we could get to the end of the gallery, we heard the door of the great chamber clap behind us, but we did not dare turn back to see if the giant was following us— Yet now I think on it, we must have heard him if he had pursued us—But for heaven's sake, good my lord, send for the chaplain and have the castle exorcised, for, for certain, it is enchanted. Ay, pray do, my lord, cried all the servants at once, or we must leave your highness's service.—Peace, dotards! said Manfred, and follow me; I will know what all this means. We! my lord! cried they with one voice; we would not go up to the gallery for your highness's revenue.[26] The young peasant, who had stood silent, now spoke. Will your highness, said he, permit me to try this adventure? My life is of consequence to nobody: I fear no bad angel, and have offended no good one. Your behaviour is above your seeming,[27] said Manfred; viewing him with surprise and admiration—hereafter I will reward your bravery—but now, continued he with a sigh, I am so circumstanced, that I dare trust no eyes but my own—However, I give you leave to accompany me.

Manfred, when he first followed Isabella from the gallery, had gone directly to the apartment of his wife, concluding the princess had retired thither. Hippolita, who knew his step, rose with anxious fondness to meet her lord, whom she had not seen since the death of their son. She would have flown in a transport mixed of joy and grief to his bosom; but he pushed her rudely off, and said, Where is Isabella? Isabella! my lord! said the astonished Hippolita. Yes, Isabella; cried Manfred imperiously; I want Isabella. My lord, replied Matilda, who perceived how much his behaviour had

---

[26] Annual income from land-rents.

[27] Appearance (as a peasant).

shocked her mother, she has not been with us since your highness summoned her to your apartment. Tell me where she is, said the prince; I do not want to know where she has been. My good lord, says Hippolita, your daughter tells you the truth: Isabella left us by your command, and has not returned since:—but, my good lord, compose yourself: retire to your rest: this dismal day has disordered you. Isabella shall wait your orders in the morning. What, then you know where she is? cried Manfred: tell me directly, for I will not lose an instant—And you, woman, speaking to his wife, order your chaplain to attend me forthwith. Isabella, said Hippolita calmly, is retired I suppose to her chamber: she is not accustomed to watch at this late hour. Gracious my lord, continued she, let me know what has disturbed you: has Isabella offended you? Trouble me not with questions, said Manfred, but tell me where she is. Matilda shall call her, said the princess—sit down, my lord, and resume your wonted fortitude.—What, art thou jealous of Isabella? replied he, that you wish to be present at our interview? Good heavens! my lord, said Hippolita, what is it your highness means? Thou wilt know ere many minutes are passed, said the cruel prince. Send your chaplain to me, and wait my pleasure here. At these words he flung out of the room in search of Isabella; leaving the amazed ladies thunder-struck with his words and frantic deportment, and lost in vain conjectures on what he was meditating.

Manfred was now returning from the vault, attended by the peasant and a few of his servants whom he had obliged to accompany him. He ascended the stair-case without stopping till he arrived at the gallery, at the door of which he met Hippolita and her chaplain. When Diego had been dismissed by Manfred, he had gone directly to the princess's apartment with the alarm of what he had seen. That excellent lady, who no more than Manfred doubted of the reality of the vision, yet affected to treat it as a delirium of the servant. Willing, however, to save her lord from any additional shock, and prepared by a series of griefs not to tremble at any accession to it; she determined to make herself the first sacrifice, if fate had marked the present hour for their destruction. Dismissing the reluctant Matilda to her rest, who in vain sued for leave to accompany her mother, and attended only by her chaplain, Hippolita had visited the gallery and great chamber: and now, with more serenity of soul than she had felt for many hours, she met her lord, and assured him that the vision of the gigantic leg and foot was all a fable; and no doubt an impression made by fear, and the dark and dismal hour of the night, on the minds of his servants: She and the chaplain had examined the chamber, and found everything in the usual order.

Manfred, though persuaded, like his wife, that the vision had been no work of fancy, recovered a little from the tempest of mind into which so many strange events had thrown him. Ashamed too of his inhuman treatment of a princess, who returned every injury with new marks of tenderness and duty, he felt returning love forcing itself into his eyes—but not less ashamed of feeling remorse towards one, against whom he was inwardly meditating a yet more bitter outrage, he curbed the yearnings of his heart, and did not dare to lean even towards pity. The next transition of his soul was to exquisite villainy. Presuming on the unshaken submission of Hippolita, he flattered himself that she would not only acquiesce with patience to a divorce, but would obey, if it was his pleasure, in endeavouring to persuade Isabella to give him her hand—But ere he could indulge this horrid hope, he reflected that Isabella was not to be found. Coming to himself, he gave orders that every avenue to the castle should be strictly guarded, and charged his domestics on pain of their lives to suffer nobody to pass out. The young peasant, to whom he spoke favourably, he ordered to remain in a small chamber on the stairs, in which there was a pallet-bed,[28] and the key of which he took away himself, telling the youth he would talk with him in the morning. Then dismissing his attendants, and bestowing a sullen kind of half-nod on Hippolita, he retired to his own chamber.

[28]Meager straw bed.

Chapter II

Matilda, who by Hippolita's order had retired to her apartment, was ill-disposed to take any rest. The shocking fate of her brother had deeply affected her. She was surprised at not seeing Isabella; but the strange words which had fallen from her father, and his obscure menace to the princess his wife, accompanied by the most furious behaviour, had filled her gentle mind with terror and alarm. She waited anxiously for the return of Bianca, a young damsel that attended her, whom she had sent to learn what was become of Isabella. Bianca soon appeared, and informed her mistress of what she had gathered from the servants, that Isabella was nowhere to be found. She related the adventure of the young peasant who had been discovered in the vault, though with many simple additions from the incoherent accounts of the domestics; and she dwelt principally on the gigantic leg and foot which had been seen in the gallery-chamber. This last circumstance had terrified Bianca so much, that she was rejoiced when Matilda told her that she would not go to rest, but would watch till the princess should rise.

The young princess wearied herself in conjectures on the flight of Isabella, and on the threats of Manfred to her mother. But what business could he have so urgent with the chaplain? said Matilda. Does he intend to have my brother's body interred privately in the chapel? Oh! madam, said Bianca, now I guess. As you are become his heiress, he is impatient to have you married: he has always been raving for more sons; I warrant he is now impatient for grandsons. As sure as I live, Madam, I shall see you a bride at last. Good madam, you won't cast off your faithful Bianca: you won't put Donna Rosara over me, now you are a great princess. My poor Bianca, said Matilda, how fast your thoughts amble! I a great princess! What hast thou seen in Manfred's behaviour since my brother's death that bespeaks any increase of tenderness to me? No, Bianca, his heart was ever a stranger to me—but he is my father, and I must not complain. Nay, if heaven shuts my father's heart against me, it over-pays my little merit in the tenderness of my mother—O that dear mother! Yes, Bianca, 'tis there I feel the rugged temper of Manfred. I can support his harshness to me with patience; but it wounds my soul when I am witness to his causeless severity towards her. Oh, madam, said Bianca, all men use their wives so, when they are weary of them.—And yet you congratulated me but now, said Matilda, when you fancied my father intended to dispose of me! I would have you a great lady, replied Bianca, come what will. I do not wish to see you moped[1] in a convent, as you would be if you had your will, and if my lady your mother, who knows that a bad husband is better than no husband at all, did not hinder you.—Bless me! what noise is that! Saint Nicholas forgive me! I was but in jest. It is the wind, said Matilda, whistling through the battlements in the tower above: you have heard it a thousand times. Nay, said Bianca, there was no harm neither in what I said: it is no sin to talk of matrimony—And so, madam, as I was saying, if my lord Manfred should offer you a handsome young prince for a bridegroom, you would drop him a curtsey, and tell him you would rather take the veil? Thank Heaven! I am in no such danger, said Matilda: you know how many proposals for me he has rejected.—And you thank him, like a dutiful daughter, do you, madam?—But come, madam; suppose, tomorrow morning he was to send for you to the great council-chamber, and there you should find at his elbow a lovely young prince, with large black eyes, a smooth white forehead, and manly curling locks like jet; in short, madam, a young hero resembling the picture of the good Alfonso in the gallery, which you sit and gaze at for hours together.—Do not speak lightly of that picture, interrupted Matilda sighing: I know the adoration with which I look at that picture is uncommon—but I am not in love with a coloured pannel. The character of that virtuous prince, the veneration with which my mother has inspired me for his memory, the orisons[2] which, I know not why, she has enjoined me to pour forth at his tomb, all have concurred to persuade me that somehow or other my destiny is linked with something relating to him.—Lord! madam, how should that be? said Bianca: I have always heard that your family was in no way related to his: and I am sure I cannot conceive why my lady, the princess, sends you in a cold morning, or a damp evening, to pray at his tomb: he is no saint by the almanack. If you must pray, why does she not bid you address yourself to our great saint Nicholas? I am sure he is the saint I pray to

[1]Moping about.
[2]Prayers.

for a husband. Perhaps my mind would be less affected, said Matilda, if my mother would explain her reasons to me: but it is the mystery she observes, that inspires me with this—I know not what to call it. As she never acts from caprice, I am sure there is some fatal secret at bottom—nay, I know there is: in her agony of grief for my brother's death she dropped some words that intimated as much. Oh, dear madam, cried Bianca, what were they? No, said Matilda: if a parent lets fall a word, and wishes it recalled, it is not for a child to utter it. What! was she sorry for what she had said? asked Bianca—I am sure, madam, you may trust me.—With my own little secrets when I have any, I may, said Matilda; but never with my mother's: a child ought to have no ears or eyes but as a parent directs. Well! to be sure, madam, you were born to be a saint, said Bianca, and there is no resisting one's vocation: you will end in a convent at last. But there is my lady Isabella would not be so reserved to me: she will let me talk to her of young men; and when a handsome cavalier has come to the castle, she has owned to me that she wished your brother Conrad resembled him. Bianca, said the princess, I do not allow you to mention my friend disrespectfully. Isabella is of a cheerful disposition, but her soul is pure as virtue itself. She knows your idle babbling humour, and perhaps has now and then encouraged it, to divert melancholy, and to enliven the solitude in which my father keeps us.—Blessed Mary! said Bianca starting, there it is again!—Dear madam, do you hear nothing?—This castle is certainly haunted!—Peace! said Matilda, and listen! I did think I heard a voice—but it must be fancy; your terrors I suppose have infected me. Indeed! indeed! madam, said Bianca, half-weeping with agony, I am sure I heard a voice. Does any body lie in the chamber beneath? said the princess. Nobody has dared to lie there, answered Bianca, since the great astrologer that was your brother's tutor drowned himself. For certain, madam, his ghost and the young prince's are now met in the chamber below—for heaven's sake let us fly to your mother's apartment! I charge you not to stir, said Matilda. If they are spirits in pain, we may ease their sufferings by questioning them. They can mean no hurt to us, for we have not injured them—and if they should, shall we be more safe in one chamber than in another? Reach me my beads; we will say a prayer, and then speak to them. Oh! dear lady, I would not speak to a ghost for the world, cried Bianca—As she said those words, they heard the casement of the little chamber below Matilda's open. They listened attentively, and in a few minutes thought they heard a person sing, but could not distinguish the words. This can be no evil spirit, said the princess in a low voice: it is undoubtedly one of the family[3]—open the window, and we shall know the voice. I dare not indeed, madam, said Bianca. Thou art a very fool, said Matilda, opening the window gently herself. The noise the princess made was however heard by the person beneath, who stopped, and, they concluded, had heard the casement open. Is anybody below? said the princess: if there is, speak. Yes, said an unknown voice. Who is it? said Matilda. A stranger, replied the voice. What stranger? said she; and how didst thou come there at this unusual hour, when all the gates of the castle are locked? I am not here willingly, answered the voice—but pardon me, lady, if I have disturbed your rest: I knew not that I was overheard. Sleep had forsaken me: I left a restless couch, and came to waste the irksome hours with gazing on the fair approach of morning, impatient to be dismissed from this castle. Thy words and accents, said Matilda, are of melancholy cast; if thou art unhappy, I pity thee. If poverty afflicts thee, let me know it; I will mention thee to the princess, whose beneficent soul ever melts for the distressed; and she will relieve thee. I am indeed unhappy, said the stranger; and I know not what wealth is: but I do not complain of the lot which heaven has cast for me: I am young and healthy, and am not ashamed of owing my support to myself—yet think me not proud, or that I disdain your generous offers. I will remember you in my orisons, and will pray for blessings on your gracious self and your noble mistress—If I sigh, lady, it is for others, not for myself. Now I have it, madam, said Bianca, whispering the princess. This is certainly the young peasant; and by my conscience he is in love!— Well, this is a charming adventure!—Do, madam, let us sift him. He does not know you, but takes you for one of my lady Hippolita's women. Art thou not ashamed, Bianca? said the princess: what right have we to pry into the secrets of this young man's heart? He seems virtuous and frank, and tells us he is unhappy: are those circumstances that authorize us to make a property of him?[4] How

---

[3]All the residents of the household, including retainers and servants.
[4]Pry.

are we entitled to his confidence? Lord! madam, how little you know of love! replied Bianca: why, lovers have no pleasure equal to talking of their mistress. And would you have *me* become a peasant's confidante? said the princess. Well then, let me talk to him, said Bianca: though I have the honour of being your highness's maid of honour, I was not always so great: besides, if love levels ranks, it raises them too: I have a respect for any young man in love. Peace, simpleton! said the princess. Though he said he was unhappy, it does not follow that he must be in love. Think of all that has happened today, and tell me if there are no misfortunes but what love causes. Stranger, resumed the princess, if thy misfortunes have not been occasioned by thy own fault, and are within the compass of the princess Hippolita's power to redress, I will take upon me to answer that she will be thy protectress. When thou art dismissed from this castle, repair to holy father Jerome at the convent adjoining to the church of saint Nicholas, and make thy story known to him, as far as thou thinkest meet: he will not fail to inform the princess, who is the mother of all that want her assistance. Farewell; it is not seemly for me to hold farther converse with a man at this unwonted hour. May the saints guard thee, gracious lady! replied the peasant—but oh, if a poor and worthless stranger might presume to beg a minute's audience farther—am I so happy?—the casement is not shut—might I venture to ask—Speak quickly, said Matilda; the morning dawns apace: should the labourers come into the fields and perceive us—What wouldst thou ask—I know not how—I know not if I dare, said the young stranger, faltering—yet the humanity with which you have spoken to me emboldens—Lady! dare I trust you?—Heavens! said Matilda, what dost thou mean? with what wouldst thou trust me? Speak boldly, if thy secret is fit to be entrusted to a virtuous breast.—I would ask, said the peasant, recollecting himself, whether what I have heard from the domestics is true, that the princess is missing from the castle? What imports it to thee to know? replied Matilda. Thy first words bespoke a prudent and becoming gravity. Dost thou come hither to pry into the secrets of Manfred? Adieu. I have been mistaken in thee.—Saying these words she shut the casement hastily, without giving the young man time to reply. I had acted more wisely, said the princess to Bianca, with some sharpness, if I had let thee converse with this peasant;

his inquisitiveness seems of a piece with thy own. It is not fit for me to argue with your highness, replied Bianca; but perhaps the questions I should have put to him, would have been more to the purpose, than those you have been pleased to ask him. Oh, no doubt, said Matilda; you are a very discreet personage! May I know what *you* would have asked him? A by-stander often sees more of the game than those that play, answered Bianca. Does your highness think, madam, that this question about my lady Isabella was the result of mere curiosity? No, no, madam, there is more in it than you great folks are aware of. Lopez told me that all the servants believe this young fellow contrived my lady Isabella's escape—Now, pray, madam, observe—You and I both know that my Lady Isabella never much fancied the prince your brother.—Well! he is killed just in a critical minute—I accuse nobody. A helmet falls from the moon—so my lord your father says; but Lopez and all the servants say that this young spark[5] is a magician, and stole it from Alfonso's tomb.—Have done with this rhapsody of impertinence, said Matilda. Nay, madam, as you please, cried Bianca—yet it is very particular though, that my lady Isabella should be missing the very same day, and that this young sorcerer should be found at the mouth of the trap-door—I accuse nobody—but if my young lord came honestly by his death—Dare not on thy duty, said Matilda, to breathe a suspicion on the purity of my dear Isabella's fame.— Purity, or not purity, said Bianca, gone she is: a stranger is found that nobody knows: you question him yourself: he tells you he is in love, or unhappy, it is the same thing—nay, he owned he was unhappy about others; and is any body unhappy about another, unless they are in love with them? And at the very next word he asks innocently, pour soul! if my lady Isabella is missing.—To be sure, said Matilda, thy observations are not totally without foundation— Isabella's flight amazes me: the curiosity of this stranger is very particular—yet Isabella never concealed a thought from me.—So she told you, said Bianca, to fish out your secrets—but who knows, madam, but this stranger may be some prince in disguise? Do, madam, let me open the window, and ask him a few questions. No, replied Matilda, I will ask him myself, if he knows aught of Isabella: he is not worthy I should converse farther with him. She

[5]Attention-getter.

was going to open the casement, when they heard the bell ring at the postern-gate[6] of the castle, which is on the right hand of the tower, where Matilda lay. This prevented the princess from renewing the conversation with the stranger.

After continuing silent for some time; I am persuaded, said she to Bianca, that whatever be the cause of Isabella's flight it had no unworthy motive. If this stranger was accessory to it, she must be satisfied with his fidelity and worth. I observed, did not you, Bianca? that his words were tinctured with an uncommon infusion of piety. It was no ruffian's speech; his phrases were becoming a man of gentle birth.[7] I told you, Madam, said Bianca, that I was sure he was some prince in disguise.—Yet, said Matilda, if he was privy to her escape, how will you account for his not accompanying her in her flight? Why expose himself unnecessarily and rashly to my father's resentment? As for that, madam, replied she, if he could get from under the helmet, he will find ways of eluding your father's anger. I do not doubt but he has some talisman or other about him.—You resolve everything into magic, said Matilda—but a man who has any intercourse with infernal spirits does not dare to make use of those tremendous and holy words which he uttered. Didst thou not observe with what fervour he vowed to remember *me* to heaven in his prayers? Yes, Isabella was undoubtedly convinced of his piety.—Commend me to the piety of a young fellow and a damsel that consult to elope! said Bianca. No, no, madam; my lady Isabella is of another guess mould[8] than you take her for. She used indeed to sigh and lift up her eyes in your company, because she knows you are a saint—but when your back was turned—You wrong her, said Matilda; Isabella is no hypocrite: she has a due sense of devotion, but never affected a call she has not. On the contrary, she always combated my inclination for the cloister: and though I own the mystery she has made to me of her flight confounds me; though it seems inconsistent with the friendship between us; I cannot forget the disinterested warmth with which she always opposed my taking the veil: she wished to see me married, though my dower would have been a loss to her and my brother's

[6]Back gate.
[7]Nobility.
[8]Type.

GARDEN GATE.

Garden Gate, Strawberry Hill (King Library, Miami University)

children.[9] For her sake I will believe well of this young peasant. Then you do think there is some liking between them? said Bianca.—While she was speaking, a servant came hastily into the chamber and told the princess that the lady Isabella was found.

[9]A bride typically brought money and/or lands to her husband's family; by the early 18th c., such dowries were considerable fortunes.

Where? said Matilda. She has taken sanctuary in saint Nicholas's church, replied the servant: father Jerome has brought the news himself; he is below with his highness. Where is my mother? said Matilda. She is in her own chamber, madam, and has asked for you.

Manfred had risen at the first dawn of light, and gone to Hippolita's apartment, to enquire if she knew aught of Isabella. While he was questioning her, word was brought that Jerome demanded to speak with him. Manfred, little suspecting the cause of the Friar's arrival, and knowing he was employed by Hippolita in her charities, ordered him to be admitted, intending to leave them together, while he pursued his search after Isabella. Is your business with me or the princess? said Manfred. With both, replied the holy man. The lady Isabella—What of her? interrupted Manfred eagerly—is at saint Nicholas's altar, replied Jerome. That is no business of Hippolita, said Manfred with confusion: let us retire to my chamber, father; and inform me how she came thither. No, my lord, replied the good man, with an air of firmness and authority that daunted even the resolute Manfred, who could not help revering the saint-like virtues of Jerome: my commission is to both, and with your highness's good-liking, in the presence of both I shall deliver it—But first, my lord, I must interrogate the princess, whether she is acquainted with the cause of the lady Isabella's retirement from your castle.—No, on my soul, said Hippolita; does Isabella charge me with being privy to it?—Father, interrupted Manfred, I pay due reverence to your holy profession; but I am sovereign here, and will allow no meddling priest to interfere in the affairs of my domestic.[10] If you have aught to say attend me to my chamber; I do not use to let my wife be acquainted with the secret affairs of my state; they are not within a woman's province. My lord, said the holy man, I am no intruder into the secrets of families. My office is to promote peace, to heal divisions, to preach repentance, and teach mankind to curb their headstrong passions. I forgive your highness's uncharitable apostrophe: I know my duty, and am the minister of a mightier prince than Manfred. Hearken to him who speaks through my organs. Manfred trembled with rage and shame. Hippolita's countenance declared her astonishment, and impatience to know where this would end: her silence more strongly spoke her observance of Manfred.

[10]Domestic affairs.

The lady Isabella, resumed Jerome, commends herself to both your highnesses; she thanks both for the kindness with which she has been treated in your castle: she deplores the loss of your son, and her own misfortune in not becoming the daughter of such wise and noble princes, whom she shall always respect as *parents*: she prays for uninterrupted union and felicity between you: [Manfred's colour changed] but as it is no longer possible for her to be allied to you, she entreats your consent to remain in sanctuary till she can learn news of her father; or, by the certainty of his death, be at liberty, with the approbation of her guardians, to dispose of herself in suitable marriage. I shall give no such consent, said the prince; but insist on her return to the castle without delay: I am answerable for her person to her guardians, and will not brook her being in any hands but my own. Your highness will recollect whether that can any longer be proper, replied the Friar. I want no monitor, said Manfred, colouring. Isabella's conduct leaves room for strange suspicions—and that young villain, who was at least the accomplice of her flight, if not the cause of it—The cause! interrupted Jerome: was a *young* man the cause? This is not to be borne! cried Manfred. Am I to be bearded[11] in my own palace by an insolent monk? Thou art privy, I guess, to their amours. I would pray to heaven to clear up your uncharitable surmises, said Jerome, if your highness were not satisfied in your conscience how unjustly you accuse me. I do pray to heaven to pardon that uncharitableness: and I implore your highness to leave the princess at peace in that holy place, where she is not liable to be disturbed by such vain and worldly fantasies as discourses of love from any man. Cant[12] not to me, said Manfred, but return and bring the princess to her duty. It is my duty to prevent her return hither, said Jerome. She is where orphans and virgins are safest from the snares and wiles of this world; and nothing but a parent's authority shall take her thence. I am her parent, cried Manfred, and demand her. She wished to have you for her parent, said the friar; but heaven that forbad that connexion, has for ever dissolved all ties betwixt you: and I announce to your highness—Stop! audacious man, said Manfred, and dread my displeasure. Holy father, said Hippolita, it is your office to be no respecter of

[11]Defied, attacked.
[12]Sermonize, hypocritically.

persons: you must speak as your duty prescribes: but it is my duty to hear nothing that it pleases not my lord I should hear. I will retire to my oratory,[13] and pray to the blessed Virgin to inspire you with her holy counsels, and to restore the heart of my gracious lord to its wonted peace and gentleness. Excellent woman! said the friar.—My lord, I attend your pleasure.

Manfred, accompanied by the friar, passed to his own apartment; where shutting the door, I perceive, father, said he, that Isabella has acquainted you with my purpose. Now hear my resolve, and obey. Reasons of state, most urgent reasons, my own and the safety of my people, demand that I should have a son. It is in vain to expect an heir from Hippolita. I have made choice of Isabella. You must bring her back; and you must do more. I know the influence you have with Hippolita: her conscience is in your hands. She is, I allow, a faultless woman: her soul is set on heaven, and scorns the little grandeur of this world: you can withdraw her from it entirely. Persuade her to consent to the dissolution of our marriage, and to retire into a monastery—she shall endow one if she will; and she shall have the means of being as liberal[14] to your order as she or you can wish. Thus you will divert the calamities that are hanging over our heads, and have the merit of saving the principality of Otranto from destruction. You are a prudent man; and though the warmth of my temper betrayed me into some unbecoming expressions, I honour your virtue, and wish to be indebted to you for the repose of my life and the preservation of my family.

The will of heaven be done! said the friar. I am but its worthless instrument. It makes use of my tongue to tell thee, prince, of thy unwarrantable designs. The injuries of the virtuous Hippolita have mounted to the throne of pity. By me thou art reprimanded for thy adulterous intention of repudiating her: by me thou art warned not to pursue the incestuous design on thy contracted daughter. Heaven, that delivered her from thy fury, when the judgments so recently fallen on thy house ought to have inspired thee with other thoughts, will continue to watch over her. Even I, a poor and despised friar, am able to protect her from thy violence.—I, sinner as I am, and uncharitably reviled by your highness as an accomplice

---

[13]Private chapel.

[14]Financially generous.

of I know not what amours,[15] scorn the allurements with which it
has pleased thee to tempt mine honesty. I love my order; I honour
devout souls; I respect the piety of thy princess—but I will not betray the confidence she reposes in me, nor serve even the cause of
religion by foul and sinful compliances—But forsooth![16] the welfare of the state depends on your highness having a son! Heaven
mocks the short-sighted views of man. But yester-morn, whose
house was so great, so flourishing as Manfred's?—Where is young
Conrad now?—My lord, I respect your tears—but I mean not to
check them—Let them flow, prince! they will weigh more with
heaven towards the welfare of thy subjects, than a marriage, which,
founded on lust or policy, could never prosper. The sceptre, which
passed from the race of Alfonso to thine, cannot be preserved by a
match which the church will never allow. If it is the will of the Most
High that Manfred's name must perish, resign yourself, my lord, to
its decrees; and thus deserve a crown that can never pass away.—
Come, my lord, I like this sorrow—Let us return to the princess:
she is not apprized of your cruel intentions; nor did I mean more
than to alarm you. You saw with what gentle patience, with what
efforts of love, she heard, she rejected hearing the extent of your
guilt. I know she longs to fold you in her arms, and assure you of
her unalterable affection. Father, said the prince, you mistake my
compunction: true, I honour Hippolita's virtues; I think her a saint;
and wish it were for my soul's health to tie faster the knot that has
united us.—But alas! father, you know not the bitterest of my
pangs! It is some time that I have had scruples on the legality of our
union: Hippolita is related to me in the fourth degree—It is true, we
had a dispensation;[17] but I have been informed that she had also
been contracted to another. This it is that sits heavy at my heart: to
this state of unlawful wedlock I impute the visitation that has fallen
on me in the death of Conrad!—Ease my conscience of this burden;
dissolve our marriage, and accomplish the work of godliness which
your divine exhortations have commenced in my soul.

How cutting was the anguish which the good man felt, when he
perceived this turn in the wily prince! He trembled for Hippolita,

[15]Lovers' trysts.

[16]In truth!

[17]At only four removes within the family, their marriage would have been regarded
as illegitimate, and incestuous, unless there were a Papal dispensation.

whose ruin he saw was determined; and he feared, if Manfred had no hope of recovering Isabella, that his impatience for a son would direct him to some other object, who might not be equally proof against the temptation of Manfred's rank. For some time the holy man remained absorbed in thought. At length, conceiving some hopes from delay, he thought the wisest conduct would be to prevent the prince from despairing of recovering Isabella. Her the friar knew he could dispose, from her affection to Hippolita, and from the aversion she had expressed to him for Manfred's addresses, to second his views, till the censures of the church could be fulminated against a divorce. With this intention, as if struck with the prince's scruples, he at length said, My lord, I have been pondering on what your highness has said; and if in truth it is delicacy of conscience that is the real motive of your repugnance to your virtuous lady, far be it from me to endeavour to harden your heart! The church is an indulgent mother; unfold your griefs to her: she alone can administer comfort to your soul, either by satisfying your conscience, or upon examination of your scruples, by setting you at liberty, and indulging you in the lawful means of continuing your lineage. In the latter case, if the lady Isabella can be brought to consent— Manfred, who concluded that he had either over-reached the good man, or that his first warmth had been but a tribute paid to appearance, was overjoyed at this sudden turn, and repeated the most magnificent promises, if he should succeed by the friar's mediation. The well-meaning priest suffered him to deceive himself, fully determined to traverse[18] his views, instead of seconding them.

Since we now understand one another, resumed the prince, I expect, father, that you satisfy me in one point. Who is the youth that I found in the vault? He must have been privy to Isabella's flight: tell me truly; is he her lover? or is he an agent for another's passion? I have often suspected Isabella's indifference to my son: a thousand circumstances crowd on my mind that confirm that suspicion. She herself was so conscious of it, that, while I discoursed her in the gallery, she outran my suspicions, and endeavoured to justify herself from coolness to Conrad. The friar, who knew nothing of the youth, but what he had learnt occasionally from the princess, ignorant what was become of him, and not sufficiently

---

[18]Thwart.

reflecting on the impetuosity of Manfred's temper, conceived that it might not be amiss to sow the seeds of jealousy in his mind: they might be turned to some use hereafter, either by prejudicing the prince against Isabella, if he persisted in that union; or, by diverting his attention to a wrong scent, and employing his thoughts on a visionary intrigue, prevent his engaging in any new pursuit. With this unhappy[19] policy, he answered in a manner to confirm Manfred in the belief of some connexion between Isabella and the youth. The prince, whose passions wanted little fuel to throw them into a blaze, fell into a rage at the idea of what the friar suggested. I will fathom to the bottom of this intrigue, cried he; and quitting Jerome abruptly, with a command to remain there till his return, he hastened to the great hall of the castle, and ordered the peasant to be brought before him.

Thou hardened young impostor! said the prince, as soon as he saw the youth; what becomes of thy boasted veracity now? It was Providence, was it, and the light of the moon, that discovered the lock of the trap-door to thee? Tell me, audacious boy, who thou art, and how long thou hast been acquainted with the princess— and take care to answer with less equivocation[20] than thou didst last night, or tortures shall wring the truth from thee. The young man, perceiving that his share in the flight of the princess was discovered, and concluding that anything he should say could no longer be of any service or detriment to her, replied, I am no impostor, my lord, nor have I deserved opprobrious[21] language. I answered to every question your highness put to me last night with the same veracity that I shall speak now: and that will not be from fear of your tortures, but because my soul abhors a falsehood. Please to repeat your questions, my lord; I am ready to give you all the satisfaction in my power. You know my questions, replied the prince, and only want time to prepare an evasion. Speak directly; who art thou? and how long hast thou been known to the princess? I am a labourer at the next village, said the peasant; my name is Theodore. The princess found me in the vault last night: before that hour I never was in her presence.—I may believe as much or as lit-

---

[19]Unlucky.
[20]Artful evasion.
[21]Defamatory.

tle as I please of this, said Manfred; but I will hear thy own story, before I examine into the truth of it. Tell me, what reason did the princess give thee for making her escape? Thy life depends on thy answer. She told me, replied Theodore, that she was on the brink of destruction; and that, if she could not escape from the castle, she was in danger in a few moments of being made miserable for ever. And on this slight foundation, on a silly girl's report, said Manfred, thou didst hazard my displeasure? I fear no man's displeasure, said Theodore, when a woman in distress puts herself under my protection.[22]—During this examination, Matilda was going to the apartment of Hippolita. At the upper end of the hall, where Manfred sat, was a boarded gallery with latticed windows, through which Matilda and Bianca were to pass. Hearing her father's voice, and seeing the servants assembled round him, she stopped to learn the occasion. The prisoner soon drew her attention: the steady and composed manner in which he answered, and the gallantry of his last reply, which were the first words she heard distinctly, interested her in his favour. His person was noble, handsome, and commanding, even in that situation: but his countenance soon engrossed her whole care. Heavens! Bianca, said the princess softly, do I dream? or is not that youth the exact resemblance of Alfonso's picture in the gallery? She could say no more, for her father's voice grew louder at every word. This bravado, said he, surpasses all thy former insolence. Thou shalt experience the wrath with which thou darest to trifle. Seize him, continued Manfred, and bind him—the first news the princess hears of her champion shall be, that he has lost his head for her sake. The injustice of which thou art guilty towards me, said Theodore, convinces me that I have done a good deed in delivering the princess from thy tyranny. May she be happy, whatever becomes of me!—This is a lover! cried Manfred in a rage: a peasant within sight of death is not animated by such sentiments. Tell me, tell me, rash boy, who thou art, or the rack shall force thy secret from thee. Thou hast threatened me with death already, said the youth, for the truth I have told thee: if that is all the encouragement I am to expect for sincerity, I am not tempted to indulge thy vain curiosity farther. Then thou wilt not speak? said Manfred. I

[22]The categorical defense of female honor and damsels in distress was specified in the medieval code of chivalry, recently itemized in Walpole's day by Richard Hurd's *Letters on Chivalry and Romance* (1762). See p. 231.

will not, replied he. Bear him away into the court-yard, said Manfred; I will see his head this instant severed from his body.— Matilda fainted at hearing those words. Bianca shrieked, and cried, Help! help! the princess is dead! Manfred started at this ejaculation, and demanded what was the matter. The young peasant, who heard it too, was struck with horror, and asked eagerly the same question; but Manfred ordered him to be hurried into the court, and kept there for execution, till he had informed himself of the cause of Bianca's shrieks. When he learned the meaning, he treated it as a womanish panic; and ordering Matilda to be carried to her apartment, he rushed into the court, and calling for one of his guards, bade Theodore kneel down, and prepare to receive the fatal blow.

The undaunted youth received the bitter sentence with a resignation that touched every heart but Manfred's. He wished earnestly to know the meaning of the words he had heard relating to the princess; but fearing to exasperate the tyrant more against her, he desisted. The only boon he deigned to ask was, that he might be permitted to have a confessor, and make his peace with heaven. Manfred, who hoped by the confessor's means to come at the youth's history, readily granted his request; and being convinced that father Jerome was now in his interest,[23] he ordered him to be called and shrieve[24] the prisoner. The holy man, who had little foreseen the catastrophe that his imprudence occasioned, fell on his knees to the prince, and adjured him in the most solemn manner not to shed innocent blood. He accused himself in the bitterest terms for his indiscretion, endeavoured to disculpate the youth, and left no method untried to soften the tyrant's rage. Manfred, more incensed than appeased by Jerome's intercession, whose retraction now made him suspect he had been imposed upon by both, commanded the friar to do his duty, telling him he would not allow the prisoner many minutes for confession. Nor do I ask many, my lord, said the unhappy young man. My sins, thank heaven! have not been numerous; nor exceed what might be expected at my years. Dry your tears, good father, and let us dispatch:[25] this is a bad world; nor have I had cause to leave it with regret. Oh! wretched

[23]Cooperating.
[24]Hear the confession of.
[25]Hurry.

youth! said Jerome; how canst thou bear the sight of me with patience? I am thy murderer! It is I have brought this dismal hour upon thee!—I forgive thee from my soul, said the youth, as I hope heaven will pardon me. Hear my confession, father; and give me thy blessing. How can I prepare thee for thy passage, as I ought? said Jerome. Thou canst not be saved without pardoning thy foes— and canst thou forgive that impious man there? I can, said Theodore; I do.—And does not this touch thee, cruel prince? said the friar. I sent for thee to confess him, said Manfred sternly; not to plead for him. Thou didst first incense me against him—his blood be upon thy head! It will! it will! said the good man, in an agony of sorrow. Thou and I must never hope to go where this blessed youth is going.—Dispatch! said Manfred: I am no more to be moved by the whining of priests, than by the shrieks of women. What! said the youth, is it possible that my fate could have occasioned what I heard! Is the princess then again in thy power?—Thou dost but remember me[26] of my wrath, said Manfred: prepare thee, for this moment is thy last. The youth, who felt his indignation rise, and who was touched with the sorrow which he saw he had infused into all the spectators, as well as into the friar, suppressed his emotions, and, putting off his doublet, and unbuttoning his collar, knelt down to his prayers. As he stooped, his shirt slipped down below his shoulder, and discovered the mark of a bloody arrow. Gracious heaven! cried the holy man, starting, what do I see? It is my child! my Theodore!

The passions that ensued must be conceived; they cannot be painted. The tears of the assistants were suspended by wonder, rather than stopped by joy. They seemed to inquire in the eyes of their lord what they ought to feel. Surprise, doubt, tenderness, respect, succeeded each other in the countenance of the youth. He received with modest submission the effusion of the old man's tears and embraces: yet afraid of giving a loose to[27] hope, and suspecting from what had passed the inflexibility of Manfred's temper, he cast a glance towards the prince, as if to say, Canst thou be unmoved at such a scene as this?

Manfred's heart was capable of being touched. He forgot his anger in his astonishment; yet his pride forbad his owning himself

---

[26]Remind me.

[27]Indulging.

affected. He even doubted whether this discovery was not a contrivance of the friar to save the youth. What may this mean? said he. How can he be thy son? Is it consistent with thy profession or reputed sanctity to avow a peasant's offspring for the fruit of thy irregular amours?[28]—Oh God! said the holy man, dost thou question his being mine? Could I feel the anguish I do, if I were not his father? Spare him! good prince, spare him! and revile me as thou pleasest.—Spare him! spare him! cried the attendants, for this good man's sake!—Peace! said Manfred, sternly: I must know more, ere I am disposed to pardon. A saint's bastard may be no saint himself.—Injurious lord! said Theodore: add not insult to cruelty. If I am this venerable man's son, though no prince as thou art, know, the blood that flows in my veins—Yes, said the Friar, interrupting him, his blood is noble: nor is he that abject thing, my lord, you speak him.[29] He is my lawful son; and Sicily can boast of few houses more ancient than that of Falconara—But alas! my lord, what is blood? what is nobility? We are all reptiles, miserable sinful creatures. It is piety alone that can distinguish us from the dust whence we sprung, and whither we must return.—Truce to your sermon, said Manfred; you forget you are no longer friar Jerome, but the count of Falconara. Let me know your history; you will have time to moralize hereafter, if you should not happen to obtain the grace of that sturdy criminal there. Mother of God! said the friar, is it possible my lord can refuse a father the life of his only, his long lost child? Trample me, my lord, scorn, afflict me, accept my life for his, but spare my son!—Thou canst feel then, said Manfred, what it is to lose an only son? A little hour ago thou didst preach up resignation to me: *my* house, if fate so pleased, must perish—but the count of Falconara—Alas! my lord, said Jerome, I confess I have offended; but aggravate not an old man's sufferings. I boast not of my family, nor think of such vanities—it is nature that pleads for this boy; it is the memory of the dear woman that bore him—Is she, Theodore, is she dead?—Her soul has long been with the blessed, said Theodore. Oh how? cried Jerome, tell me—No—she is happy! Thou art all my care now!—Most dread lord! will you—

---

[28]Vows of clerical celibacy had been decreed by the first and second Lateran councils, 1123 and 1139.

[29]A bastard (Father Jerome could not be thus charged if he had been married, taking vows and retiring to a convent after his wife's death).

will you grant me my poor boy's life? Return to thy convent, answered Manfred; conduct the princess hither; obey me in what else thou knowest; and I promise thee the life of thy son.—Oh! my lord, said Jerome, is honesty the price I must pay for this dear youth's safety?—For me! cried Theodore: let me die a thousand deaths, rather than stain thy conscience. What is it the tyrant would exact of thee? Is the princess still safe from his power? Protect her, thou venerable old man! and let all his wrath fall on me. Jerome endeavoured to check the impetuosity of the youth; and ere Manfred could reply, the trampling of horses was heard, and a brazen[30] trumpet, which hung without the gate of the castle, was suddenly sounded. At the same instant the sable plumes on the enchanted helmet, which still remained at the other end of the court, were tempestuously agitated, and nodded thrice, as if bowed by some invisible wearer.

[30]Brass.

Chapter III

Manfred's heart misgave him when he beheld the plumage on the miraculous casque shaken in concert with the sounding of the brazen trumpet. Father! said he to Jerome, whom he now ceased to treat as count of Falconara, what mean these portents? If I have offended—[the plumes were shaken with greater violence than before] Unhappy prince that I am! cried Manfred—Holy father! will you not assist me with your prayers?—My lord, replied Jerome, heaven is no doubt displeased with your mockery of its servants. Submit yourself to the church; and cease to persecute her ministers. Dismiss this innocent youth; and learn to respect the holy character I wear: heaven will not be trifled with: you see—[the trumpet sounded again] I acknowledge I have been too hasty, said Manfred. Father, do you go to the wicket,[1] and demand who is at the gate. Do you grant me the life of Theodore? replied the friar. I do, said Manfred; but enquire who is without.

Jerome, falling on the neck of his son, discharged a flood of tears, that spoke the fulness of his soul. You promised to go to the gate, said Manfred. I thought, replied the friar, your highness would excuse my thanking you first in this tribute of my heart. Go, dearest sir, said Theodore, obey the prince; I do not deserve that you should delay his satisfaction for me.

Jerome, enquiring who was without, was answered, A herald. From whom? said he. From the knight of the gigantic sabre, said the herald: and I must speak with the usurper of Otranto. Jerome returned to the prince, and did not fail to repeat the message in the very words it had been uttered. The first sounds struck Manfred with terror; but when he heard himself styled[2] usurper, his rage rekindled, and all his courage revived. Usurper!—Insolent villain! cried he, who dares to question my title? Retire, father; this is no business for monks: I will meet this presumptuous man myself. Go to your convent, and prepare the princess's return: your son shall be a hostage for your fidelity: his life depends on your obedience.— Good heaven! my lord, cried Jerome, your highness did but this instant freely pardon my child—have you so soon forgot the interpo-

---

[1] A small hole for communicating with those outside.

[2] Described as.

sition of heaven?—Heaven, replied Manfred, does not send heralds to question the title of a lawful prince—I doubt whether it even notifies its will through friars—but that is your affair, not mine. At present you know my pleasure; and it is not a saucy[3] herald that shall save your son, if you do not return with the princess.

It was in vain for the holy man to reply. Manfred commanded him to be conducted to the postern-gate, and shut out from the castle: and he ordered some of his attendants to carry Theodore to the top of the black tower, and guard him strictly; scarce permitting the father and son to exchange a hasty embrace at parting. He then withdrew to the hall, and, seating himself in princely state, ordered the herald to be admitted to his presence.

Well, thou insolent, said the prince, what wouldst thou with me? I come, replied he, to thee, Manfred, usurper of the principality of Otranto, from the renowned and invincible knight, the knight of the gigantic sabre: in the name of his lord, Frederic, marquis of Vicenza, he demands the lady Isabella, daughter of that prince, whom thou hast basely and traitorously got into thy power, by bribing her false guardians during his absence: and he requires thee to resign the principality of Otranto, which thou hast usurped from the said lord Frederic, the nearest of blood to the last rightful lord Alfonso the Good. If thou dost not instantly comply with these just demands, he defies thee to single combat to the last extremity. And so saying, the herald cast down his warder.[4]

And where is this braggart who sends thee? said Manfred. At the distance of a league, said the herald: he comes to make good his lord's claim against thee, as he is a true knight, and thou an usurper and ravisher.

Injurious as this challenge was, Manfred reflected that it was not his interest to provoke the marquis. He knew how wellfounded the claim of Frederic was; nor was this the first time he had heard of it. Frederic's ancestors had assumed the style[5] of princes of Otranto, from the death of Alfonso the Good without

---

[3]Impertinent.

[4]Via his herald, Frederic challenges Manfred to ordeal by combat, throwing down a gauntlet (glove), or as here, a warder (a staff to prevent flight). According to laws introduced in England by William the Conqueror, legal disputes could be thus settled, trusting Heaven to favor the just man with victory.

[5]Title.

issue: but Manfred, his father, and grandfather, had been too powerful for the house of Vicenza to dispossess them. Frederic, a martial and amorous young prince, had married a beautiful young lady, of whom he was enamoured, and who had died in childbed of Isabella. Her death affected him so much that he had taken the cross and gone to the Holy Land, where he was wounded in an engagement against the infidels,[6] made prisoner, and reported to be dead. When the news reached Manfred's ears, he bribed the guardians of the lady Isabella to deliver her up to him as a bride for his son Conrad; by which alliance he had purposed to unite the claims of the two houses. This motive, on Conrad's death, had co-operated to make him so suddenly resolve on espousing her himself; and the same reflection determined him now to endeavour at obtaining the consent of Frederic to this marriage. A like policy inspired him with the thought of inviting Frederic's champion[7] into the castle, lest he should be informed of Isabella's flight, which he strictly enjoined his domestics not to disclose to any of the knight's retinue.

Herald, said Manfred, as soon as he had digested these reflections, return to thy master, and tell him, ere we liquidate our differences by the sword, Manfred would hold some converse with him. Bid him welcome to my castle, where by my faith, as I am a true knight, he shall have courteous reception, and full security for himself and followers.[8] If we cannot adjust our quarrel by amicable means, I swear he shall depart in safety, and shall have full satisfaction according to the laws of arms: so help me God and his holy Trinity!—The herald made three obeisances,[9] and retired.

During this interview Jerome's mind was agitated by a thousand contrary passions. He trembled for the life of his son, and his first thought was to persuade Isabella to return to the castle. Yet he was scarce less alarmed at the thought of her union with Manfred. He dreaded Hippolita's unbounded submission to the will of her lord: and though he did not doubt but he could alarm her piety not to consent to a divorce, if he could get access to her; yet should Manfred discover that the obstruction came from him, it might be

[6]On a Crusade, against the "unfaithful."

[7]For these rites of combat, one could hire a "champion" to fight on one's behalf. Manfred assumes that Frederic has sent one of his knights in this office.

[8]The codes of chivalry enjoined hospitality, even to the ambassadors of one's enemies.

[9]Low bows.

equally fatal to Theodore. He was impatient to know whence came the herald, who with so little management[10] had questioned the title of Manfred: yet he did not dare absent himself from the convent, lest Isabella should leave it, and her flight be imputed to him. He returned disconsolately to the monastery, uncertain on what conduct to resolve. A monk, who met him in the porch and observed his melancholy air, said, Alas! brother, is it then true that we have lost our excellent princess Hippolita? The holy man started, and cried, What meanest thou, brother? I come this instant from the castle, and left her in perfect health. Martelli, replied the other friar, passed by the convent but a quarter of an hour ago on his way from the castle, and reported that her highness was dead. All our brethren are gone to the chapel to pray for her happy transit to a better life, and willed me to wait thy arrival. They know thy holy attachment to that good lady, and are anxious for the affliction it will cause in thee—Indeed we have all reason to weep; she was a mother to our house—But this life is but a pilgrimage; we must not murmur—we shall all follow her; may our end be like hers!—Good brother, thou dreamest, said Jerome: I tell thee I come from the castle, and left the princess well—Where is the lady Isabella? Poor gentlewoman! replied the friar; I told her the sad news, and offered her spiritual comfort; I reminded her of the transitory condition of mortality, and advised her to take the veil: I quoted the example of the holy princess Sanchia of Arragon.[11]—Thy zeal was laudable, said Jerome impatiently; but at present it was unnecessary: Hippolita is well—at least I trust in the Lord she is; I heard nothing to the contrary—Yet methinks the prince's earnestness—Well, brother, but where is the lady Isabella?—I know not, said the friar: she wept much, and said she would retire to her chamber. Jerome left his comrade abruptly, and hastened to the princess, but she was not in her chamber. He inquired of the domestics of the convent, but could learn no news of her. He searched in vain throughout the monastery and the church, and dispatched messengers round the neighbourhood, to get intelligence if she had been seen; but to no purpose. Nothing could equal the good man's perplexity. He judged that Isabella, suspecting Manfred of having precipitated his

[10]Courtesy.

[11]Sanchia Castile of Aragon (northeastern Spain), wife of Alfonso I, lived from 1154 to 1208.

wife's death, had taken the alarm, and withdrawn herself to some more secret place of concealment. This new flight would probably carry the prince's fury to the height. The report of Hippolita's death, though it seemed almost incredible, increased his consternation; and though Isabella's escape bespoke her aversion of Manfred for a husband, Jerome could feel no comfort from it, while it endangered the life of his son. He determined to return to the castle, and made several of his brethren accompany him to attest his innocence to Manfred, and, if necessary, join their intercession with his for Theodore.

The prince, in the mean time, had passed into the court, and ordered the gates of the castle to be flung open for the reception of the stranger knight and his train. In a few minutes the cavalcade arrived. First came two harbingers with wands.[12] Next a herald, followed by two pages and two trumpets. Then a hundred foot-guards. These were attended by as many horse. After them fifty footmen, clothed in scarlet and black, the colours of the knight. Then a led horse. Two heralds on each side of a gentleman on horseback bearing a banner with the arms of Vicenza and Otranto quarterly—a circumstance that much offended Manfred—but he stifled his resentment.[13] Two more pages. The knight's confessor telling his beads.[14] Fifty more footmen clad as before. Two knights habited in complete armour, their beavers[15] down, comrades to the principal knight. The 'squires of the two knights, carrying their shields and devices.[16] The knight's own squire. A hundred gentlemen bearing an enormous sword, and seeming to faint under the weight of it. The knight himself on a chestnut steed, in complete armour, his lance in the rest, his face entirely concealed by his vizor, which was surmounted by a large plume of scarlet and black feathers. Fifty foot-guards with drums and trumpets closed the procession, which wheeled off to the right and left to make room for the principal knight.

As soon as he approached the gate he stopped; and the herald advancing, read again the words of the challenge. Manfred's eyes

---

[12]Signs of office.

[13]The banner flaunts the insignia of Vicenza and Otranto in two of its quarters, implying sovereignty of both.

[14]Rosary.

[15]Visors.

[16]An esquire ('squire) is a comrade honored with the office of arms-bearer.

were fixed on the gigantic sword, and he scarce seemed to attend to the cartel:[17] but his attention was soon diverted by a tempest of wind that rose behind him. He turned and beheld the plumes of the enchanted helmet agitated in the same extraordinary manner as before. It required intrepidity like Manfred's not to sink under a concurrence of circumstances that seemed to announce his fate. Yet scorning in the presence of strangers to betray the courage he had always manifested, he said boldly, Sir knight, whoever thou art, I bid thee welcome. If thou art of mortal mould, thy valour shall meet its equal: and if thou art a true knight, thou wilt scorn to employ sorcery to carry thy point. Be these omens from heaven or hell, Manfred trusts to the righteousness of his cause and to the aid of saint Nicholas, who has ever protected his house. Alight, sir knight, and repose thyself. To-morrow thou shalt have a fair field, and heaven befriend the juster side!

The knight made no reply, but, dismounting, was conducted by Manfred to the great hall of the castle. As they traversed the court, the knight stopped to gaze on the miraculous casque; and kneeling down, seemed to pray inwardly for some minutes. Rising, he made a sign to the prince to lead on. As soon as they entered the hall, Manfred proposed to the stranger to disarm, but the knight shook his head in token of refusal. Sir knight, said Manfred, this is not courteous; but by my good faith I will not cross thee! nor shalt thou have cause to complain of the prince of Otranto. No treachery is designed on my part: I hope none is intended on thine. Here take my gage:[18] [giving him his ring] your friends and you shall enjoy the laws of hospitality. Rest here until refreshments are brought: I will but give orders for the accommodation of your train, and return to you. The three knights bowed as accepting his courtesy. Manfred directed the stranger's retinue to be conducted to an adjacent hospital,[19] founded by the princess Hippolita for the reception of pilgrims. As they made the circuit of the court to return towards the gate, the gigantic sword burst from the supporters, and, falling to the ground opposite to the helmet, remained immovable. Manfred, almost hardened to preternatural appearances, surmounted

---

[17]Written challenge, with the terms for combat.

[18]Something valuable given as a pledge.

[19]A place of hospitality for travelers.

the shock of this new prodigy; and returning to the hall, where by this time the feast was ready, he invited his silent guests to take their places. Manfred, however ill his heart was at ease, endeavoured to inspire the company with mirth. He put several questions to them, but was answered only by signs. They raised their vizors but sufficiently to feed themselves, and that sparingly. Sirs, said the prince, ye are the first guests I ever treated within these walls who scorned to hold any intercourse[20] with me: nor has it oft been customary, I ween,[21] for princes to hazard their state and dignity against strangers and mutes. You say you come in the name of Frederic of Vicenza; I have ever heard that he was a gallant and courteous knight; nor would he, I am bold to say, think it beneath him to mix in social converse with a prince that is his equal, and not unknown by deeds in arms.—Still ye are silent—Well! be it as it may—by the laws of hospitality and chivalry ye are masters under this roof: ye shall do your pleasure—but come, give me a goblet of wine; ye will not refuse to pledge me to the healths of your fair mistresses. The principal knight sighed and crossed himself, and was rising from the board[22]—Sir knight, said Manfred, what I said was but in sport: I shall constrain you in nothing; use your good liking. Since mirth is not your mood, let us be sad. Business may hit your fancies better: let us withdraw; and hear if what I have to unfold may be better relished than the vain efforts I have made for your pastime.

Manfred, then, conducting the three knights into an inner chamber, shut the door, and, inviting them to be seated, began thus, addressing himself to the chief personage:

You come, sir knight, as I understand, in the name of the Marquis of Vicenza, to re-demand the lady Isabella, his daughter, who has been contracted in the face of holy church to my son, by the consent of her legal guardians; and to require me to resign my dominions to your lord, who gives himself for the nearest of blood to prince Alfonso, whose soul God rest! I shall speak to the latter article of your demands first. You must know, your lord knows, that I enjoy the principality of Otranto from my father, Don Manuel, as

---

[20]Conversation.
[21]Believe.
[22]Table.

he received it from his father, Don Ricardo. Alfonso, their predecessor, dying childless in the Holy Land, bequeathed his estates to my grandfather, Don Ricardo, in consideration of his faithful services. [The stranger shook his head]—Sir Knight, said Manfred warmly, Ricardo was a valiant and upright man; he was a pious man; witness his munificent[23] foundation of the adjoining church and two converts. He was peculiarly patronised by saint Nicholas—My grandfather was incapable—I say, sir, Don Ricardo was incapable—Excuse me, your interruption has disordered me—I venerate the memory of my grandfather—Well, sirs, he held this estate; he held it by his good sword and by the favour of saint Nicholas— so did my father; and so, sirs, will I, come what come will.—But Frederic, your lord, is nearest in blood—I have consented to put my title to the issue of the sword—does that imply a vitious[24] title? I might have asked, where is Frederic your lord? Report speaks him dead in captivity. You say, your actions say, he lives—I question it not—I might, sirs, I might—but I do not. Other princes would bid Frederic take his inheritance by force, if he can: they would not stake their dignity on a single combat: they would not submit it to the decision of unknown mutes! Pardon me, gentlemen, I am too warm: but suppose yourselves in my situation: as ye are stout knights, would it not move your choler[25] to have your own and the honour of your ancestors called in question?—But to the point. Ye require me to deliver up the lady Isabella. Sirs, I must ask if ye are authorized to receive her? [The Knight nodded.] Receive her—continued Manfred: Well! you are authorized to receive her—But, gentle knight, may I ask if you have full powers? [The Knight nodded.] 'Tis well, said Manfred: then hear what I have to offer—Ye see, gentlemen, before you the most unhappy of men! [he began to weep] afford me your compassion; I am entitled to it; indeed I am. Know, I have lost my only hope, my joy, the support of my house— Conrad died yester morning. [The Knights discovered signs of surprise.] Yes, sirs, fate has disposed of my son. Isabella is at liberty.— Do you then restore her? cried the chief knight, breaking silence. Afford me your patience, said Manfred. I rejoice to find, by this

[23]Financially generous.
[24]Illicit.
[25]Anger.

testimony of your good-will, that this matter may be adjusted without blood. It is no interest of mine dictates what little I have farther to say. Ye behold in me a man disgusted with the world: the loss of my son has weaned me from earthly cares. Power and greatness have no longer any charms in my eyes. I wished to transmit the sceptre I had received from my ancestors with honour to my son—but that is over! Life itself is so indifferent to me, that I accepted your defiance[26] with joy: a good knight cannot go to the grave with more satisfaction than when falling in his vocation. Whatever is the will of heaven, I submit; for, alas! sirs, I am a man of many sorrows. Manfred is no object of envy—but no doubt you are acquainted with my story. [The knight made signs of ignorance, and seemed curious to have Manfred proceed.] Is it possible, sirs, continued the prince, that my story should be a secret to you? Have you heard nothing relating to me and the princess Hippolita? [They shook their heads]—No! Thus then, sirs, it is. You think me ambitious: ambition, alas, is composed of more rugged materials. If I were ambitious, I should not for so many years have been a prey to all the hell of conscientious scruples—But I weary your patience: I will be brief. Know then, that I have long been troubled in mind on my union with the princess Hippolita.—Oh! sirs, if ye were acquainted with that excellent woman! if ye knew that I adore her like a mistress, and cherish her as a friend—But man was not born for perfect happiness! She shares my scruples, and with her consent I have brought this matter before the church, for we are related within the forbidden degrees. I expect every hour the definitive sentence that must separate us for ever. I am sure you feel for me—I see you do—pardon these tears! [The knights gazed on each other, wondering where this would end.] Manfred continued: The death of my son betiding while my soul was under this anxiety, I thought of nothing but resigning my dominions, and retiring for ever from the sight of mankind. My only difficulty was to fix on a successor, who would be tender of my people, and to dispose of the lady Isabella, who is dear to me as my own blood. I was willing to restore the line of Alfonso, even in his most distant kindred: and though, pardon me, I am satisfied it was his will that Ricardo's lineage should take place of his own relations; yet where was I to search for

[26]Challenge.

those relations? I knew of none but Frederic, your lord: he was a captive to the infidels, or dead; and were he living, and at home, would he quit the flourishing state of Vicenza for the inconsiderable principality of Otranto? If he would not, could I bear the thought of seeing a hard, unfeeling viceroy[27] set over my poor faithful people?—for, sirs, I love my people, and thank heaven am beloved by them.—But ye will ask, Whither tends this long discourse? Briefly then, thus, sirs. Heaven in your arrival seems to point out a remedy for these difficulties and my misfortunes. The lady Isabella is at liberty: I shall soon be so. I would submit to anything for the good of my people. Were it not the best, the only way to extinguish the feuds between our families, if I was to take the lady Isabella to wife?—You start—But though Hippolita's virtues will ever be dear to me, a prince must not consider himself; he is born for his people.—A servant at that instant entering the chamber apprised Manfred that Jerome and several of his brethren demanded immediate access to him.

The prince, provoked at this interruption, and fearing that the friar would discover to the strangers that Isabella had taken sanctuary, was going to forbid Jerome's entrance. But recollecting that he was certainly arrived to notify the princess's return, Manfred began to excuse himself to the knights for leaving them for a few moments, but was prevented by the arrival of the friars. Manfred angrily reprimanded them for their intrusion, and would have forced them back from the chamber; but Jerome was too much agitated to be repulsed. He declared aloud the flight of Isabella, with protestations of his own innocence. Manfred, distracted at the news, and not less at its coming to the knowledge of the strangers, uttered nothing but incoherent sentences, now upbraiding the friar, now apologizing to the knights, earnest to know what was become of Isabella, yet equally afraid of their knowing, impatient to pursue her, yet dreading to have them join in the pursuit. He offered to dispatch messengers in quest of her:—but the chief knight, no longer keeping silence, reproached Manfred in bitter terms for his dark and ambiguous dealing, and demanded the cause of Isabella's first absence from the castle. Manfred, casting a stern look at Jerome, implying a command of silence, pretended that on Conrad's death

[27]Ruler by proxy.

he had placed her in sanctuary until he could determine how to dispose of her. Jerome, who trembled for his son's life, did not dare contradict this falsehood, but one of his brethren, not under the same anxiety, declared frankly that she had fled to their church in the preceding night. The prince in vain endeavoured to stop this discovery, which overwhelmed him with shame and confusion. The principal stranger, amazed at the contradictions he heard, and more than half persuaded that Manfred had secreted the princess, notwithstanding the concern he expressed at her flight, rushing to the door, said, Thou traitor prince! Isabella shall be found. Manfred endeavoured to hold him; but the other knights assisting their comrade, he broke from the prince, and hastened into the court, demanding his attendants. Manfred, finding it vain to divert him from the pursuit, offered to accompany him; and summoning his attendants, and taking Jerome and some of the friars to guide them, they issued from the castle; Manfred privately giving orders to have the knight's company secured, while to the knight he affected to dispatch a messenger to require their assistance.

The company had no sooner quitted the castle, than Matilda, who felt herself deeply interested for the young peasant, since she had seen him condemned to death in the hall, and whose thoughts had been taken up with concerting measures to save him, was informed by some of the female attendants that Manfred had dispatched all his men various ways in pursuit of Isabella. He had in his hurry given this order in general terms, not meaning to extend it to the guard he had set upon Theodore, but forgetting it. The domestics, officious[28] to obey so peremptory[29] a prince, and urged by their own curiosity and love of novelty to join in any precipitate chace, had to a man left the castle. Matilda disengaged herself from her women, stole up to the black tower, and unbolting the door, presented herself to the astonished Theodore. Young man, said she, though filial duty and womanly modesty condemn the step I am taking, yet holy charity, surmounting all other ties, justifies this act. Fly; the doors of thy prison are open: my father and his domestics are absent; but they may soon return: begone in safety; and may the angels of heaven direct thy course!—Thou art surely one of those

[28]Too eager.
[29]Dictatorial.

angels! said the enraptured Theodore: none but a blessed saint could speak, could act, could look like thee!—May I not know the name of my divine protectress? Methought thou namedst thy father: is it possible? can Manfred's blood feel holy pity?—Lovely lady, thou answerest not—But how art thou here thyself? Why dost thou neglect thy own safety, and waste a thought on a wretch like Theodore? Let us fly together: the life thou bestowest shall be dedicated to thy defence. Alas! thou mistakest, said Matilda, sighing: I am Manfred's daughter, but no dangers await me. Amazement! said Theodore: but last night I blessed myself for yielding thee the service thy gracious compassion so charitably returns me now. Still thou art in an error, said the princess; but this is no time for explanation. Fly, virtuous youth, while it is in my power to save thee: should my father return, thou and I both should indeed have cause to tremble. How? said Theodore: thinkest thou, charming maid, that I will accept of life at the hazard of aught calamitous to thee? Better I endured a thousand deaths[30]—I run no risk, said Matilda, but by thy delay. Depart: it cannot be known that I have assisted thy flight. Swear by the saints above, said Theodore, that thou canst not be suspected; else here I vow to await whatever can befall me. Oh! thou art too generous, said Matilda; but rest assured that no suspicion can alight on me. Give me thy beauteous hand in token that thou dost not deceive me, said Theodore; and let me bathe it with the warm tears of gratitude.—Forbear,[31] said the princess: this must not be.—Alas! said Theodore, I have never known but calamity until this hour—perhaps shall never know other fortune again: suffer the chaste raptures of holy gratitude: 'tis my soul would print its effusions on thy hand.—Forbear, and begone, said Matilda: how would Isabella approve of seeing thee at my feet? Who is Isabella? said the young man with surprise. Ah, me! I fear, said the princess, I am serving a deceitful one! Hast thou forgot thy curiosity this morning?—Thy looks, thy actions, all thy beauteous self seem an emanation of divinity, said Theodore; but thy words are dark and mysterious—Speak, lady, speak to thy servant's comprehension.—Thou understandest but too well, said Matilda: but once more I command thee to be gone: thy blood, which I may

---

[30]The extravagant rhetoric of chivalry.
[31]Resist.

preserve, will be on my head, if I waste the time in vain discourse. I go, lady, said Theodore, because it is thy will, and because I would not bring the grey hairs of my father with sorrow to the grave. Say but, adored lady, that I have thy gentle pity.—Stay, said Matilda; I will conduct thee to the subterraneous vault by which Isabella escaped; it will lead thee to the church of saint Nicholas, where thou mayst take sanctuary.—What! said Theodore, was it another, and not thy lovely self, that I assisted to find the subterraneous passage? It was, said Matilda: but ask no more; I tremble to see thee still abide here; fly to the sanctuary.—To sanctuary! said Theodore: No, princess; sanctuaries are for helpless damsels, or for criminals. Theodore's soul is free from guilt, nor will wear the appearance of it. Give me a sword, lady, and thy father shall learn that Theodore scorns an ignominious[32] flight. Rash youth! said Matilda, thou wouldst not dare to lift thy presumptuous arm against the prince of Otranto? Not against *thy* father; indeed I dare not, said Theodore: excuse me, lady; I had forgotten—but could I gaze on thee, and remember thou art sprung from the tyrant Manfred?—But he is thy father, and from this moment my injuries are buried in oblivion. A deep and hollow groan, which seemed to come from above, startled the princess and Theodore. Good heaven! we are overheard! said the princess. They listened; but perceiving no further noise, they both concluded it the effect of pent-up vapours: and the princess, preceding Theodore softly, carried him to her father's armoury; where equipping him with a complete suit, he was conducted by Matilda to the postern-gate. Avoid the town, said the princess, and all the western side of the castle. 'Tis there the search must be making by Manfred and the strangers: but hie[33] thee to the opposite quarter. Yonder, behind that forest to the east is a chain of rocks, hollowed into a labyrinth of caverns that reach to the sea coast. There thou mayst lie concealed, till thou canst make signs to some vessel to put on shore and take thee off. Go! heaven be thy guide!—and sometimes in thy prayers remember—Matilda!— Theodore flung himself at her feet, and seizing her lily hand, which with struggles she suffered him to kiss, he vowed on the earliest opportunity to get himself knighted, and fervently entreated her per-

[32]Cowardly.
[33]Hurry.

mission to swear himself eternally her knight.—Ere the princess could reply, a clap of thunder was suddenly heard that shook the battlements. Theodore, regardless of the tempest, would have urged his suit; but the princess, dismayed, retreated hastily into the castle, and commanded the youth to be gone with an air that would not be disobeyed. He sighed, and retired, but with eyes fixed on the gate, until Matilda, closing it, put an end to an interview, in which the hearts of both had drunk so deeply of a passion, which both now tasted for the first time.

Theodore went pensively to the convent, to acquaint his father with his deliverance. There he learned the absence of Jerome, and the pursuit that was making after the lady Isabella, with some particulars of whose story he now first became acquainted. The generous gallantry of his nature prompted him to wish to assist her; but the monks could lend him no lights to guess at the route she had taken. He was not tempted to wander far in search of her, for the idea of Matilda had imprinted itself so strongly on his heart, that he could not bear to absent himself at much distance from her abode. The tenderness Jerome had expressed for him concurred to confirm this reluctance; and he even persuaded himself that filial affection was the chief cause of his hovering between the castle and monastery. Until Jerome should return at night, Theodore at length determined to repair to the forest that Matilda had pointed out to him. Arriving there, he sought the gloomiest shades, as best suited to the pleasing melancholy that reigned in his mind. In this mood he roved insensibly to the caves which had formerly served as a retreat to hermits, and were now reported round the country to be haunted by evil spirits. He recollected to have heard this tradition; and being of a brave and adventurous disposition, he willingly indulged his curiosity in exploring the secret recesses of this labyrinth. He had not penetrated far before he thought he heard the steps of some person who seemed to retreat before him. Theodore, though firmly grounded in all our holy faith enjoins[34] to be believed, had no apprehension that good men were abandoned without cause to the malice of the powers of darkness. He thought the place more likely to be infested by robbers than by those infernal agents who are reported to molest and bewilder travellers. He

[34]Requires.

had long burned with impatience to approve[35] his valour. Drawing his sabre, he marched sedately onwards, still directing his steps as the imperfect rustling sound before him led the way. The armour he wore was a like indication to the person who avoided him. Theodore, now convinced that he was not mistaken, redoubled his pace, and evidently gained on the person that fled, whose haste increasing, Theodore came up just as a woman fell breathless before him. He hasted to raise her; but her terror was so great that he apprehended she would faint in his arms. He used every gentle word to dispel her alarms, and assured her that, far from injuring, he would defend her at the peril of his life. The lady recovering her spirits from his courteous demeanour, and gazing on her protector, said, Sure, I have heard that voice before?—Not to my knowledge, replied Theodore, unless, as I conjecture, thou art the lady Isabella.—Merciful heaven! cried she, thou art not sent in quest of me, art thou? And saying those words, she threw herself at his feet, and besought him not to deliver her up to Manfred. To Manfred! cried Theodore—No, lady: I have once already delivered thee from his tyranny, and it shall fare hard with me now, but I will place thee out of the reach of his daring. Is it possible, said she, that thou shouldst be the generous unknown whom I met last night in the vault of the castle? Sure thou art not a mortal, but my guardian angel: on my knees, let me thank—Hold,[36] gentle princess, said Theodore, nor demean thyself before a poor and friendless young man. If heaven has selected me for thy deliverer, it will accomplish its work, and strengthen my arm in thy cause. But come, lady, we are too near the mouth of the cavern; let us seek its inmost recesses: I can have no tranquillity till I have placed thee beyond the reach of danger.—Alas! what mean you, sir? said she. Though all your actions are noble, though your sentiments speak the purity of your soul, is it fitting that I should accompany you alone into these perplexed retreats? Should we be found together, what would a censorious world think of my conduct?[37]—I respect your virtuous delicacy, said Theodore; nor do you harbour a suspicion that wounds

---

[35]Prove.

[36]Stop.

[37]A proper young woman, careful of her reputation, would not be alone in this remote retreat with a man, even of Theodore's character.

my honour. I meant to conduct you into the most private cavity of these rocks; and then, at the hazard of my life, to guard their entrance against every living thing. Besides, lady, continued he, drawing a deep sigh, beauteous and all perfect as your form is, and though my wishes are not guiltless of aspiring, know, my soul is dedicated to another; and although—A sudden noise prevented Theodore from proceeding. They soon distinguished these sounds, Isabella! What ho! Isabella!—The trembling princess relapsed into her former agony of fear. Theodore endeavoured to encourage her, but in vain. He assured her he would die rather than suffer her to return under Manfred's power; and begging her to remain concealed, he went forth to prevent the person in search of her from approaching.

At the mouth of the cavern he found an armed knight, discoursing with a peasant, who assured him he had seen a lady enter the passes of the rock. The knight was preparing to seek her, when Theodore, placing himself in his way, with his sword drawn, sternly forbad him at his peril to advance. And who art thou who darest to cross my way? said the knight haughtily. One who does not dare more than he will perform, said Theodore. I seek the lady Isabella, said the knight; and understand she has taken refuge among these rocks. Impede me not, or thou wilt repent having provoked my resentment.—Thy purpose is as odious as thy resentment is contemptible, said Theodore. Return whence thou camest, or we shall soon know whose resentment is most terrible.—The stranger, who was the principal knight that had arrived from the marquis of Vicenza, had galloped from Manfred as he was busied in getting information of the princess, and giving various orders to prevent her falling into the power of the three knights. Their chief had suspected Manfred of being privy to the princess's absconding, and this insult from a man, who he concluded was stationed by that prince to secrete her, confirming his suspicions, he made no reply, but discharging a blow with his sabre at Theodore, would soon have removed all obstruction, if Theodore, who took him for one of Manfred's captains, and who had no sooner given the provocation than prepared to support it, had not received the stroke on his shield. The valour that had so long been smothered in his breast broke forth at once: he rushed impetuously on the knight, whose pride and wrath were not less powerful incentives to hardy deeds.

The combat was furious, but not long. Theodore wounded the knight in three several places, and at last disarmed him as he fainted by the loss of blood. The peasant, who had fled on the first onset, had given the alarm to some of Manfred's domestics, who by his orders, were dispersed through the forest in pursuit of Isabella. They came up as the knight fell, whom they soon discovered to be the noble stranger. Theodore, notwithstanding his hatred to Manfred, could not behold the victory he had gained without emotions of pity and generosity: but he was more touched, when he learned the quality of his adversary, and was informed that he was no retainer, but an enemy of Manfred. He assisted the servants of the latter in disarming the knight, and in endeavouring to staunch the blood that flowed from his wounds. The knight, recovering his speech, said in a faint and faltering voice, Generous foe, we have both been in an error: I took thee for an instrument of the tyrant; I perceive thou hast made the like mistake—It is too late for excuses—I faint.—If Isabella is at hand, call her—I have important secrets to—He is dying! said one of the attendants; has nobody a crucifix about them? Andrea, do thou pray over him.—Fetch some water, said Theodore, and pour it down his throat, while I hasten to the princess. Saying this, he flew to Isabella, and in few words told her modestly that he had been so unfortunate by mistake as to wound a gentleman from her father's court, who wished ere he died to impart something of consequence to her. The princess, who had been transported at hearing the voice of Theodore, as he called to her to come forth, was astonished at what she heard. Suffering herself to be conducted by Theodore, the new proof of whose valour recalled her dispersed spirits, she came where the bleeding knight lay speechless on the ground—but her fears returned when she beheld the domestics of Manfred. She would again have fled if Theodore had not made her observe that they were unarmed, and had not threatened them with instant death, if they should dare to seize the princess. The stranger, opening his eyes, and beholding a woman, said, Art thou—pray tell me truly—art thou Isabella of Vicenza? I am, said she; good heaven restore thee!—Then thou—then thou—said the knight, struggling for utterance—seest—thy father!—Give me one—Oh! amazement! horror! what do I hear! what do I see! cried Isabella. My father! You my father! How came you here, sir? For heaven's sake, speak!—Oh! run for help, or he will expire!—'Tis most true, said the wounded knight, exerting all his force; I am Frederic thy father—Yes, I came to deliver thee—It will not be—Give me a parting kiss, and take—Sir, said Theodore, do not exhaust yourself: suffer us to convey you to the castle.—To the castle! said Isabella: Is there no help nearer than the castle? Would you expose my father to the tyrant? If he goes thither, I dare not accompany him.—And yet, can I leave him? My child, said Frederic, it matters not for me whither I am carried: few minutes will place me beyond danger: but while I have eyes to dote on thee, forsake me not, dear Isabella! This brave knight—I know not who he is—will protect thy innocence. Sir, you will not abandon my child, will you?—Theodore, shedding tears over his victim, and vowing to guard the princess at the expence of his life, persuaded Frederic to suffer himself to be conducted to the castle. They placed him on a horse belonging to one of the domestics, after binding up his wounds as well as they were able. Theodore marched by his side; and the afflicted Isabella, who could not bear to quit him, followed mournfully behind.

Chapter IV

The sorrowful troop no sooner arrived at the castle, than they were met by Hippolita and Matilda, whom Isabella had sent one of the domestics before to advertise of their approach. The ladies, causing Frederic to be conveyed into the nearest chamber, retired, while the surgeons examined his wounds. Matilda blushed at seeing Theodore and Isabella together; but endeavoured to conceal it by embracing the latter, and condoling with her on her father's mischance. The surgeons soon came to acquaint Hippolita that none of the Marquis's wounds were dangerous; and that he was desirous of seeing his daughter and the princesses. Theodore, under pretence of expressing his joy at being freed from his apprehensions of the combat being fatal to Frederic, could not resist the impulse of following Matilda. Her eyes were so often cast down on meeting his, that Isabella, who regarded Theodore as attentively as he gazed on Matilda, soon divined who the object was that he had told her in the cave engaged his affections. While this mute scene passed, Hippolita demanded of Frederic the cause of his having taken that mysterious course for reclaiming his daughter; and threw in various apologies to excuse her lord for the match contracted between their children. Frederic, however incensed against Manfred, was not insensible to the courtesy and benevolence of Hippolita: but he was still more struck with the lovely form of Matilda. Wishing to detain them by his bedside, he informed Hippolita of his story. He told her that, while prisoner to the infidels, he had dreamed that his daughter, of whom he had learned no news since his captivity, was detained in a castle, where she was in danger of the most dreadful misfortunes; and that if he obtained his liberty, and repaired to a wood near Joppa,[1] he would learn more. Alarmed at this dream, and incapable of obeying the direction given by it, his chains became more grievous than ever. But while his thoughts were occupied on the means of obtaining his liberty, he received the agreeable news that the confederate princes who were warring in Palestine had paid his ransom. He instantly set out for the wood that had been marked in his dream. For three days he and his attendants had

[1]The port city of Jaffa in ancient Palestine, conquered by Richard the Lion-hearted in the Third Crusade of 1191, became the headquarters of "the confederate princes" of Christian Europe, including France, England, and the Holy Roman Emperor.

wandered in the forest without seeing a human form: but on the evening of the third they came to a cell, in which they found a venerable hermit in the agonies of death. Applying rich cordials, they brought the saint-like man to his speech. My sons, said he, I am bounden to your charity—but it is in vain—I am going to my eternal rest—yet I die with the satisfaction of performing the will of heaven. When first I repaired to this solitude, after seeing my country become a prey to unbelievers [it is, alas! above fifty years since I was witness to that dreadful scene!] saint Nicholas appeared to me, and revealed a secret, which he bade me never disclose to mortal man, but on my death-bed. This is that tremendous hour, and ye are no doubt the chosen warriors to whom I was ordered to reveal my trust. As soon as ye have done the last offices to this wretched corse, dig under the seventh tree on the left hand of this poor cave, and your pains will—Oh! good heaven receive my soul! With those words the devout man breathed his last. By break of day, continued Frederic, when we had committed the holy relics to earth,[2] we dug according to direction—But what was our astonishment, when about the depth of six feet we discovered an enormous sabre—the very weapon yonder in the court. On the blade, which was then partly out of the scabbard, though since closed by our efforts in removing it, were written the following lines—No; excuse me, madam, added the marquis, turning to Hippolita; if I forbear to repeat them: I respect your sex and rank, and would not be guilty of offending your ear with sounds injurious to aught that is dear to you.—He paused. Hippolita trembled. She did not doubt but Frederic was destined by heaven to accomplish the fate that seemed to threaten her house. Looking with anxious fondness at Matilda, a silent tear stole down her cheek; but recollecting herself, she said, Proceed, my lord; heaven does nothing in vain: mortals must receive its divine behests with lowliness and submission. It is our part to deprecate[3] its wrath, or bow to its decrees. Repeat the sentence, my lord: we listen resigned.—Frederic was grieved that he had proceeded so far. The dignity and patient firmness of Hippolita penetrated him with respect, and the tender silent affection, with which the princess and her daughter regarded each other,

[2] Buried the corpse ("corse").
[3] Pray for deliverance from.

melted him almost to tears. Yet apprehensive that his forbearance[4] to obey would be more alarming, he repeated in a faltering and low voice the following lines:

> Where'er a casque that suits this sword is found,
> With perils is thy daughter compass'd round:
> *Alfonso's* blood alone can save the maid,
> And quiet a long restless prince's shade.

What is there in these lines, said Theodore impatiently, that affects these princesses? Why were they to be shocked by a mysterious delicacy, that has so little foundation? Your words are rude, young man, said the marquis; and though fortune has favoured you once—My honoured lord, said Isabella, who resented Theodore's warmth, which she perceived was dictated by his sentiments for Matilda, discompose not yourself for the glosing[5] of a peasant's son: he forgets the reverence he owes you; but he is not accustomed—Hippolita, concerned at the heat that had arisen, checked Theodore for his boldness, but with an air acknowledging his zeal; and, changing the conversation, demanded of Frederic where he had left her lord? As the marquis was going to reply, they heard a noise without, and rising to inquire the cause, Manfred, Jerome, and part of the troop, who had met an imperfect rumour of what had happened, entered the chamber. Manfred advanced hastily towards Frederic's bed to condole with him on his misfortune, and to learn the circumstances of the combat; when starting in an agony of terror and amazement, he cried, Ha! what art thou, thou dreadful spectre! Is my hour come?—My dearest, gracious lord, cried Hippolita, clasping him in her arms, what is it you see? Why do you fix your eye-balls thus?—What! cried Manfred breathless; dost thou see nothing, Hippolita? Is this ghastly phantom sent to me alone—to me, who did not—For mercy's sweetest self, my lord, said Hippolita, resume your soul, command your reason. There is none here, but us, your friends. What, is not that Alfonso? cried Manfred. Dost thou not see him? Can it be my brain's delirium?[6]

---

[4]Hesitation.

[5]Interpretation.

[6]These exchanges evoke Macbeth's guilty vision of murdered Banquo's ghost (*Macbeth* 3.4).

This! my lord, said Hippolita; this is Theodore, the youth who has been so unfortunate—Theodore! said Manfred mournfully, and striking his forehead—Theodore, or a phantom, he has unhinged the soul of Manfred. But how comes he here? and how comes he in armour? I believe he went in search of Isabella, said Hippolita. Of Isabella! said Manfred, relapsing into rage—Yes, yes, that is not doubtful—But how did he escape from durance[7] in which I left him? Was it Isabella, or this hypocritical old friar, that procured his enlargement?[8]—And would a parent be criminal, my lord, said Theodore, if he meditated the deliverance of his child? Jerome, amazed to hear himself in a manner accused by his son, and without foundation, knew not what to think. He could not comprehend how Theodore had escaped, how he came to be armed, and to encounter Frederic. Still he would not venture to ask any questions that might tend to inflame Manfred's wrath against his son. Jerome's silence convinced Manfred that he had contrived Theodore's release.—And is it thus, thou ungrateful old man, said the prince, addressing himself to the friar, that thou repayest mine and Hippolita's bounties? And not content with traversing my heart's nearest wishes, thou armest thy bastard, and bringest him into my own castle to insult me!—My lord, said Theodore, you wrong my father: nor he nor I are capable of harbouring a thought against your peace. Is it insolence thus to surrender myself to your highness's pleasure? added he, laying his sword respectfully at Manfred's feet. Behold my bosom; strike, my lord, if you suspect that a disloyal thought is lodged there. There is not a sentiment engraven on my heart that does not venerate you and yours. The grace and fervour with which Theodore uttered these words, interested every person present in his favour. Even Manfred was touched—yet still possessed with[9] his resemblance to Alfonso, his admiration was dashed with secret horror. Rise, said he; thy life is not my present purpose.—But tell me thy history, and how thou camest connected with this old traitor here. My lord, said Jerome eagerly.—Peace, impostor! said Manfred; I will not have him prompted. My lord, said Theodore, I want no assistance; my story

[7]Imprisonment.
[8]Freedom.
[9]Gripped by.

is very brief. I was carried at five years of age to Algiers with my mother, who had been taken by corsairs[10] from the coast of Sicily. She died of grief in less than a twelvemonth.—The tears gushed from Jerome's eyes, on whose countenance a thousand anxious passions stood expressed. Before she died, continued Theodore, she bound a writing about my arm under my garments, which told me I was the son of the Count Falconara.—It is most true, said Jerome; I am that wretched father.—Again I enjoin thee silence,[11] said Manfred: proceed. I remained in slavery, said Theodore, until within these two years, when attending on my master in his cruizes, I was delivered by a christian vessel, which overpowered the pirate; and discovering myself to the captain, he generously put me on shore in Sicily. But alas! instead of finding a father, I learned that his estate, which was situated on the coast, had, during his absence, been laid waste by the rover[12] who had carried my mother and me into captivity: that his castle had been burnt to the ground, and that my father on his return had sold what remained, and was retired into religion in the kingdom of Naples, but where, no man could inform me. Destitute and friendless, hopeless almost of attaining the transport of a parent's embrace, I took the first opportunity of setting sail for Naples; from whence, within these six days, I wandered into this province, still supporting myself by the labour of my hands; nor until yester-morn did I believe that heaven had reserved any lot for me but peace of mind and contented poverty. This, my lord, is Theodore's story. I am blessed beyond my hope in finding a father; I am unfortunate beyond my desert in having incurred your highness's displeasure. He ceased. A murmur of approbation gently arose from the audience. This is not all, said Frederic; I am bound in honour to add what he suppresses. Though he is modest, I must be generous—he is one of the bravest youths on christian ground. He is warm[13] too; and from the short knowledge I have of him, I will pledge myself for his veracity: if what he reports of himself were not true, he would not utter it—and for me, youth, I honour a frankness which becomes thy birth. But now, and thou didst offend

---

[10]Pirates licensed by Muslim governments to attack Christian ships.

[11]Be quiet.

[12]Pirate.

[13]Ardent.

me; yet the noble blood which flows in thy veins may well be allowed to boil out, when it has so recently traced itself to its source. Come, my lord, [turning to Manfred], if I can pardon him, surely you may: it is not the youth's fault, if you took him for a spectre. This bitter taunt galled the soul of Manfred. If beings from another world, replied he haughtily, have power to impress my mind with awe, it is more than living man can do; nor could a stripling's arm.—My lord, interrupted Hippolita, your guest has occasion for repose; shall we not leave him to his rest? Saying this, and taking Manfred by the hand, she took leave of Frederic, and led the company forth. The prince, not sorry to quit a conversation which recalled to mind the discovery he had made of his most secret sensations, suffered himself to be conducted to his own apartment, after permitting Theodore, though under engagement to return to the castle on the morrow [a condition the young man gladly accepted] to retire with his father to the convent. Matilda and Isabella were too much occupied with their own reflections, and too little content with each other, to wish for farther converse that night. They separated each to her chamber, with more expressions of ceremony, and fewer of affection, than had passed between them since their childhood.

If they parted with small cordiality, they did but meet with greater impatience, as soon as the sun was risen. Their minds were in a situation that excluded sleep, and each recollected a thousand questions which she wished she had put to the other overnight. Matilda reflected that Isabella had been twice delivered by Theodore in very critical situations, which she could not believe accidental. His eyes, it was true, had been fixed on her in Frederic's chamber; but that might have been to disguise his passion for Isabella from the fathers of both. It were better to clear this up. She wished to know the truth, lest she should wrong her friend by entertaining a passion for Isabella's lover. Thus jealousy prompted, and at the same time borrowed an excuse from friendship to justify its curiosity.

Isabella, not less restless, had better foundation for her suspicions. Both Theodore's tongue and eyes had told her his heart was engaged, it was true—yet perhaps, Matilda might not correspond to[14] his passion—She had ever appeared insensible to love; all her

[14]Return.

thoughts were set on heaven—Why did I dissuade her? said Isabella to herself; I am punished for my generosity—But when did they meet? where?—It cannot be; I have deceived myself—Perhaps last night was the first time they ever beheld each other—it must be some other object that has prepossessed his affections—If it is, I am not so unhappy as I thought; if it is not my friend Matilda—How! can I stoop to wish for the affection of a man, who rudely and unnecessarily acquainted me with his indifference? and that at the very moment in which common courtesy demanded at least expressions of civility. I will go to my dear Matilda, who will confirm me in this becoming pride—Man is false—I will advise with her on taking the veil: she will rejoice to find me in this disposition; and I will acquaint her that I no longer oppose her inclination for the cloister. In this frame of mind, and determined to open her heart entirely to Matilda, she went to that princess's chamber, whom she found already dressed, and leaning pensively on her arm. This attitude, so correspondent to what she felt herself, revived Isabella's suspicions, and destroyed the confidence she had purposed to place in her friend. They blushed at meeting, and were too much novices to disguise their sensations with address.[15] After some unmeaning questions and replies, Matilda demanded of Isabella the cause of her flight. The latter, who had almost forgotten Manfred's passion, so entirely was she occupied by her own, concluding that Matilda referred to her last escape from the convent, which had occasioned the events of the preceding evening, replied, Martelli brought word to the convent that your mother was dead.—Oh! said Matilda, interrupting her, Bianca has explained that mistake to me: on seeing me faint, she cried out, The princess is dead! and Martelli, who had come for the usual dole to the castle—And what made you faint? said Isabella, indifferent to the rest. Matilda blushed, and stammered—My father—he was sitting in judgment on a criminal.— What criminal? said Isabella eagerly. A young man, said Matilda— I believe—I think it was that young man that—What, Theodore? said Isabella. Yes, answered she; I never saw him before; I do not know how he had offended my father—but, as he has been of service to you, I am glad my lord has pardoned him. Served me? replied Isabella: do you term it serving me, to wound my father,

---

[15]Skill.

and almost occasion his death? Though it is but since yesterday that I am blessed with knowing a parent, I hope Matilda does not think I am such a stranger to filial tenderness as not to resent the boldness of that audacious youth, and that it is impossible for me ever to feel any affection for one who dared to lift his arm against the author of my being. No, Matilda, my heart abhors him; and if you still retain the friendship for me that you have vowed from your infancy, you will detest a man who has been on the point of making me miserable for ever. Matilda held down her head, and replied, I hope my dearest Isabella does not doubt her Matilda's friendship: I never beheld that youth until yesterday; he is almost a stranger to me: but as the surgeons have pronounced your father out of danger, you ought not to harbour uncharitable resentment against one who I am persuaded did not know the marquis was related to you. You plead his cause very pathetically, said Isabella, considering he is so much a stranger to you! I am mistaken, or he returns your charity. What mean you? said Matilda. Nothing, said Isabella; repenting that she had given Matilda a hint of Theodore's inclination for her. Then changing the discourse, she asked Matilda what occasioned Manfred to take Theodore for a spectre? Bless me, said Matilda, did not you observe his extreme resemblance to the portrait of Alfonso in the gallery? I took notice of it to Bianca even before I saw him in armour; but with the helmet on, he is the very image of that picture. I do not much observe pictures, said Isabella; much less have I examined this young man so attentively as you seem to have done.—Ah! Matilda, your heart is in danger—but let me warn you as a friend—He has owned to me that he is in love: it cannot be with you, for yesterday was the first time you ever met—was it not? Certainly, replied Matilda. But why does my dearest Isabella conclude from anything I have said, that—She paused—then continuing, He saw you first, and I am far from having the vanity to think that my little portion of charms could engage a heart devoted to you. May you be happy, Isabella, whatever is the fate of Matilda!—My lovely friend, said Isabella, whose heart was too honest to resist a kind expression, it is you that Theodore admires; I saw it; I am persuaded of it; nor shall a thought of my own happiness suffer me to interfere with yours. This frankness drew tears from the gentle Matilda; and jealousy, that for a moment had raised a coolness between these amiable maidens, soon gave way to the natural sincerity and candour of their souls. Each confessed to the other the impression that Theodore had made on her; and this confidence was followed by a struggle of generosity, each insisting on yielding her claim to her friend. At length, the dignity of Isabella's virtue reminding her of the preference which Theodore had almost declared for her rival, made her determine to conquer her passion, and cede the beloved object to her friend.

During this contest of amity, Hippolita entered her daughter's chamber. Madam, said she to Isabella, you have so much tenderness for Matilda, and interest yourself so kindly in whatever affects our wretched house, that I can have no secrets with my child which are not proper for you to hear. The princesses were all attention and anxiety. Know then, madam, continued Hippolita, and you my dearest Matilda, that being convinced by all the events of these two last ominous days, that heaven purposes the sceptre of Otranto should pass from Manfred's hands into those of the marquis Frederic, I have been perhaps inspired with the thought of averting our total destruction by the union of our rival houses. With this view I have been proposing to Manfred, my lord, to tender this dear dear child to Frederic, your father.—Me to lord Frederic! cried Matilda—Good heavens! my gracious mother—and have you named it to my father? I have, said Hippolita: he listened benignly to my proposal, and is gone to break it to the marquis. Ah! wretched princess! cried Isabella, what hast thou done! What ruin has thy inadvertent goodness been preparing for thyself, for me, and for Matilda! Ruin from me to you and to my child! said Hippolita: What can this mean? Alas! said Isabella, the purity of your own heart prevents your seeing the depravity of others. Manfred, your lord, that impious man—Hold, said Hippolita; you must not in my presence, young lady, mention Manfred with disrespect: he is my lord and husband, and—Will not long be so, said Isabella, if his wicked purposes can be carried into execution. This language amazes me, said Hippolita. Your feeling, Isabella, is warm; but until this hour I never knew it betray you into intemperance. What deed of Manfred authorizes you to treat him as a murderer, an assassin? Thou virtuous, and too credulous princess! replied Isabella; it is not thy life he aims at—it is to separate himself from thee! to divorce thee! To—to divorce me! To divorce my mother! cried Hippolita and Matilda at once.—Yes, said Isabella; and to complete his crime, he meditates—I cannot speak it! What can surpass what thou hast already uttered? said Matilda. Hippolita was silent. Grief choked her speech: and the recollection of Manfred's late ambiguous discourses confirmed what she heard. Excellent, dear lady! madam! mother! cried Isabella, flinging herself at Hippolita's feet in a transport of passion; trust me, believe me, I will die a thousand deaths sooner than consent to injure you, than yield to so odious— oh!—This is too much! cried Hippolita: what crimes does one crime suggest! Rise, dear Isabella; I do not doubt your virtue. Oh! Matilda, this stroke is too heavy for thee! Weep not, my child; and not a murmur, I charge thee. Remember, he is *thy* father still! But you are my mother too, said Matilda fervently; and *you* are virtuous, *you* are guiltless!—Oh! must not I, must not I complain? You must not, said Hippolita—Come, all will yet be well. Manfred, in the agony for the loss of thy brother, knew not what he said: perhaps Isabella misunderstood him: his heart is good—and, my child, thou knowest not all. There is a destiny hangs over us; the hand of Providence is stretched out—Oh! could I but save thee from the wreck!—Yes, continued she in a firmer tone, perhaps the sacrifice of myself may atone for all—I will go and offer myself to this divorce—it boots not[16] what becomes of me. I will withdraw into the neighbouring monastery, and waste the remainder of life in prayers and tears for my child and—the prince! Thou art as much too good for this world, said Isabella, as Manfred is execrable—But think not, lady, that thy weakness shall determine for me. I swear, hear me all ye angels—Stop, I adjure thee, cried Hippolita; remember, thou dost not depend on thyself; thou hast a father.—My father is too pious, too noble, interrupted Isabella, to command an impious deed. But should he command it, can a father enjoin a cursed act?[17] I was contracted to the son, can I wed the father?—No, madam, no; force should not drag me to Manfred's hated bed. I loathe him, I abhor him: divine and human laws forbid.—And my friend, my dearest Matilda! would I wound her tender soul by injuring her adored mother? my own mother—I never have known another.— Oh! she is the mother of both! cried Matilda. Can we, can we, Isabella, adore her too much? My lovely children, said the touched

---

[16]Doesn't matter.

[17]The "incest" of marrying Manfred.

Hippolita, your tenderness overpowers me—but I must not give way to it. It is not ours to make election[18] for ourselves; heaven, our fathers, and our husbands must decide for us. Have patience until you hear what Manfred and Frederic have determined. If the marquis accepts Matilda's hand, I know she will readily obey. Heaven may interpose and prevent the rest. What means my child? continued she, seeing Matilda fall at her feet with a flood of speechless tears—But no; answer me not, my daughter; I must not hear a word against the pleasure of thy father. Oh! doubt not my obedience, my dreadful obedience to him and to you! said Matilda. But can I, most respected of women, can I experience all this tenderness, this world of goodness, and conceal a thought from the best of mothers? What art thou going to utter? said Isabella trembling. Recollect thyself, Matilda. No, Isabella, said the princess, I should not deserve this incomparable parent, if the inmost recesses of my soul harboured a thought without her permission—Nay, I have offended her; I have suffered a passion to enter my heart without her avowal[19]—But here I disclaim it; here I vow to heaven and her— My child! my child! said Hippolita, what words are these? What new calamities has fate in store for us? Thou, a passion? thou, in this hour of destruction—Oh! I see all my guilt! said Matilda. I abhor myself, if I cost my mother a pang. She is the dearest thing I have on earth—Oh! I will never, never behold him more! Isabella, said Hippolita, thou art conscious to this unhappy secret, whatever it is. Speak! What! cried Matilda, have I so forfeited my mother's love, that she will not permit me even to speak my own guilt? Oh! wretched, wretched Matilda!—Thou art too cruel, said Isabella to Hippolita: canst thou behold this anguish of a virtuous mind, and not commiserate it? Not pity my child! said Hippolita, catching Matilda in her arms—Oh! I know she is good, she is all virtue, all tenderness, and duty. I do forgive thee, my excellent, my only hope! The princesses then revealed to Hippolita their mutual inclination for Theodore, and the purpose of Isabella to resign him to Matilda. Hippolita blamed their imprudence, and showed them the improbability that either father would consent to bestow his heiress on so poor a man, though nobly born. Some comfort it gave her to find

18Choice.
19Approval.

their passion of so recent a date, and that Theodore had had but little cause to suspect it in either. She strictly enjoined them to avoid all correspondence[20] with him. This Matilda fervently promised: but Isabella, who flattered herself that she meant no more than to promote his union with her friend, could not determine to avoid him; and made no reply. I will go to the convent, said Hippolita, and order new masses to be said for a deliverance from these calamities.—Oh! my mother, said Matilda, you mean to quit us: you mean to take sanctuary, and to give my father an opportunity of pursuing his fatal intention. Alas! on my knees I supplicate you to forbear—Will you leave me a prey to Frederic? I will follow you to the convent.—Be at peace, my child, said Hippolita: I will return instantly. I will never abandon thee, until I know it is the will of heaven, and for thy benefit. Do not deceive me, said Matilda. I will not marry Frederic until thou commandest it. Alas! what will become of me?—Why that exclamation? said Hippolita. I have promised thee to return.—Ah! my mother, replied Matilda, stay and save me from myself. A frown from thee can do more than all my father's severity. I have given away my heart, and you alone can make me recall it. No more, said Hippolita: thou must not relapse, Matilda. I can quit Theodore, said she, but must I wed another? Let me attend thee to the altar, and shut myself from the world for ever.[21] Thy fate depends on thy father, said Hippolita: I have ill-bestowed my tenderness, if it has taught thee to revere aught beyond him. Adieu, my child! I go to pray for thee.

Hippolita's real purpose was to demand of Jerome, whether in conscience she might not consent to the divorce. She had oft urged Manfred to resign the principality, which the delicacy of her conscience rendered an hourly burthen to her. These scruples concurred to make the separation from her husband appear less dreadful to her than it would have seemed in any other situation.

Jerome, at quitting the castle overnight, had questioned Theodore severely why he had accused him to Manfred of being privy to his escape. Theodore owned it had been with design to prevent Manfred's suspicion from alighting on Matilda; and added, the holiness of Jerome's life and character secured him from the

---

[20]Communication.

[21]Enter a convent and take vows.

tyrant's wrath. Jerome was heartily grieved to discover his son's inclination for that princess; and, leaving him to his rest, promised in
the morning to acquaint him with important reasons for conquer-
ing his passion. Theodore, like Isabella, was too recently acquainted with parental authority to submit to its decisions against
the impulse of his heart. He had little curiosity to learn the Friar's
reasons, and less disposition to obey them. The lovely Matilda had
made stronger impressions on him than filial affection. All night he
pleased himself with visions of love; and it was not till late after the
morning-office, that he recollected the friar's commands to attend
him at Alfonso's tomb.

Young man, said Jerome, when he saw him, this tardiness does
not please me. Have a father's commands already so little weight?
Theodore made awkward excuses, and attributed his delay to having overslept himself. And on whom were thy dreams employed?
said the friar sternly. His son blushed. Come, come, resumed the
friar, inconsiderate youth, this must not be; eradicate this guilty
passion from thy breast.—Guilty passion! cried Theodore: can guilt
dwell with innocent beauty and virtuous modesty? It is sinful,
replied the friar, to cherish those whom heaven has doomed to destruction. A tyrant's race must be swept from the earth to the third
and fourth generation. Will heaven visit the innocent for the crimes
of the guilty? said Theodore. The fair Matilda has virtues enough—
To undo thee, interrupted Jerome. Hast thou so soon forgotten that
twice the savage Manfred has pronounced thy sentence?[22] Nor
have I forgotten, sir, said Theodore, that the charity of his daughter
delivered me from his power. I can forget injuries, but never benefits. The injuries thou hast received from Manfred's race, said the
friar, are beyond what thou canst conceive.—Reply not, but view
this holy image! Beneath this marble monument rest the ashes of
the good Alfonso; a prince adorned with every virtue: the father of
his people! the delight of mankind! Kneel, head-strong boy, and
list,[23] while a father unfolds a tale of horror that will expel every
sentiment from thy soul, but sensations of sacred vengeance.—
Alfonso! much-injured prince! let thy unsatisfied shade sit awful on
the troubled air, while these trembling lips—Ha! who comes there?

[22]Sentenced you to death.
[23]Listen.

Chapel, Strawberry Hill (King Library, Miami University)

The most wretched of women, said Hippolita, entering the choir. Good father, art thou at leisure?—But why this kneeling youth? what means the horror imprinted on each countenance? why at this venerable tomb—Alas! hast thou seen aught? We were pouring forth our orisons to heaven, replied the friar, with some confusion, to put an end to the woes of this deplorable province. Join with us, lady! thy spotless soul may obtain an exemption from the judgments which the portents of these days but too speakingly denounce against thy house. I pray fervently to heaven to divert them, said the pious princess. Thou knowest it has been the occupation of my life to wrest a blessing for my lord and my harmless children— One, alas! is taken from me! Would heaven but hear me for my poor Matilda! Father, intercede for her! Every heart will bless her, cried Theodore with rapture.—Be dumb,[24] rash youth! said Jerome. And thou, fond princess, contend not with the powers above! the Lord giveth, and the Lord taketh away: bless his holy name, and submit to his decrees. I do most devoutly, said Hippolita: but will he not spare my only comfort? must Matilda perish too?—Ah! father, I came—But dismiss thy son. No ear but thine must hear what I have to utter. May heaven grant thy every wish, most excellent princess! said Theodore retiring. Jerome frowned.

Hippolita then acquainted the friar with the proposal she had suggested to Manfred, his approbation of it, and the tender[25] of Matilda that he was gone to make to Frederic. Jerome could not conceal his dislike of the motion, which he covered under pretence of the improbability that Frederic, the nearest of blood to Alfonso, and who was come to claim his succession, would yield to an alliance with the usurper of his right. But nothing could equal the perplexity of the friar, when Hippolita confessed her readiness not to oppose the separation, and demanded his opinion on the legality of her acquiescence. The friar catched eagerly at her request of his advice, and without explaining his aversion to the proposed marriage of Manfred and Isabella, he painted to Hippolita in the most alarming colours the sinfulness of her consent, denounced judgments against her if she complied, and enjoined her in the severest terms to treat any such proposition with every mark of indignation and refusal.

[24]Silent.
[25]Offer.

Manfred, in the mean time, had broken[26] his purpose to Frederic, and proposed the double marriage. That weak prince, who had been struck with the charms of Matilda, listened but too eagerly to the offer. He forgot his enmity to Manfred, whom he saw but little hope of dispossessing by force; and flattering himself that no issue might succeed from the union of his daughter with the tyrant, he looked upon his own succession to the principality as facilitated by wedding Matilda. He made faint opposition to the proposal; affecting, for form only, not to acquiesce unless Hippolita should consent to the divorce. Manfred took that upon himself. Transported with his success, and impatient to see himself in a situation to expect sons, he hastened to his wife's apartment, determined to extort her compliance. He learned with indignation that she was absent at the convent. His guilt suggested to him that she had probably been informed by Isabella of his purpose. He doubted whether[27] her retirement to the convent did not import an intention of remaining there, until she could raise obstacles to their divorce; and the suspicions he had already entertained of Jerome, made him apprehend that the friar would not only traverse his views, but might have inspired Hippolita with the resolution of talking sanctuary. Impatient to unravel this clue, and to defeat its success, Manfred hastened to the convent, and arrived there as the friar was earnestly exhorting the princess never to yield to the divorce.

Madam, said Manfred, what business drew you hither? Why did you not await my return from the marquis? I came to implore a blessing on your councils, replied Hippolita. My councils do not need a friar's intervention, said Manfred—and of all men living is that hoary[28] traitor the only one whom you delight to confer with? Profane prince! said Jerome: is it at the altar that thou choosest to insult the servants of the altar?—But, Manfred, thy impious schemes are known. Heaven and this virtuous lady know them. Nay, frown not, prince. The church despises thy menaces. Her[29] thunders will be heard above thy wrath. Dare to proceed in thy cursed purpose of a divorce, until her sentence be known, and here

[26]Explained.
[27]Was unsure if.
[28]White-haired (elderly).
[29]The Church's.

I lance her anathema[30] at thy head. Audacious rebel! said Manfred, endeavouring to conceal the awe with which the friar's words inspired him; dost thou presume to threaten thy lawful prince? Thou art no lawful prince, said Jerome; thou art no prince—Go, discuss thy claim with Frederic; and when that is done—It is done, replied Manfred: Frederic accepts Matilda's hand, and is content to waive his claim, unless I have no male issue.—As he spoke those words three drops of blood fell from the nose of Alfonso's statue. Manfred turned pale, and the princess sank on her knees. Behold! said the friar: mark this miraculous indication that the blood of Alfonso will never mix with that of Manfred! My gracious lord, said Hippolita, let us submit ourselves to heaven. Think not thy ever obedient wife rebels against thy authority. I have no will but that of my lord and the church. To that revered tribunal let us appeal. It does not depend on us to burst the bonds that unite us. If the church shall approve the dissolution of our marriage, be it so—I have but few years, and those of sorrow, to pass. Where can they be worn away so well as at the foot of this altar, in prayers for thine and Matilda's safety? But thou shalt not remain here until then, said Manfred. Repair with me to the castle, and there I will advise on the proper measures for a divorce.—But this meddling friar comes not thither; my hospitable roof shall never more harbour a traitor—and for thy reverence's offspring, continued he, I banish him from my dominions. He, I ween, is no sacred personage, nor under the protection of the church. Whoever weds Isabella, it shall not be Father Falconara's started-up son.[31] They start up, said the friar, who are suddenly beheld in the seat of lawful princes; but they wither away like the grass, and their place knows them no more. Manfred, casting a look of scorn at the friar, led Hippolita forth; but at the door of the church whispered one of his attendants to remain concealed about the convent, and bring him instant notice, if any one from the castle should repair thither.

[30]Thrust her excommunication.
[31]Upstart, an illicit rise in status.

Chapter V

Every reflection which Manfred made on the friar's behaviour, conspired to persuade him that Jerome was privy to an amour between Isabella and Theodore. But Jerome's new presumption, so dissonant from his former meekness, suggested still deeper apprehensions. The prince even suspected that the friar depended on some secret support from Frederic, whose arrival coinciding with the novel appearance of Theodore seemed to bespeak a correspondence. Still more was he troubled with the resemblance of Theodore to Alfonso's portrait. The latter he knew had unquestionably died without issue. Frederic had consented to bestow Isabella on him. These contradictions agitated his mind with numberless pangs. He saw but two methods of extricating himself from his difficulties. The one was to resign his dominions to the marquis.—Pride, ambition, and his reliance on ancient prophecies, which had pointed out a possibility of his preserving them to his posterity, combated that thought. The other was to press his marriage with Isabella. After long ruminating on these anxious thoughts, as he marched silently with Hippolita to the castle, he at last discoursed with that princess on the subject of his disquiet, and used every insinuating and plausible argument to extract her consent to, even her promise of promoting, the divorce. Hippolita needed little persuasions to bend her to his pleasure. She endeavoured to win him over to the measure of resigning his dominions; but finding her exhortations fruitless, she assured him, that as far as her conscience would allow, she would raise no opposition to a separation, though, without better founded scruples than what he yet alleged, she would not engage to be active in demanding it.

This compliance, though inadequate, was sufficient to raise Manfred's hopes. He trusted that his power and wealth would easily advance his suit at the court of Rome, whither he resolved to engage Frederic to take a journey on purpose. That prince had discovered so much passion for Matilda, that Manfred hoped to obtain all he wished by holding out or withdrawing his daughter's charms, according as the marquis should appear more or less disposed to co-operate in his views. Even the absence of Frederic would be a material point gained, until he could take further measures for his security.

Dismissing Hippolita to her apartment, he repaired to that of the marquis; but crossing the great hall through which he was to pass, he met Bianca. That damsel he knew was in the confidence of both the young ladies. It immediately occurred to him to sift her on the subject of Isabella and Theodore. Calling her aside into the recess of the oriel window[1] of the hall, and soothing her with many fair words and promises, he demanded of her whether she knew aught of the state of Isabella's affections. I! my lord? No, my lord—Yes, my lord—Poor lady! she is wonderfully alarmed about her father's wounds; but I tell her he will do well; don't your highness think so? I do not ask you, replied Manfred, what she thinks about her father: but you are in her secrets: come, be a good girl and tell me, is there any young man—ha?—you understand me. Lord bless me! understand your highness? No, not I: I told her a few vulnerary[2] herbs and repose—I am not talking, replied the prince, impatiently, about her father: I know he will do well. Bless me, I rejoice to hear your highness say so; for though I thought it not right to let my young lady despond, methought his greatness had a wan look, and a something—I remember when young Ferdinand was wounded by the Venetian. Thou answerest from the point,[3] interrupted Manfred; but here, take this jewel, perhaps that may fix thy attention—Nay, no reverences;[4] my favour shall not stop here—Come, tell me truly; how stands Isabella's heart? Well, your highness has such a way, said Bianca—to be sure—but can your highness keep a secret? If it should ever come out of your lips—It shall not, it shall not, cried Manfred. Nay, but swear, your highness—by my halidame,[5] if it should ever be known that I said it—Why, truth is truth, I do not think my Lady Isabella ever much affectioned my young lord your son: yet he was a sweet youth as one should see. I am sure, if I had been a princess—But bless me! I must attend my lady Matilda; she will marvel what is become of me.—Stay, cried Manfred, thou hast not satisfied my question. Hast thou ever carried any message, any letter? I! Good gracious! cried Bianca: I carry a letter? I would not to be a queen. I hope your highness thinks, though I am poor, I am honest. Did your highness never hear what

---

[1] A decorative bay window on the upper story.
[2] Curative.
[3] You are digressing.
[4] Signs of deference, gratefulness.
[5] Holy dame (Virgin Mary).

Count Marsigli offered me, when he came a-wooing to my lady Matilda?—I have not leisure, said Manfred, to listen to thy tales. I do not question thy honesty; but it is thy duty to conceal nothing from me. How long has Isabella been acquainted with Theodore?—Nay, there is nothing can escape your highness, said Bianca—not that I know any thing of the matter. Theodore, to be sure, is a proper young man, and, as my lady Matilda says, the very image of good Alfonso: Has not your highness remarked it? Yes, yes—No—thou torturest me, said Manfred: Where did they meet? when?—Who, my lady Matilda? said Bianca. No, no, not Matilda; Isabella: when did Isabella first become acquainted with this Theodore?—Virgin Mary! said Bianca, how should I know? Thou dost know, said Manfred; and I must know; I will.—Lord! your highness is not jealous of young Theodore!? said Bianca.—Jealous! No, no: why should I be jealous?—Perhaps I mean to unite them— if I were sure Isabella would have no repugnance.—Repugnance! No, I'll warrant[6] her, said Bianca: he is as comely[7] a youth as ever trod on christian ground: we are all in love with him: there is not a soul in the castle but would be rejoiced to have him for our prince—I mean, when it shall please heaven to call your highness to itself.—Indeed! said Manfred: has it gone so far! Oh! this cursed friar!—But I must not lose time—Go, Bianca, attend Isabella; but I charge thee, not a word of what has passed. Find out how she is affected towards Theodore; bring me good news, and that ring has a companion. Wait at the foot of the winding staircase: I am going to visit the marquis, and will talk farther with thee at my return.

Manfred, after some general conversation, desired Frederic to dismiss the two knights, his companions, having to talk with him on urgent affairs. As soon as they were alone, he began in artful guise to sound the marquis on the subject of Matilda; and finding him disposed to his wish, he let drop hints on the difficulties that would attend the celebration of their marriage, unless—At that instant Bianca burst into the room, with a wildness in her look and gestures that spoke the utmost terror. Oh! my lord, my lord! cried she; we are all undone! It is come again! it is come again!—What is come again? cried Manfred amazed.—Oh! the hand! the giant! the

[6]Vouch for.
[7]Handsome.

hand!—Support me! I am terrified out of my senses, cried Bianca: I will not sleep in the castle to-night. Where shall I go? My things may come after me to-morrow.—Would I had been content to wed Francesco! This comes of ambition!—What has terrified thee thus, young woman? said the marquis: thou art safe here; be not alarmed. Oh! your greatness is wonderfully good, said Bianca, but I dare not—No, pray let me go—I had rather leave every thing behind me, than stay another hour under this roof. Go to, thou hast lost thy senses, said Manfred. Interrupt us not; we were communing on important matters.—My lord, this wench is subject to fits—Come with me, Bianca.—Oh! the saints! No, said Bianca—for certain it comes to warn your highness; why should it appear to me else? I say my prayers morning and evening—Oh! if your highness had believed Diego! 'Tis the same hand that he saw the foot to in the gallery-chamber—Father Jerome has often told us the prophecy would be out one of these days—Bianca, said he, mark my words.—Thou ravest, said Manfred, in a rage: Begone, and keep these fooleries to frighten thy companions.—What! my lord, cried Bianca, do you think I have seen nothing? Go to the foot of the great stairs yourself—As I live I saw it. Saw what? tell us, fair maid, what thou hast seen, said Frederic. Can your highness listen, said Manfred, to the delirium of a silly wench, who has heard stories of apparitions until she believes them? This is more than fancy, said the marquis; her terror is too natural and too strongly impressed to be the work of imagination. Tell us, fair maiden, what it is has moved thee thus? Yes, my lord, thank your greatness, said Bianca— I believe I look very pale; I shall be better when I have recovered myself.—I was going to my lady Isabella's chamber, by his highness's order—We do not want the circumstances, interrupted Manfred: since his highness will have it so, proceed; but be brief.— Lord, your highness thwarts one so! replied Bianca—I fear my hair—I am sure I never in my life—Well! as I was telling your greatness, I was going by his highness's order to my lady Isabella's chamber: she lies in the watchet-coloured[8] chamber, on the right hand, one pair of stairs: so when I came to the great stairs—I was looking on his highness's present here. Grant me patience! said Manfred, will this wench never come to the point? What imports it to the

---

[8]Light blue.

marquis, that I gave thee a bawble for thy faithful attendance on my daughter? We want to know what thou sawest. I was going to tell your highness, said Bianca, if you would permit me.—So, as I was rubbing the ring—I am sure I had not gone up three steps, but I heard the rattling of armour; for all the world such a clatter, as Diego says he heard when the giant turned him about in the gallery-chamber. What does she mean, my lord? said the marquis. Is your castle haunted by giants and goblins?—Lord! what, has not your greatness heard the story of the giant in the gallery-chamber? cried Bianca. I marvel his highness has not told you—mayhap you do not know there is a prophecy—This trifling is intolerable, interrupted Manfred. Let us dismiss this silly wench, my lord: we have more important affairs to discuss. By your favour, said Frederic, these are no trifles: the enormous sabre I was directed to in the wood; yon casque, its fellow—are these visions of this poor maiden's brain? So Jaquez thinks, may it please your greatness, said Bianca. He says this moon will not be out without our seeing some strange revolution. For my part, I should not be surprised if it was to happen to-morrow; for, as I was saying, when I heard the clattering of armour, I was all in a cold sweat—I looked up, and, if your greatness will believe me, I saw upon the uppermost banister of the great stairs a hand in armour as big, as big—I thought I should have swooned—I never stopped until I came hither—Would I were well out of this castle! My lady Matilda told me but yester-morning that her highness Hippolita knows something—Thou art an insolent! cried Manfred—Lord marquis, it much misgives me[9] that this scene is concerted to affront me. Are my own domestics suborned[10] to spread tales injurious to my honour? Pursue your claim by manly daring; or let us bury our feuds, as was proposed, by the intermarriage of our children: but trust me, it ill becomes a prince of your bearing to practise on mercenary wenches.—I scorn your imputation, said Frederic; until this hour I never set eyes on this damsel: I have given her no jewel!—My lord, my lord, your conscience, your guilt accuses you, and would throw the suspicion on me—But keep your daughter, and think no more of Isabella: the judgments already fallen on your house forbid me matching into it.

[9]I suspect.
[10]Bribed.

Manfred, alarmed at the resolute tone in which Frederic delivered these words, endeavoured to pacify him. Dismissing Bianca, he made such submissions to the marquis, and threw in such artful encomiums on Matilda, that Frederic was once more staggered. However, as his passion was of so recent a date, it could not at once surmount the scruples he had conceived. He had gathered enough from Bianca's discourse to persuade him that heaven declared itself against Manfred. The proposed marriages too removed his claim to a distance: and the principality of Otranto was a stronger temptation, than the contingent reversion of it with Matilda.[11] Still he would not absolutely recede from his engagements; but purposing to gain time, he demanded of Manfred if it was true in fact that Hippolita consented to the divorce. The prince, transported to find no other obstacle, and depending on his influence over his wife, assured the marquis it was so, and that he might satisfy himself of the truth from her own mouth.

As they were thus discoursing, word was brought that the banquet was prepared. Manfred conducted Frederic to the great hall, where they were received by Hippolita and the young princesses. Manfred placed the marquis next to Matilda, and seated himself between his wife and Isabella. Hippolita comported herself with an easy gravity; but the young ladies were silent and melancholy. Manfred, who was determined to pursue his point with the marquis in the remainder of the evening, pushed on the feast until it waxed late; affecting unrestrained gaiety, and plying Frederic with repeated goblets of wine. The latter, more upon his guard than Manfred wished, declined his frequent challenges, on pretence of his late loss of blood; while the prince, to raise his own disordered spirits, and to counterfeit unconcern, indulged himself in plentiful draughts, though not to the intoxication of his senses.

The evening being far advanced, the banquet concluded. Manfred would have withdrawn with Frederic; but the latter, pleading weakness and want of repose, retired to his chamber, gallantly telling the prince that his daughter should amuse his highness until himself could attend him. Manfred accepted the party, and to the no small grief of Isabella, accompanied her to her apartment.

[11]Frederic would rather inherit the principality from Alfonso than hazard the chance of Manfred dying without a male heir, the title reverting to Matilda (and thus her husband).

Matilda waited on her mother to enjoy the freshness of the evening on the ramparts of the castle.

Soon as the company were dispersed their several ways, Frederic, quitting his chamber, inquired if Hippolita was alone, and was told by one of her attendants, who had not noticed her going forth, that at that hour she generally withdrew to her oratory, where he probably would find her. The marquis during the repast[12] had beheld Matilda with increase of passion. He now wished to find Hippolita in the disposition her lord had promised. The portents that had alarmed him were forgotten in his desires. Stealing softly and unobserved to the apartment of Hippolita, he entered it with a resolution to encourage her acquiescence to the divorce, having perceived that Manfred was resolved to make the possession of Isabella an unalterable condition, before he would grant Matilda to his wishes.

The marquis was not surprised at the silence that reigned in the princess's apartment. Concluding her, as he had been advertised,[13] in her oratory, he passed on. The door was a-jar; the evening gloomy and overcast. Pushing open the door gently, he saw a person kneeling before the altar. As he approached nearer, it seemed not a woman, but one in a long woollen weed, whose back was towards him. The person seemed absorbed in prayer. The marquis was about to return,[14] when the figure rising, stood some moments fixed in meditation, without regarding him. The marquis, expecting the holy person to come forth, and meaning to excuse his uncivil interruption, said, Reverend Father, I sought the Lady Hippolita.— Hippolita! replied a hollow voice: camest thou to this castle to seek Hippolita?—And then the figure, turning slowly round, discovered to Frederic the fleshless jaws and empty sockets of a skeleton, wrapt in a hermit's cowl. Angels of grace, protect me! cried Frederic recoiling. Deserve their protection, said the spectre. Frederic, falling on his knees, adjured[15] the phantom to take pity on him. Dost thou not remember me? said the apparition. Remember the wood of Joppa! Art thou that holy hermit? cried Frederic trembling—can I do aught for thy eternal peace?—Wast thou delivered

[12]Meal.
[13]Told.
[14]Turn away.
[15]Begged.

from bondage, said the spectre, to pursue carnal delights? Hast thou forgotten the buried sabre, and the behest of heaven engraven on it?—I have not, I have not, said Frederic—But say, blest spirit, what is thy errand to me? what remains to be done? To forget Matilda! said the apparition—and vanished.

Frederic's blood froze in his veins. For some minutes he remained motionless. Then falling prostrate on his face before the altar, he besought the intercession of every saint for pardon. A flood of tears succeeded to this transport; and the image of the beauteous Matilda rushing in spite of him on his thoughts, he lay on the ground in a conflict of penitence and passion. Ere he could recover from this agony of his spirits, the princess Hippolita with a taper in her hand entered the oratory alone. Seeing a man without motion on the floor, she gave a shriek, concluding him dead. Her fright brought Frederic to himself. Rising suddenly, his face bedewed with tears, he would have rushed from her presence; but Hippolita stopping him, conjured him in the most plaintive accents to explain the cause of his disorder, and by what strange chance she had found him there in that posture. Ah, virtuous princess! said the marquis, penetrated with grief—and stopped. For the love of heaven, my lord, said Hippolita, disclose the cause of this transport! What mean these doleful sounds, this alarming exclamation on my name? What woes has heaven still in store for the wretched Hippolita?—Yet silent! By every pitying angel, I adjure thee, noble prince, continued she, falling at his feet, to disclose the purport of what lies at thy heart—I see thou feelest for me; thou feelest the sharp pangs that thou inflictest—Speak, for pity!—Does aught thou knowest concern my child?—I cannot speak, cried Frederic, bursting from her.—Oh! Matilda!

Quitting the princess thus abruptly, he hastened to his own apartment. At the door of it he was accosted by Manfred, who, flushed by wine and love had come to seek him, and to propose to waste some hours of the night in music and revelling. Frederic, offended at an invitation so dissonant from[16] the mood of his soul, pushed him rudely aside, and, entering his chamber, flung the door intemperately against Manfred, and bolted it inwards. The haughty prince, enraged at this unaccountable behaviour, withdrew in a frame of mind capable of the most fatal excesses. As he crossed the court, he was met by the domes-

---

[16]Contradictory to.

tic whom he had planted at the convent as a spy on Jerome and Theodore. This man, almost breathless with the haste he had made, informed his lord that Theodore and some lady from the castle were at that instant in private conference at the tomb of Alfonso in St. Nicholas's church. He had dogged Theodore thither, but the gloominess of the night had prevented his discovering who the woman was.

Manfred, whose spirits were inflamed, and whom Isabella had driven from her on his urging his passion with too little reserve, did not doubt but the inquietude she had expressed had been occasioned by her impatience to meet Theodore. Provoked by this conjecture, and enraged at her father, he hastened secretly to the great church. Gliding softly between the aisles, and guided by an imperfect gleam of moonshine that shone faintly through the illuminated windows, he stole towards the tomb of Alfonso, to which he was directed by indistinct whispers of the persons he sought. The first sounds he could distinguish were—Does it, alas! depend on me? Manfred will never permit our union.—No, this shall prevent it! cried the tyrant, drawing his dagger, and plunging it over her shoulder into the bosom of the person that spoke—Ah, me, I am slain! cried Matilda, sinking. Good heaven, receive my soul!—Savage, inhuman monster, what hast thou done? cried Theodore, rushing on him, and wrenching his dagger from him.—Stop, stop thy impious hand! cried Matilda; it is my father!—Manfred, waking as from a trance, beat his breast, twisted his hands in his locks, and endeavoured to recover his dagger from Theodore to dispatch himself. Theodore, scarce less distracted, and only mastering the transports of his grief to assist Matilda, had now by his cries drawn some of the monks to his aid. While part of them endeavoured in concert with the afflicted Theodore to stop the blood of the dying princess, the rest prevented Manfred from laying violent hands on himself.

Matilda, resigning herself patiently to her fate, acknowledged with looks of grateful love the zeal of Theodore. Yet oft as her faintness would permit her speech its way, she begged the assistants to comfort her father. Jerome, by this time, had learnt the fatal news, and reached the church. His looks seemed to reproach Theodore, but turning to Manfred, he said, Now, tyrant! behold the completion of woe fulfilled on thy impious and devoted head! The blood of Alfonso cried to heaven for vengeance; and heaven has permitted its altar to be polluted by assassination, that thou mightest shed thy own blood at the foot of that prince's sepulchre!—Cruel man! cried Matilda, to aggravate the woes of a parent! May heaven bless my father, and forgive him as I do! My lord, my gracious sire, dost thou forgive thy child? Indeed, I came not hither to meet Theodore. I found him praying at this tomb, whither my mother sent me to intercede for thee, for her—Dearest father, bless your child, and say you forgive her.—Forgive thee! Murderous monster! cried Manfred—can assassins forgive? I took thee for Isabella; but heaven directed my bloody hand to the heart of my child!—Oh, Matilda—I cannot utter it—canst thou forgive the blindness of my rage?—I can, I do, and may heaven confirm it! said Matilda—But while I have life to ask it—oh, my mother! what will she feel?—Will you comfort her, my lord? Will you not put her away? Indeed she loves you—Oh, I am faint! bear me to the castle—can I live to have her close my eyes?

Theodore and the monks besought her earnestly to suffer herself to be borne into the convent; but her instances were so pressing[17] to be carried to the castle, that, placing her on a litter, they conveyed her thither as she requested. Theodore, supporting her head with his arm, and hanging over her in an agony of despairing love, still endeavoured to inspire her with hopes of life. Jerome on the other side comforted her with discourses of heaven, and holding a crucifix before her, which she bathed with innocent tears, prepared her for her passage to immortality. Manfred, plunged in the deepest affliction, followed the litter in despair.

Ere they reached the castle, Hippolita, informed of the dreadful catastrophe, had flown to meet her murdered child; but when she saw the afflicted procession, the mightiness of her grief deprived her of her senses, and she fell lifeless to the earth in a swoon. Isabella and Frederic, who attended her, were overwhelmed in almost equal sorrow. Matilda alone seemed insensible to her own situation: every thought was lost in tenderness for her mother. Ordering the litter to stop, as soon as Hippolita was brought to herself, she asked for her father. He approached, unable to speak. Matilda, seizing his hand and her mother's, locked them in her own, and then clasped them to her heart. Manfred could not support this act of pathetic piety. He dashed himself on the ground, and cursed the

[17]Insistent.

day he was born. Isabella, apprehensive that these struggles of passion were more than Matilda could support, took upon herself to order Manfred to be borne to his apartment, while she caused Matilda to be conveyed to the nearest chamber. Hippolita, scarce more alive than her daughter, was regardless of everything but her: but when the tender Isabella's care would have likewise removed her, while the surgeons examined Matilda's wound, she cried, Remove me? Never! never! I lived but in her, and will expire with her. Matilda raised her eyes at her mother's voice, but closed them again without speaking. Her sinking pulse and the damp coldness of her hand soon dispelled all hopes of recovery. Theodore followed the surgeons into the outer chamber, and heard them pronounce the fatal sentence with a transport equal to phrenzy—Since she cannot live mine, cried he, at least she shall be mine in death!—Father! Jerome! will you not join our hands? cried he to the friar, who, with the marquis, had accompanied the surgeons. What means thy distracted rashness? said Jerome: is this an hour for marriage? It is; it is, cried Theodore: alas! there is no other! Young man, thou art too unadvised, said Frederic: dost thou think we are to listen to thy fond transports in this hour of fate? What pretensions hast thou to the princess? Those of a prince, said Theodore; of the sovereign of Otranto. This reverend man, my father, has informed me who I am. Thou ravest, said the marquis: there is no prince of Otranto but myself, now Manfred, by murder, by sacrilegious murder, has forfeited all pretensions. My lord, said Jerome, assuming an air of command, he tells you true. It was not my purpose the secret should have been divulged so soon, but fate presses onward to its work. What his hot-headed passion has revealed, my tongue confirms. Know, prince, that when Alfonso set sail for the Holy Land—Is this a season for explanations? cried Theodore. Father, come and unite me to the princess: she shall be mine—in every other thing I will dutifully obey you. My life! my adored Matilda! continued Theodore, rushing back into the inner chamber, will you not be mine? will you not bless your—Isabella made signs to him to be silent, apprehending the princess was near her end. What, is she dead? cried Theodore: is it possible? The violence of his exclamations brought Matilda to herself. Lifting up her eyes, she looked round for her mother—Life of my soul, I am here! cried Hippolita: think not I will quit thee!—Oh! you are too good, said Matilda—

but weep not for me, my mother! I am going where sorrow never dwells.—Isabella, thou hast loved me; wot[18] thou not supply my fondness to this dear, dear woman? Indeed I am faint!—Oh! my child! my child! said Hippolita in a flood of tears, can I not withhold thee a moment?—It will not be, said Matilda—Commend me to heaven—Where is my father? Forgive him, dearest mother—forgive him my death; it was an error—Oh! I had forgotten—Dearest mother, I vowed never to see Theodore more—Perhaps that has drawn down this calamity—but it was not intentional—can you pardon me? Oh! wound not my agonizing soul! said Hippolita; thou never couldst offend me.—Alas, she faints! Help! help!—I would say something more, said Matilda, struggling, but it wonnot be—Isabella—Theodore—for my sake—oh!—She expired. Isabella and her women tore Hippolita from the corse; but Theodore threatened destruction to all who attempted to remove him from it. He printed a thousand kisses on her clay-cold hands, and uttered every expression that despairing love could dictate.

Isabella, in the meantime, was accompanying the afflicted Hippolita to her apartment; but in the middle of the court they were met by Manfred, who, distracted with his own thoughts, and anxious once more to behold his daughter, was advancing to the chamber where she lay. As the moon was now at its height, he read in the countenances of this unhappy company the event[19] he dreaded. What! is she dead? cried he in wild confusion—A clap of thunder at that instant shook the castle to its foundations; the earth rocked, and the clank of more than mortal armour was heard behind. Frederic and Jerome thought the last day was at hand. The latter, forcing Theodore along with them, rushed into the court. The moment Theodore appeared, the walls of the castle behind Manfred were thrown down with a mighty force, and the form of Alfonso, dilated to an immense magnitude, appeared in the centre of the ruins. Behold in Theodore, the true heir of Alfonso! said the vision: and having pronounced those words, accompanied by a clap of thunder, it ascended solemnly towards heaven, where the clouds parting asunder, the form of saint Nicholas was seen; and receiving Alfonso's shade, they were soon wrapt from mortal eyes in a blaze of glory.

[18]Will.
[19]Outcome.

The beholders fell prostrate on their faces, acknowledging the divine will. The first that broke silence was Hippolita. My lord, said she to the desponding Manfred, behold the vanity of human greatness! Conrad is gone! Matilda is no more! in Theodore we view the true prince of Otranto. By what miracle he is so, I know not—suffice it to us, our doom is pronounced! Shall we not, can we but dedicate the few deplorable hours we have to live, in deprecating the further wrath of heaven? Heaven ejects us—whither can we fly,[20] but to yon holy cells that yet offer us a retreat?—Thou guiltless but unhappy woman! unhappy by my crimes! replied Manfred, my heart at last is open to thy devout admonitions. Oh! could—but it cannot be—ye are lost in wonder—let me at last do justice on myself! To heap shame on my own head is all the satisfaction I have left to offer to offended heaven. My story has drawn down these judgments: let my confession atone—But, ah! what can atone for usurpation and a murdered child? a child murdered in a consecrated place?—List, sirs, and may this bloody record be a warning to future tyrants!

Alfonso, ye all know, died in the Holy Land—Ye would interrupt me; ye would say he came not fairly to his end—It is most true—why else this bitter cup which Manfred must drink to the dregs. Ricardo, my grandfather, was his chamberlain[21]—I would draw a veil over my ancestor's crimes—but it is in vain: Alfonso died by poison. A fictitious will declared Ricardo his heir. His crimes pursued him—yet he lost no Conrad, no Matilda! I pay the price of usurpation for all! A storm overtook him. Haunted by his guilt he vowed to saint Nicholas to found a church and two convents, if he lived to reach Otranto. The sacrifice was accepted: the saint appeared to him in a dream, and promised that Ricardo's posterity should reign in Otranto until the rightful owner should be grown too large to inhabit the castle, and as long as issue male from Ricardo's loins should remain to enjoy it.—Alas! alas! nor male nor female, except myself, remains of all his wretched race!—I have done—the woes of these three days speak the rest. How this young man can be Alfonso's heir I know not—yet I do not doubt it. His are these dominions; I resign them—yet I knew not Alfonso had an heir—I question

[20]Hippolita casts Manfred in the lineage of Milton's Satan: "Me miserable! which way shall I fly [i.e., flee from] / Infinite wrath, and infinite despair? / Which way I fly is Hell; myself am Hell" (*Paradise Lost* 4.73–75).

[21]Steward, chief executive assistant.

not the will of heaven—poverty and prayer must fill up the woeful space, until Manfred shall be summoned to Ricardo.

What remains is my part to declare, said Jerome. When Alfonso set sail for the Holy Land he was driven by a storm to the coast of Sicily. The other vessel, which bore Ricardo and his train, as your *lordship* must have heard, was separated from him. It is most true, said Manfred; and the title you give me is more than an out-cast can claim—Well, be it so—proceed. Jerome blushed, and continued. For three months lord Alfonso was wind-bound in Sicily. There he became enamoured of a fair virgin named Victoria. He was too pious to tempt her to forbidden pleasures. They were married. Yet deeming this amour incongruous with the holy vow of arms by which he was bound, he determined to conceal their nuptials until his return from the crusado, when he purposed to seek and acknowledge her for his lawful wife. He left her pregnant. During his absence she was delivered of a daughter: but scarce had she felt a mother's pangs, ere she heard the fatal rumour of her lord's death, and the succession of Ricardo. What could a friendless, helpless woman do? would her testimony avail?—Yet, my lord, I have an authentic writing.—It needs not, said Manfred; the horrors of these days, the vision we have but now seen, all corroborate thy evidence beyond a thousand parchments. Matilda's death and my expulsion—Be composed, my lord, said Hippolita; this holy man did not mean to recall your griefs. Jerome proceeded.

I shall not dwell on what is needless. The daughter of which Victoria was delivered, was at her maturity bestowed in marriage on me. Victoria died; and the secret remained locked in my breast. Theodore's narrative has told the rest.

The friar ceased. The disconsolate company retired to the remaining part of the castle. In the morning Manfred signed his abdication of the principality, with the approbation of Hippolita, and each took on them the habit of religion in the neighbouring convents. Frederic offered his daughter to the new prince, which Hippolita's tenderness for Isabella concurred to promote: but Theodore's grief was too fresh to admit the thought of another love; and it was not until after frequent discourses with Isabella of his dear Matilda, that he was persuaded he could know no happiness but in the society of one with whom he could for ever indulge the melancholy that had taken possession of his soul.

The Man of Feeling

by Henry Mackenzie

The MAN of FEELING

THE SECOND EDITION, CORRECTED (LONDON: T. CADELL, 1771)

Introduction

My dog had made a point on a piece of fallow-ground,[1] and led the curate and me two or three hundred yards over that and some stubble adjoining, in a breathless state of expectation, on a burning first of September.

It was a false point, and our labour was vain: yet, to do Rover justice (for he's an excellent dog, though I have lost his pedigree[2]) the fault was none of his, the birds were gone; the curate showed me the spot where they had lain basking, at the root of an old hedge.

I stopped and cried Hem! The curate is fatter than I; he wiped the sweat from his brow.

There is no state where one is apter to pause and look round one, than after such a disappointment. It is even so in life. When we have been hurrying on, impelled by some warm wish or other, looking neither to the right hand nor to the left—we find of a sudden that all our gay hopes are flown; and the only slender consolation that some friend can give us, is to point where they were once to be found. And lo! if we are not of that combustible race, who will rather beat their heads in spite, than wipe their brows with the curate, we look round and say, with the nauseated listlessness of the king of Israel, "All is vanity and vexation of spirit."[3]

I looked round with some such grave apothegm[4] in my mind when I discovered, for the first time, a venerable pile, to which the enclosure belonged.[5] An air of melancholy hung about it. There was a languid stillness in the day, and a single crow, that perched

[1]Pointed to prey on untilled acreage.

[2]Papers certifying a purebred.

[3]The words of the Preacher, the son of David, Ecclesiasties 1.14; vanity: emptiness.

[4]Maxim.

[5]The ruins of the landlord's residence; enclosure is private land, off-limits to hunting, except by license.

on an old tree by the side of the gate, seemed to delight in the echo of its own croaking.

I leaned on my gun and looked; but I had not breath enough to ask the curate a question. I observed carving on the bark of some of the trees: 'twas indeed the only mark of human art about the place, except that some branches appeared to have been lopped, to give a view of the cascade, which was formed by a little rill at some distance.

Just at that instant I saw pass between the trees, a young lady with a book in her hand. I stood upon a stone to observe her; but the curate sat him down on the grass, and leaning his back where I stood, told me, "That was the daughter of a neighbouring gentleman of the name of WALTON, whom he had seen walking there more than once.

"Some time ago," he said, "one HARLEY lived there, a whimsical sort of man I am told, but I was not then in the cure;[6] though, if I had a turn for those things, I might know a good deal of his history, for the greatest part of it is still in my possession."

"His history!" said I. "Nay, you may call it what you please, said the curate; for indeed it is no more a history than it is a sermon. The way I came by it was this: Some time ago, a grave, oddish kind of a man, boarded at a farmer's in this parish: The country people called him The Ghost; and he was known by the slouch in his gait, and the length of his stride. I was but little acquainted with him, for he never frequented any of the clubs[7] hereabouts. Yet for all he used to walk a-nights, he was as gentle as a lamb at times; for I have seen him playing at te-totum[8] with the children, on the great stone at the door of our churchyard.

"Soon after I was made curate, he left the parish, and went nobody knows whither; and in his room was found a bundle of papers, which was brought to me by his landlord. I began to read them, but I soon grew weary of the task; for, besides that the hand is intolerably bad, I could never find the author in one strain for two chapters together: and I don't believe there's a single syllogism from beginning to end."

[6]In charge of the parish.

[7]Tavern societies.

[8]Game of chance played with a four-sided disk or die.

"I should be glad to see this medley," said I. "You shall see it now," answered the curate, "for I always take it along with me a-shooting." "How came it so torn?" "'Tis excellent wadding," said the curate.—This was a plea of expediency I was not in a condition to answer; for I had actually in my pocket great part of an edition of one of the German Illustrissimi,[9] for the very same purpose. We exchanged books; and by that means (for the curate was a strenuous[10] logician) we probably saved both.

When I returned to town, I had leisure to peruse the acquisition I had made: I found it a bundle of little episodes, put together without art, and of no importance on the whole, with something of nature, and little else in them. I was a good deal affected with some very trifling passages in it; and had the name of a Marmontel,[11] or a Richardson, been on the title-page—'tis odds that I should have wept: But

One is ashamed to be pleased with the works of one knows not whom.

---

[9]The Italian designates the nobility; the "most illustrious" Germans are the difficult modern philosophers.

[10]Exacting (Christian Wolff's *Logic* was translated into English in 1770).

[11]18th-c. tragedian Jean-François Marmontel published *Moral Tales*.

Chapter XI[1]

Of bashfulness.—A character.—His opinion on that subject.

There is some rust[2] about every man at the beginning; though in some nations (among the French, for instance) the ideas of the inhabitants from climate, or what other cause you will, are so vivacious, so eternally on the wing, that they must, even in small societies, have a frequent collision; the rust therefore will wear off sooner: but in Britain, it often goes with a man to his grave; nay, he dares not even pen a *hic jacet*[3] to speak out for him after his death.

"Let them rub it off by travel," said the baronet's brother, who was a striking instance of excellent metal, shamefully rusted. I had drawn my chair near his. Let me paint the honest old man: 'tis but one passing sentence to preserve his image in my mind.

He sat in his usual attitude, with his elbow rested on his knee, and his fingers pressed on his cheek. His face was shaded by his hand; yet it was a face that might once have been well accounted handsome; its features were manly and striking, a dignity resided on his eyebrows, which were the largest I remember to have seen. His person was tall and well-made; but the indolence of his nature had now inclined it to corpulency.

His remarks were few, and made only to his familiar friends; but they were such as the world might have heard with veneration: and his heart, uncorrupted by its ways, was ever warm in the cause of virtue and his friends.

He is now forgotten and gone! The last time I was at Silton hall, I saw his chair stand in its corner by the fire-side; there was an additional cushion on it, and it was occupied by my young lady's favourite lap-dog. I drew near unperceived, and pinched its ears in the bitterness of my soul; the creature howled, and ran to its mistress. She did not suspect the author of its misfortune, but she bewailed it in the most pathetic terms; and kissing its lips, laid it gen-

---

[1]The Reader will remember, that the Editor is accountable only for scattered chapters, and fragments of chapters; the curate must answer for the rest. The number at the top, when the chapter was entire, he has given as it originally stood, with the title which its author had affixed to it. [Mackenzie's note; the curate has used some pages to clean his gun.]

[2]Local corrosion, imperfection.

[3]Latin: *here lies*—the first words of a gravestone epitaph.

tly on her lap, and covered it with a cambric handkerchief. I sat in my old friend's seat; I heard the roar of mirth and gaiety around me: poor Ben Silton! I gave thee a tear then: accept of one cordial drop that falls to thy memory now.

"They should wear it off by travel."—Why, it is true, said I, that will go far; but then it will often happen, that in the velocity of a modern tour, and amidst the materials through which it is commonly made, the friction is so violent, that not only the rust, but the metal too is lost in the progress.

Give me leave to correct the expression of your metaphor," said Mr. Silton: "that is not always rust which is acquired by the inactivity of the body on which it preys; such, perhaps, is the case with me, though indeed I was never cleared from my youth; but (taking it in its first stage) it is rather an encrustation, which nature has given for purposes of the greatest wisdom."

You are right, I returned; and sometimes, like certain precious fossils, there may be hid under it gems of the purest brilliancy.[4]

Nay, farther, continued Mr. Silton, there are two distinct sorts of what we call bashfulness; this, the awkwardness of a booby,[5] which a few steps into the world will convert into the pertness of a coxcomb;[6] that, a consciousness, which the most delicate feelings produce, and the most extensive knowledge cannot always remove.

From the incidents I have already related, I imagine it will be concluded that Harley was of the latter species of bashful animals; at least, if Mr. Silton's principle is just, it may be argued on this side: for the gradation of the first mentioned sort, it is certain, he never attained. Some part of his external appearance was modelled from the company of those gentlemen, whom the antiquity of a family, now possessed of bare 250 l. a year,[7] entitled its representative to approach; these indeed were not many; great part of the property in his neighbourhood being in the hands of merchants, who had got rich by their lawful calling abroad, and the sons of

---

[4]A glance at Thomas Gray's *Elegy Written in a Country Church-Yard* (1751): "Full many a gem of purest ray serene, / The dark unfathom'd caves of ocean bear" (53–54).

[5]Dull boy.

[6]Dandy.

[7]Aristocratic by birth, Harley is broke; in 1750, £250 was a lower-middle-class income.

stewards, who had got rich by their lawful calling at home: persons so perfectly versed in the ceremonial of thousands, tens of thousands, and hundreds of thousands (whose degrees of precedency are plainly demonstrable from the first page of the Compleat Accomptant, or Young Man's Best Pocket Companion[8]) that a bow at church from them to such a man as Harley,—would have made the parson look back into his sermon for some precept of Christian humility.

---

[8]A second edition of John Duncombe's *A new arithmetical dictionary, or the accomptant's compleat assistant; . . . chiefly designed for the use of schools* was published in 1774. "The young man's companion" was a popular genre for aspiring young men. From 1735 to 1772, *The Instructor: or, Young Man's Best Companion,* by "accomptant" (accountant) George Fisher, went through 21 London editions.

Chapter XII

Of worldly interests.

There are certain interests which the world supposes every man to have, and which therefore are properly enough termed worldly; but the world is apt to make an erroneous estimate: ignorant of the dispositions which constitute our happiness or misery, they bring to an undistinguished[1] scale the means of the one, as connected with power, wealth, or grandeur, and of the other with their contraries.[2] Philosophers and poets have often protested against this decision; but their arguments have been despised as declamatory, or ridiculed as romantic.

There are never wanting[3] to a young man some grave and prudent friends to set him right in this particular, if he need it: to watch his ideas as they arise, and point them to those objects which a wise man should never forget.

Harley did not want for some monitors[4] of this sort. He was frequently told of men, whose fortunes enabled them to command all the luxuries of life, whose fortunes were of their own acquirement: his envy was invited by a description of their happiness, and his emulation by a recital of the means which had procured it.

Harley was apt to hear those lectures with indifference; nay, sometimes they got the better of his temper; and as the instances[5] were not always amiable, provoked, on his part, some reflections,[6] which I am persuaded his good-nature would else have avoided.

Indeed I have observed one ingredient, somewhat necessary in a man's composition[7] towards happiness, which people of feeling would do well to acquire; a certain respect for the follies of mankind: for there are so many fools whom the opinion of the world entitles to regard, whom accident has placed in heights of which they are unworthy, that he who cannot restrain his contempt or indignation at the sight, will be too often quarrelling with the

---

[1]Undifferentiated.
[2]Absences.
[3]Lacking.
[4]Mentors.
[5]Particulars.
[6]Criticisms.
[7]Actions.

disposal of things, to relish that share which is allotted to himself. I do not mean, however, to insinuate this to have been the case with Harley; on the contrary, if we might rely on his own testimony, the conceptions he had of pomp and grandeur, served to endear the state which Providence had assigned him.

He lost his father, the last surviving of his parents, as I have already related, when he was a boy. The good man, from a fear of offending, as well as a regard to his son, had named him a variety of guardians; one consequence of which was, that they seldom met at all to consider the affairs of their ward; and when they did meet, their opinions were so opposite, that the only possible method of conciliation was the mediatory power of a dinner and a bottle, which commonly interrupted, not ended, the dispute; and after that interruption ceased, left the consulting parties in a condition not very proper for adjusting it. His education therefore had been but indifferently attended to; and after being taken from a country school, at which he had been boarded, the young gentleman was suffered to be his own master in the subsequent branches of literature, with some assistance from the parson of the parish in languages and philosophy, and from the exciseman[8] in arithmetic and book-keeping. One of his guardians, indeed, who, in his youth, had been an inhabitant of the Temple, set him to read Coke upon Lyttelton;[9] a book which is very properly put into the hands of beginners in that science, as its simplicity is accommodated to their understandings, and its size to their inclination. He profited but little by the perusal; but it was not without its use in the family: for his maiden aunt applied it commonly to the laudable purpose of pressing her rebellious linens to the folds she had allotted them.

There were particularly two ways of increasing his fortune, which might have occurred to people of less foresight than the counsellors we have mentioned. One of these was the prospect of his succeeding to an old lady, a distant relation, who was known to be possessed of a very large sum in the stocks:[10] but in this their hopes were

---

[8]Tax collector.

[9]Temple: one of the Inns of Court (a legal institution). Sir Edward Coke's *The First Part of the Institutes of the Laws of England. Or, a Commentary upon Littleton, not the name of a lawyer onely, but of the law it selfe*, a 17th-c. treatise on property laws, was influential well into the 18th c.

[10]As now, income-producing investments.

disappointed; for the young man was so untoward[11] in his disposition, that, notwithstanding the instructions he daily received, his visits rather tended to alienate than gain the good-will of his kinswoman. He sometimes looked grave when the old lady told the jokes of her youth; he often refused to eat when she pressed him, and was seldom or never provided with sugar-candy or liquorice when she was seized with a fit of coughing: nay, he had once the rudeness to fall asleep while she was describing the composition and virtues of her favourite cholic-water.[12] In short, he accommodated himself so ill to her humour, that she died, and did not leave him a farthing.

The other method pointed out to him was, an endeavour to get a lease of some crown-lands, which lay contiguous to his little paternal estate. This, it was imagined, might be easily procured, as the crown did not draw so much rent as Harley could afford to give, with very considerable profit to himself; and the then lessee had rendered himself so obnoxious to the ministry, by the disposal of his vote at an election, that he could not expect a renewal.[13] This, however, needed some interest with the great,[14] which Harley or his father never possessed.

His neighbour, Mr. Walton, having heard of this affair, generously offered his assistance to accomplish it. He told him, that though he had long been a stranger to courtiers, yet he believed there were some of them who might pay regard to his recommendation; and that, if he thought it worth the while to take a London journey upon the business, he would furnish him with a letter of introduction to a baronet of his acquaintance, who had a great deal to say with the first lord of the treasury.

When his friends heard of this offer, they pressed him with the utmost earnestness to accept of it. They did not fail to enumerate the many advantages which a certain degree of spirit and assurance gives a man who would make a figure in the world: they repeated their instances of good fortune in others, ascribed them all to a happy forwardness[15] of disposition; and made so copious a recital

[11]Unappealing.

[12]For gastrointestinal distress.

[13]Even though voting was private, a voter's choice would be well-known.

[14]An important person's support.

[15]Gregariousness.

of the disadvantages which attend the opposite weakness, that a stranger, who had heard them, would have been led to imagine, that in the British code there was some disqualifying statute against any citizen who should be convicted of—modesty.

Harley, though he had no great relish for the attempt, yet could not resist the torrent of motives[16] that assaulted him; and as he needed but little preparation for his journey, a day, not very distant, was fixed for his departure.

[16]Offers.

Chapter XIII

The Man of Feeling in love.

The day before that on which he set out, he went to take leave of Mr. Walton.—We would conceal nothing;—there was another person of the family to whom also the visit was intended, on whose account, perhaps, there were some tenderer feelings in the bosom of Harley, than his gratitude for the friendly notice of that gentleman (though he was seldom deficient in that virtue) could inspire. Mr. Walton had a daughter; and such a daughter! we will attempt some description of her by and by.

Harley's notions of the χαλον, or beautiful, were not always to be defined, nor indeed such as the world would always assent to, though we could define them. A blush, a phrase of affability to an inferior, a tear at a moving tale, were to him, like the Cestus of Cytherea,[1] unequalled in conferring beauty.[2] For all these Miss Walton was remarkable; but as these, like the above-mentioned Cestus, are perhaps still more powerful when the wearer is possessed of some degree of beauty, commonly so called; it happened, that, from this cause, they had more than usual power in the person of that young lady.

She was now arrived at that period of life which takes, or is supposed to take, from the flippancy of girlhood those sprightlinesses with which some good-natured old maids oblige the world at three-score.[3] She had been ushered into life (as that word is used in the dialect of St. Jameses[4]) at seventeen, her father being then in parliament, and living in London: at seventeen, therefore, she had been a universal toast; her health,[5] now she was four and twenty was only drank by those who knew her face at least. Her complexion was mellowed into a paleness, which certainly took from her beauty; but agreed, at least Harley used to say so, with the pensive softness of her mind. Her eyes were of that gentle hazel colour

---

[1]The silk sash of Venus, goddess of beauty (born of sea foam on the island of Cythera) had the power to make its wearer more enchantingly beautiful.

[2]The Greek χαλον, means "good." Compare Harley's definition of the beautiful with Burke's, p. 209.

[3]Sixty.

[4]In the Court.

[5]A toast to her health.

which is rather mild than piercing; and, except when they were lighted up by good-humour, which was frequently the case, were supposed by the fine gentlemen to want fire. Her air and manner were elegant in the highest degree, and were as sure of commanding respect as their mistress was far from demanding it. Her voice was inexpressibly soft; it was, according to that incomparable simile of Otway's,

> "— like the shepherd's pipe upon the mountains,
> "When all his little flock's at feed before him."[6]

The effect it had upon Harley, himself used to paint ridiculously enough; and ascribed to it powers, which few believed, and nobody cared for.

Her conversation was always cheerful, but rarely witty; and without the smallest affectation of learning, had as much sentiment in it as would have puzzled a Turk, upon his principles of female materialism, to account for. Her beneficence was unbounded; indeed the natural tenderness of her heart might have been argued, by the frigidity of a casuist,[7] as detracting from her virtue in this respect, for her humanity was a feeling, not a principle: but minds like Harley's are not very apt to make this distinction, and generally give our virtue credit for all that benevolence which is instinctive in our nature.

As her father had some years retired to the country, Harley had frequent opportunities of seeing her. He looked on her for some time merely with that respect and admiration which her appearance seemed to demand, and the opinion of others conferred upon her: from this cause perhaps, and from that extreme sensibility of which we have taken frequent notice, Harley was remarkably silent in her presence. He heard her sentiments[8] with peculiar attention, sometimes with looks very expressive of approbation; but seldom declared his opinion on the subject, much less made compliments to the lady on the justness of her remarks.

---

[6]The orphan-heroine's dying words in Thomas Otway's *The Orphan* (1680) (5.1.416–17).

[7]One skilled in deliberating moral questions.

[8]See note 6 above.

From this very reason it was, that Miss Walton frequently took more particular notice of him than of other visitors, who, by the laws of precedency,[9] were better entitled to it: it was a mode of politeness she had peculiarly studied, to bring to the line of that equality, which is ever necessary for the ease of our guests, those whose sensibility had placed them below it.

Harley saw this; for though he was a child in the drama of the world, yet was it not altogether owing to a want of knowledge on his part; on the contrary, the most delicate consciousness of propriety often kindled that blush which marred the performance of it: this raised his esteem something above what the most sanguine[10] descriptions of her goodness had been able to do; for certain it is, that notwithstanding the laboured definitions which very wise men have given us of the inherent beauty of virtue, we are always inclined to think her handsomest when she condescends to smile upon ourselves.

It would be trite to observe the easy gradation from esteem to love; in the bosom of Harley there scarce needed a transition; for there were certain seasons when his ideas were flushed to a degree much above their common complexion. In times not credulous of inspiration, we should account for this from some natural cause; but we do not mean to account for it at all; it were sufficient to describe its effects; but they were sometimes so ludicrous, as might derogate from the dignity of the sensations which produced them to describe. They were treated indeed as such by most of Harley's sober friends, who often laughed very heartily at the awkward blunders of the real Harley, when the different faculties, which should have prevented them, were entirely occupied by the ideal. In some of these paroxysms of fancy, Miss Walton did not fail to be introduced; and the picture which had been drawn amidst the surrounding objects of unnoticed levity, was now singled out to be viewed through the medium of romantic imagination:[11] it was improved of course, and esteem was a word inexpressive of the feelings which it excited.

---

[9]Persons of higher rank had precedence of social attention.
[10]Optimistic.
[11]An imagination inclined to "fancy" and illusion.

Chapter XIV

He sets out on his journey.—The beggar and his dog.

He had taken leave of his aunt on the eve of his intended departure; but the good lady's affection for her nephew interrupted her sleep, and early as it was next morning when Harley came downstairs to set out, he found her in the parlour with a tear on her cheek, and her caudle[1]-cup in her hand. She knew enough of physic to prescribe against going abroad of a morning with an empty stomach. She gave her blessing with the draught;[2] her instructions she had delivered the night before. They consisted mostly of negatives; for London, in her idea, was so replete with temptations that it needed the whole armour of her friendly cautions to repel their attacks.

Peter stood at the door. We have mentioned this faithful fellow formerly: Harley's father had taken him up an orphan, and saved him from being cast on the parish;[3] and he had ever since remained in the service of him and of his son. Harley shook him by the hand as he passed, smiling, as if he had said, "I will not weep." He sprung hastily into the chaise that waited for him; Peter folded up the step. "My dear master, said he, (shaking the solitary lock that hung on either side of his head) I have been told as how London is a sad place."—He was choked with the thought, and his benediction could not be heard:—but it shall be heard, honest Peter!—where these tears will add to its energy.

In a few hours Harley reached the inn where he proposed breakfasting; but the fulness of his heart would not suffer him to eat a morsel. He walked out on the road, and gaining a little height, stood gazing on that quarter he had left. He looked for his wonted prospect,[4] his fields, his woods, and his hills: they were lost in the distant clouds! He pencilled them on the clouds, and bade them farewell with a sigh!

He sat down on a large stone to take out a little pebble from his shoe, when he saw, at some distance, a beggar approaching him. He had on a loose sort of coat, mended with different-coloured

---

[1]A warm, sweet, spicy tonic.

[2]Drink.

[3]Meager community charity, compelled by law.

[4]Accustomed view.

rags, amongst which the blue and the russet were predominant. He had a short knotty stick in his hand, and on the top of it was stuck a ram's horn; his knees (though he was no pilgrim) had worn the stuff of his breeches; he wore no shoes, and his stockings had entirely lost that part of them which should have covered his feet and ancles: in his face, however, was the plump appearance of good-humour; he walked a good round[5] pace, and a crook-legged dog trotted at his heels.

"Our delicacies, said Harley to himself, are fantastic; they are not in nature! that beggar walks over the sharpest of these stones barefooted, whilst I have lost the most delightful dream in the world, from the smallest of them happening to get into my shoe."—The beggar had by this time come up, and pulling off a piece of hat, asked charity of Harley; the dog began to beg too:—it was impossible to resist both; and in truth, the want of shoes and stockings had made both unnecessary, for Harley had destined six-pence for him before. The beggar, on receiving it, poured forth blessings without number; and, with a sort of smile on his counte-nance, said to Harley, "that, if he wanted to have his fortune told"—Harley turned his eye briskly on the beggar: it was an un-promising look for the subject of a prediction, and silenced the prophet immediately. "I would much rather learn, said Harley, what it is in your power to tell me: your trade must be an entertain-ing one; sit down on this stone, and let me know something of your profession; I have often thought of turning fortune-teller for a week or two myself."

"Master, replied the beggar, I like your frankness much; God knows I had the humour of plain-dealing in me from a child; but there is no doing with it in this world; we must live as we can, and lying is, as you call it, my profession: but I was in some sort forced to the trade, for I dealt once in telling truth.

"I was a labourer, Sir, and gained as much as to make me live: I never laid by indeed; for I was reckoned a piece of a wag,[6] and your wags, I take it, are seldom rich, Mr. Harley."

"So," said Harley, "you seem to know me." "Ay, there are few folks in the country that I don't know something of: How should I

[5]Brisk.
[6]Jokester.

tell fortunes else?" "True; but to go on with your story: you were a labourer, you say, and a wag; your industry, I suppose, you left with your old trade, but your humour you preserve to be of use to you in your new."

"What signifies sadness, Sir? a man grows lean on't: but I was brought to my idleness by degrees; first I could not work, and it went against my stomach to work ever after. I was seized with a jail fever at the time of the assizes[7] being in the county where I lived; for I was always curious to get acquainted with the felons, because they are commonly fellows of much mirth and little thought, qualities I had ever an esteem for. In the height of this fever, Mr. Harley, the house where I lay took fire, and burnt to the ground: I was carried out in that condition, and lay all the rest of my illness in a barn. I got the better of my disease however, but I was so weak that I spit blood whenever I attempted to work. I had no relation living that I knew of, and I never kept a friend above a week, when I was able to joke; I seldom remained above six months in a parish, so that I might have died before I had found a settlement in any: thus I was forced to beg my bread, and a sorry trade I found it, Mr. Harley. I told all my misfortunes truly, but they were seldom believed; and the few who gave me a halfpenny as they passed, did it with a shake of the head, and an injunction not to trouble them with a long story. In short, I found that people don't care to give alms without some security for their money; a wooden leg or a withered arm is a sort of draught[8] upon heaven for those who choose to have their money placed to account there; so I changed my plan, and, instead of telling my own misfortunes, began to prophesy happiness to others. This I found by much the better way: folks will always listen when the tale is their own; and of many who say they do not believe in fortune telling, I have known few on whom it had not a very sensible effect. I pick up the names of their acquaintance; amours and little squabbles are easily gleaned among servants and neighbours; and indeed people themselves are the best intelligencers in the world for our purpose: they dare not puzzle us for their own sakes, for every one is anxious to hear what they wish to believe; and they who repeat it, to laugh at it when they have

---

[7]Criminal court sessions held by a circuit (traveling) judge.
[8]Bank draft or check to be cashed.

done, are generally more serious than their hearers are apt to imagine. With a tolerable good memory, and some share of cunning, with the help of walking a-nights over heaths and church-yards, with this, and showing the tricks of that there dog, whom I stole from the serjeant of a marching regiment (and by the way, he can steal too upon occasion) I make shift to pick up a livelihood. My trade, indeed, is none of the honestest; yet people are not much cheated neither, who give a few halfpence for a prospect of happiness, which I have heard some persons say is all a man can arrive at in this world.—But I must bid you good-day; Sir, for I have three miles to walk before noon, to inform some boarding-school young ladies, whether their husbands are to be peers of the realm[9] or captains in the army: a question which I promised to answer them by that time."

Harley had drawn a shilling from his pocket; but virtue bade him consider on whom he was going to bestow it.—Virtue held back his arm:—but a milder form, a younger sister of virtue's, not so severe as virtue, nor so serious as pity, smiled upon him: His fingers lost their compression;—nor did virtue offer to catch the money as it fell. It had no sooner reached the ground than the watchful cur (a trick he had been taught) snapped it up; and, contrary to the most approved method of stewardship, delivered it immediately into the hands of his master.

* * * * * * * *

---

[9]Nobility.

Chapter XIX

*He makes a second expedition to the Baronet's. The laudable
ambition of a young man to be thought something by the world.*

We have related, in a former chapter, the little success of his first
visit to the great man, for whom he had the introductory letter
from Mr. Walton. To people of equal sensibility, the influence of
those trifles we mentioned on his deportment[1] will not appear surprising; but to his friends in the country they could not be stated,
nor would they have allowed them any place in the account. In
some of their letters, therefore, which he received soon after, they
expressed their surprise at his not having been more urgent in his
application, and again recommended the blushless assiduity of successful merit.

He resolved to make another attempt at the baronet's; fortified
with higher notions of his own dignity, and with less apprehension
of repulse. In his way to Grosvenor-square[2] he began to ruminate
on the folly of mankind, who affixed those ideas of superiority to
riches, which reduced the minds of men, by nature equal with the
more fortunate, to that sort of servility which he felt in his own. By
the time he had reached the Square, and was walking along the
pavement which led to the baronet's, he had brought his reasoning
on the subject to such a point, that the conclusion, by every rule of
logic, should have led him to a thorough indifference in his approaches to a fellow-mortal, whether that fellow-mortal was possessed of six, or six thousand pounds a year.[3] It is probable, however, that the premises had been improperly formed; for it is
certain, that when he approached the great man's door he felt his
heart agitated by an unusual pulsation.

He had almost reached it, when he observed a young gentleman
coming out, dressed in a white frock, and a red laced waistcoat,
with a small switch in his hand, which he seemed to manage with a
particular good grace. As he passed him on the steps, the stranger
very politely made him a bow, which Harley returned, though he
could not remember ever having seen him before. He asked Harley,

---

[1]Behavior.

[2]One of the newer, wealthier London districts.

[3]The income that would be produced from property worth £100,000.

in the same civil manner, if he was going to wait on his friend the Baronet? "For I was just calling, said he, and am sorry to find that he is gone for some days into the country." Harley thanked him for his information; and was turning from the door, when the other observed, that it would be proper to leave his name, and very obligingly knocked for that purpose. "Here is a gentleman, Tom, who meant to have waited on your master." "Your name, if you please, Sir?" "Harley."—"You'll remember, Tom, Harley."—The door was shut. "Since we are here, said he, we shall not lose our walk if we add a little to it by a turn or two in Hyde-park."[4] He accompanied this proposal with a second bow, and Harley accepted of it by another in return.

The conversation, as they walked, was brilliant on the side of his companion. The playhouse, the opera, with every occurrence in high-life, he seemed perfectly master of; and talked of some reigning beauties of quality, in a manner the most feeling in the world. Harley admired the happiness of his vivacity; and, opposite as it was to the reserve of his own nature, began to be much pleased with its effects.

Though I am not of opinion with some wise men, that the existence of objects depends on idea;[5] yet I am convinced, that their appearance is not a little influenced by it. The optics of some minds are in so unlucky a perspective, as to throw a certain shade on every picture that is presented to them; while those of others (of which number was Harley), like the mirrors of the ladies, have a wonderful effect in bettering their complexions. Through such a medium perhaps he was looking on his present companion.

When they had finished their walk, and were returning by the corner of the Park, they observed a board hung out of a window signifying, "An excellent ORDINARY[6] on Saturdays and Sundays." It happened to be Saturday, and the table was covered for the purpose. "What if we should go in and dine here, if you happen not to be engaged, Sir? said the young gentleman. It is not impossible but we shall meet with some original or other; it is a sort of humour I

---

[4]Enclosed from 1695, Hyde Park provided a meeting and parading ground for the wealthy.

[5]The philosophy of John Locke (1632–1704) and George Berkeley (1685–1753), that the objective world is to be verified only by its impressions on a percipient mind.

[6]Restaurant meal.

like hugely." Harley made no objection; and the stranger showed him the way into the parlour.

He was placed, by the courtesy of his introductor, in an arm-chair that stood at one side of the fire. Over-against him was seated a man of a grave considering aspect, with that look of sober prudence which indicates what is commonly called a warm man. He wore a pretty large wig, which had once been white, but was now of a brownish yellow; his coat was one of those modest-coloured drabs which mock the injuries of dust and dirt; two jack-boots[7] concealed, in part, the well-mended knees of an old pair of buck-skin breeches, while the spotted handkerchief round his neck preserved at once its owner from catching cold and his neck-cloth from being dirtied. Next him sat another man, with a tankard in his hand and a quid of tobacco in his cheek, whose eye was rather more vivacious, and whose dress was something smarter.

The first-mentioned gentleman took notice that the room had been so lately washed, as not to have had time to dry; and re-marked, that wet lodging was unwholesome for man or beast. He looked round at the same time for a poker to stir the fire with, which, he at last observed to the company, the people of the house had removed, in order to save their coals. This diffi-culty, however, he overcame by the help of Harley's stick, saying, "that as they should, no doubt, pay for their fire in some shape or other, he saw no reason why they should not have the use of it while they sat."

The door was now opened for the admission of dinner. "I don't know how it is with you, gentlemen, said Harley's new acquain-tance; but I am afraid I shall not be able to get down a morsel at this horrid mechanical hour of dining." He sat down, however, and did not show any want of appetite by his eating. He took upon him the carving of the meat, and criticised on the goodness of the pudding.

When the table-cloth was removed, he proposed calling for some punch, which was readily agreed to; he seemed at first in-clined to make it himself, but afterwards changed his mind, and left that province to the waiter, telling him to have it pure West Indian, or he could not taste a drop of it.

[7]Above the knee.

When the punch was brought he undertook to fill the glasses and call the toasts.—"The king."—The toast naturally produced politics. It is the privilege of Englishmen to drink the king's health, and to talk of his conduct. The man who sat opposite to Harley (and who by this time, partly from himself, and partly from his acquaintance on his left hand, was discovered to be a grazier[8]) observed, "That it was a shame for so many pensioners to be allowed to take the bread out of the mouth of the poor." "Ay, and provisions, said his friend, were never so dear in the memory of man; I wish the king, and his counsellors, would look to that." "As for the matter of provisions, neighbour Wrightson, he replied, I am sure the prices of cattle —" A dispute would have probably ensued, but it was prevented by the spruce toastmaster, who gave a Sentiment:[9] and turning to the two politicians, "Pray, gentlemen, said he, let us have done with these musty politics: I would always leave them to the beer-suckers in Butcher Row.[10] Come, let us have something of the fine arts. That was a damn'd hard match betwixt the Nailor and Tim Bucket. The knowing ones were cursedly taken in there! I lost a cool hundred myself, faith."

At mention of the cool hundred, the grazier threw his eyes aslant, with a mingled look of doubt and surprise; while the man at his elbow looked arch, and gave a short emphatical sort of cough.

Both seemed to be silenced, however, by this intelligence; and while the remainder of the punch lasted the conversation was wholly engrossed by the gentleman with the fine waistcoat, who told a great many "immense comical stories" and "confounded smart things," as he termed them, acted and spoken by lords, ladies, and young bucks of quality, of his acquaintance. At last, the grazier, pulling out a watch, of a very unusual size, and telling the hour, said, that he had an appointment. "Is it so late? said the young gentleman; then I am afraid I have missed an appointment already; but the truth is, I am cursedly given to missing of appointments."

When the grazier and he were gone, Harley turned to the remaining personage, and asked him, If he knew that young gentle-

---

[8]Cattle feeder.

[9]Witty saying.

[10]Street in the area of Smithfield cattle market.

man. "A gentleman! said he; ay, he is one of your gentlemen at the top of an affidavit. I knew him, some years ago, in the quality of a footman; and, I believe, he had some times the honour to be a pimp. At last, some of the great folks, to whom he had been serviceable in both capacities, had him made a gauger;[11] in which station he remains, and has the assurance to pretend an acquaintance with men of quality. The impudent dog! with a few shillings in his pocket, he will talk you three times as much as my friend Mundy there, who is worth nine thousand if he's worth a farthing. But I know the rascal, and despise him, as he deserves."

Harley began to despise him too, and to conceive some indignation at having sat with patience to hear such a fellow speak nonsense. But he corrected himself, by reflecting, that he was perhaps as well entertained, and instructed too, by this same modest gauger, as he should have been by such a man as he had thought proper to personate. And surely the fault may more properly be imputed to that rank where the futility is real than where it is feigned; to that rank, whose opportunities for nobler accomplishments have only served to rear a fabric of folly, which the untutored hand of affection, even among the meanest of mankind, can imitate with success.

[11]Someone who gauges quantities (of liquor, for example) to set taxes.

Chapter XX

He visits Bedlam.—The distresses of a daughter.

Of those things called Sights, in London, which every stranger is supposed desirous to see, Bedlam is one.[1] To that place, therefore, an acquaintance of Harley's, after having accompanied him to several other shows, proposed a visit. Harley objected to it, "because, said he, I think it an inhuman practice to expose the greatest misery with which our nature is afflicted to every idle visitant who can afford a trifling perquisite to the keeper; especially as it is a distress which the humane must see with the painful reflection, that it is not in their power to alleviate it." He was overpowered, however, by the solicitations of his friend and the other persons of the party (amongst whom were several ladies); and they went in a body to Moorfields.

Their conductor led them first to the dismal mansions of those who are in the most horrid state of incurable madness. The clanking of chains, the wildness of their cries, and the imprecations which some of them uttered, formed a scene inexpressibly shocking. Harley and his companions, especially the female part of them, begged their guide to return: he seemed surprised at their uneasiness, and was with difficulty prevailed on to leave that part of the house without showing them some others; who, as he expressed it in the phrase of those that keep wild beasts for show, were much better worth seeing than any they had passed, being ten times more fierce and unmanageable.

He led them next to that quarter where those reside who, as they are not dangerous to themselves or others, enjoy a certain degree of freedom, according to the state of their distemper.

Harley had fallen behind his companions, looking at a man, who was making pendulums with bits of thread and little balls of clay. He had delineated a segment of a circle on the wall with chalk, and marked their different vibrations by intersecting it with cross lines. A decent-looking man came up, and smiling at the maniac, turned to Harley, and told him, that gentleman had once been a very celebrated mathematician. "He fell a sacrifice, said he,

---

[1]Bethlehem hospital for the insane, where a penny let one view the inmates. By the end of the century, reform movements advocated more compassionate treatment.

to the theory of comets; for, having, with infinite labour, formed a table on the conjectures of Sir Isaac Newton,[2] he was disappointed in the return of one of those luminaries, and was very soon after obliged to be placed here by his friends. If you please to follow me, Sir, continued the stranger, I believe I shall be able to give you a more satisfactory account of the unfortunate people you see here, than the man who attends your companions." Harley bowed, and accepted his offer.

The next person they came up to had scrawled a variety of figures on a piece of slate. Harley had the curiosity to take a nearer view of them. They consisted of different columns, on the top of which were marked South-sea annuities, India-stock, and Three per cent. annuities consol. "This, said Harley's instructor, was a gentleman well known in Change Alley.[3] He was once worth fifty thousand pounds, and had actually agreed for the purchase of an estate in the west, in order to realize his money; but he quarrelled with the proprietor about the repairs of the garden-wall, and so returned to town to follow his old trade of stock-jobbing a little longer; when an unlucky fluctuation of stock, in which he was engaged to an immense extent, reduced him at once to poverty and to madness. Poor wretch! he told me t'other day that against the next payment of differences, he should be some hundreds above a plum."[4]—

"It is a spondee,[5] and I will maintain it," interrupted a voice on his left hand. This assertion was followed by a very rapid recital of some verses from Homer. "That figure, said the gentleman, whose clothes are so bedaubed with snuff, was a schoolmaster of some reputation: he came hither to be resolved of some doubts he entertained concerning the genuine pronunciation of the Greek vowels. In his highest fits, he makes frequent mention of one Mr. Bentley.[6]

"But delusive ideas, Sir, are the motives of the greatest part of mankind, and a heated imagination the power by which their actions are incited: the world, in the eye of a philosopher, may be said to be a large madhouse." "It is true, answered Harley, the

---

[2]The great scientist and mathematician (1642–1727).

[3]Exchange Alley, the London stock market.

[4]£100,000; the "differences" are losses.

[5]In poetry, two consecutive stressed syllables.

[6]Esteemed classicist Richard Bentley (1662–1742) was most famous for being mocked in Alexander Pope's *The Dunciad* (1727; 1743).

passions of men are temporary madnesses; and sometimes very fatal in their effects,

From Macedonia's madman to the Swede."[7]

"It was indeed, said the stranger, a very mad thing in Charles, to think of adding so vast a country as Russia to his dominions; that would have been fatal indeed; the balance of the North would then have been lost; but the Sultan and I would never have allowed it."—"Sir!" said Harley, with no small surprise on his countenance. "Why, yes, answered the other, the Sultan and I; do you know me? I am the Chan of Tartary."[8]

Harley was a good deal struck by this discovery; he had prudence enough, however, to conceal his amazement, and bowing as low to the monarch as his dignity required, left him immediately, and joined his companions.

He found them in a quarter of the house set apart for the insane of the other sex, several of whom had gathered about the female visitors, and were examining, with rather more accuracy than might have been expected, the particulars of their dress.

Separate from the rest stood one whose appearance had something of superior dignity. Her face, though pale and wasted, was less squalid than those of the others, and showed a dejection of that decent kind, which moves our pity unmixed with horror: upon her, therefore, the eyes of all were immediately turned. The keeper who accompanied them observed it: "This, said he, is a young lady who was born to ride in her coach and six.[9] She was beloved, if the story I have heard is true, by a young gentleman, her equal in birth, though by no means her match in fortune: but Love, they say, is blind, and so she fancied him as much as he did her. Her father, it seems, would not hear of their marriage, and threatened to turn her out of doors if ever she saw him again. Upon this the young gentleman took a voyage to the West Indies, in hopes of bettering his fortune, and obtaining his mistress; but he was scarce landed, when he

---

[7]Alexander the Great (4th c. B.C.E.) and Charles XII of Sweden (1682–1718) answer the question "where Greatness lies," in Pope's *Essay on Man* (4.220).

[8]11th-c. Mongolian warlord Jenghiz Khan (1202–1227) invaded Eastern Asia and Europe.

[9]Six horses; she descends from wealthy nobility.

was seized with one of the fevers which are common in those islands, and died in a few days, lamented by every one that knew him. This news soon reached his mistress, who was at the same time pressed by her father to marry a rich miserly fellow, who was old enough to be her grandfather. The death of her lover had no effect on her inhuman parent; he was only the more earnest for her marriage with the man he had provided for her; and what between her despair at the death of the one, and her aversion to the other, the poor young lady was reduced to the condition you see her in. But God would not prosper such cruelty; her father's affairs soon after went to wreck, and he died almost a beggar."

Though this story was told in very plain language, it had particularly attracted Harley's notice: he had given it the tribute of some tears. The unfortunate young lady had till now seemed entranced in thought, with her eyes fixed on a little garnet-ring she wore on her finger: she turned them now upon Harley. "My Billy is no more! said she; do you weep for my Billy? Blessings on your tears! I would weep too, but my brain is dry; and it burns, it burns, it burns!"—She drew nearer to Harley.—"Be comforted, young Lady, said he, your Billy is in heaven." "Is he, indeed? and shall we meet again? And shall that frightful man (pointing to the keeper) not be there!—Alas! I am grown naughty of late; I have almost forgoten to think of heaven: yet I pray sometimes; when I can, I pray; and sometimes I sing; when I am saddest, I sing:—You shall hear me, hush!

"Light be the earth on Billy's breast,
"And green the sod that wraps his grave!"

There was a plaintive wildness in the air not to be withstood; and, except the keeper's, there was not an unmoistened eye around her.

"Do you weep again? said she; I would not have you weep: you are like my Billy; you are, believe me; just so he looked when he gave me this ring; poor Billy! 'twas the last time ever we met! —

"'Twas when the seas were roaring—I love you for resembling my Billy; but I shall never love any man like him."—She stretched out her hand to Harley; he pressed it between both of his, and bathed it with his tears.—"Nay, that is Billy's ring, said she, you cannot have it, indeed; but here is another, look here, which I plaited to-day of some gold-thread from this bit of stuff; will you keep it for my sake? I am a strange girl;—but my heart is harmless: my poor heart! it will burst some day; feel how it beats!"—She press'd his hand to her bosom, then holding her head in the attitude of listening—"Hark! one, two, three! be quiet, thou little trembler; my Billy is cold!—but I had forgotten the ring."—She put it on his finger.—"Farewel! I must leave you now."—She would have withdrawn her hand; Harley held it to his lips.—"I dare not stay longer; my head throbs sadly: farewel!"—She walked with a hurried step to a little apartment at some distance. Harley stood fixed in astonishment and pity! his friend gave money to the keeper.—Harley looked on his ring.—He put a couple of guineas into the man's hand: "Be kind to that unfortunate."—He burst into tears, and left them.

Chapter XXI

The Misanthrope

The friend, who had conducted him to Moorfields, called upon him again the next evening. After some talk on the adventures of the preceding day; "I carried you yesterday, said he to Harley, to visit the mad; let me introduce you to-night, at supper, to one of the wise: but you must not look for anything of the Socratic pleasantry about him; on the contrary, I warn you to expect the spirit of a Diogenes.[1] That you may be a little prepared for his extraordinary manner, I will let you into some particulars of his history.

"He is the elder of the two sons of a gentleman of considerable estate in the country. Their father died when they were young: both were remarkable at school for quickness of parts,[2] and extent of genius; this had been bred to no profession, because his father's fortune, which descended to him, was thought sufficient to set him above it; the other was put apprentice to an eminent attorney.[3] In this the expectations of his friends were more consulted than his own inclination; for both his brother and he had feelings of that warm kind that could ill brook a study so dry as the law, especially in that department of it which was allotted to him. But the difference of their tempers made the characteristical distinction between them. The younger, from the gentleness of his nature, bore with patience a situation entirely discordant to his genius and disposition. At times, indeed, his pride would suggest, of how little importance those talents were, which the partiality of his friends had often extolled: they were now incumbrances in a walk of life where the dull and the ignorant passed him at every turn; his fancy and his feeling, were invincible obstacles to eminence in a situation where his fancy had no room for exertion, and his feeling experienced perpetual disgust. But these murmurings he never suffered to be heard; and that he might not offend the prudence of those who had been con-

---

[1]Greek philosopher Socrates (5th c. B.C.E.) engaged his friends in sometimes playful dialogues; Diogenes, one of the sect known as "Cynics," practiced self-denial.

[2]Mental capacities.

[3]In order to keep estates consolidated and thus politically influential, laws of primogeniture ("first born") bequeathed all property and title to the eldest son; young sons had to train for a profession, often by apprenticeship (service in exchange for training).

cerned in the choice of his profession, he continued to labour in it several years, 'till, by the death of a relation, he succeeded to an estate of a little better than 100 l. a year, with which, and the small patrimony left him, he retired into the country, and made a love-match with a young lady of a similar temper to his own, with whom the sagacious world pitied him for finding happiness.

"But his elder brother, whom you are to see at supper, if you will do us the favour of your company, was naturally impetuous, decisive, and overbearing. He entered into life with those ardent expectations by which young men are commonly deluded: in his friendships, warm to excess; and equally violent in his dislikes. He was on the brink of marriage with a young lady, when one of those friends, for whose honour he would have pawned his life, made an elopement with that very goddess, and left him besides deeply engaged for sums which that good friend's extravagance had squandered.

"The dreams he had formerly enjoyed were now changed for ideas of a very different nature. He abjured all confidence in anything of human form; sold his lands, which still produced him a very large reversion,[4] came to town, and immured himself, with a woman who had been his nurse, in little better than a garret; and has ever since applied his talents to the vilifying of his species. In one thing I must take the liberty to instruct you: however different your sentiments may be (and different they must be), you will suffer him to go on without contradiction; otherwise, he will be silent immediately, and we shall not get a word from him all the night after." Harley promised to remember this injunction, and accepted the invitation of his friend.

When they arrived at the house, they were informed that the gentleman was come, and had been shown into the parlour. They found him sitting with a daughter of his friend's, about three years old, on his knee, whom he was teaching the alphabet from a horn-book:[5] at a little distance stood a sister of hers, some years older. "Get you away, Miss, said he to this last, you are a pert gossip, and I will have nothing to do with you." "Nay, answered she, Nancy is your favourite; you are quite in love with Nancy." "Take away that girl, said he to

[4]A future interest, or right of succession.
[5]Reading primers, so called from paper covered with translucent horn.

her father, whom he now observed to have entered the room, she has woman about her already." The children were accordingly dismissed.

Betwixt that and supper-time he did not utter a syllable. When supper came, he quarrelled with every dish at table, but eat of them all; only exempting from his censures a sallad, which you have not spoiled, said he, because you have not attempted to cook it.

When the wine was set upon the table, he took from his pocket a particular smoking apparatus, and filled his pipe, without taking any more notice of Harley or his friend, than if no such persons had been in the room.

Harley could not help stealing a look of surprize at him; but his friend, who knew his humour, returned it, by annihilating his presence in the like manner, and, leaving him to his own meditations, addressed himself entirely to Harley.

In their discourse some mention happened to be made of an amiable character, and the words *honour* and *politeness* were applied to it. Upon this the gentleman, laying down his pipe, and changing the tone of his countenance, from an ironical grin to something more intently contemptuous: "Honour, said he: Honour and Politeness! this is the coin of the world, and passes current with the fools of it. You have substituted the shadow Honour, instead of the substance Virtue; and have banished the reality of Friendship for the fictitious semblance, which you have termed Politeness: politeness, which consists in a certain ceremonious jargon, more ridiculous to the ear of reason than the voice of a puppet. You have invented sounds, which you worship, though they tyrannize over your peace: and are surrounded with empty forms, which take from the honest emotions of joy, and add to the—poignancy of misfortune."—"Sir!" said Harley—His friend winked to him, to remind him of the caution he had received. He was silenced by the thought—The philosopher turned his eye upon him: he examined him from top to toe, with a sort of triumphant contempt; Harley's coat happened to be a new one; the other's was as shabby as could possibly be supposed to be on the back of a gentleman: there was much significance in his look with regard to this coat: it spoke of the sleekness of folly and the threadbareness of wisdom.

"Truth, continued he, the most amiable, as well as the most natural of virtues, you are at pains to eradicate. Your very nurseries are seminaries of falsehood; and what is called Fashion in manhood completes the system of avowed insincerity. Mankind, in the gross, is a gaping monster, that loves to be deceived, and has seldom been disappointed: nor is their vanity less fallacious to your philosophers, who adopt modes of truth to follow them through the paths of error, and defend paradoxes merely to be singular in defending them. These are they whom ye term Ingenious; 'tis a phrase of commendation I detest; it implies an attempt to impose on my judgment, by flattering my imagination: yet these are they whose works are read by the old with delight, which the young are taught to look upon as the codes of knowledge and philosophy.

"Indeed, the education of your youth is every way preposterous: you waste at school years in improving talents, without having ever spent an hour in discovering them; one promiscuous line of instruction is followed, without regard to genius, capacity, or probable situation in the commonwealth. From this bear-garden[6] of the pedagogue, a raw, unprincipled boy is turned loose upon the world to travel; without any ideas but those of improving his dress at Paris, or starting into taste by gazing on some paintings at Rome. Ask him of the manners of the people, and he will tell you, That the skirt is worn much shorter in France, and that every body eats macaroni in Italy.[7] When he returns home, he buys a seat in parliament, and studies the constitution at Arthur's.[8]

"Nor are your females trained to any more useful purpose: they are taught, by the very rewards which their nurses propose for good behaviour, by the first thing like a jest which they hear from every male visitor of the family, that a young woman is a creature to be married; and when they are grown somewhat older, are instructed, that it is the purpose of marriage to have the enjoyment of pin-money, and the expectation of a jointure."[9]

[10]"These indeed are the effects of luxury, which is perhaps inseparable from a certain degree of power and grandeur in a nation. But it is not simply of the progress of luxury that we have to complain:

[6]Place for bear-baiting and other rough, competitive sports.

[7]A parody of the Continental tour that completed an aristocrat's education after university.

[8]Arthur's Chocolate House (est. 1755 by Robert Arthur).

[9]Pin-money is a wife's spending allowance; jointure is land owned by both husband and wife, to which she could retain title as a widow.

[10]Though the Curate could not remember having shown this chapter to any body, I strongly suspect that these political observations are the work of a later pen than the

did its votaries keep in their own sphere of thoughtless dissipation, we might despise them without emotion; but the frivolous pursuits of pleasure are mingled with the most important concerns of the state; and public enterprize shall sleep till he who should guide its operation has decided his bets at Newmarket,[11] or fulfilled his engagement with a favourite mistress in the country. We want some man of acknowledged eminence to point our counsels with that firmness which the counsels of a great people require. We have hundreds of ministers, who press forward into office, without having ever learned that art which is necessary for every business, the art of thinking; and mistake the petulance, which could give inspiration to smart sarcasms on an obnoxious measure in a popular assembly, for the ability which is to balance the interest of kingdoms, and investigate the latent sources of national superiority. With the administration of such men the people can never be satisfied; for besides that their confidence is gained only by the view of superior talents, there needs that depth of knowledge, which is not only acquainted with the just extent of power, but can also trace its connection with the expedient, to preserve its possessors from the contempt which attends irresolution, or the resentment which follows temerity."

* * * * * * * *

[Here a considerable part is wanting.]

* *"In short, man is an animal equally selfish and vain. Vanity, indeed, is but a modification of selfishness. From the latter, there are some who pretend to be free: they are generally such as declaim against the lust of wealth and power, because they have never been able to attain any high degree in either: they boast of generosity and feeling. They tell us (perhaps they tell us in rhyme) that the sensations of an honest heart, of a mind universally benevolent, make up the quiet bliss which they enjoy; but they will not, by this, be ex-

rest of this performance. There seems to have been, by some accident, a gap in the manuscript, from the words "Expectation of a jointure," to these, "In short, man is an animal," where the present blank ends; and some other person (for the hand is different, and the ink whiter) has filled part of it with sentiments of his own. Whoever he was, he seems to have caught some portion of the spirit of the man he personates. [Mackenzie's note.]

[11]Horse track.

empted from the charge of selfishness. Whence the luxurious happiness they describe in their little family-circles? Whence the pleasure which they feel, when they trim their evening fires, and listen to the howl of winter's wind? whence, but from the secret reflection of what houseless wretches feel from it?[12] Or do you administer comfort in affliction—the motive is at hand; I have had it preached to me in nineteen out of twenty of your consolatory discourses—the comparative littleness of our own misfortunes.[13]

"With vanity your best virtues are grossly tainted: your benevolence, which ye deduce immediately from the natural impulse of the heart, squints to it for its reward. There are some, indeed, who tell us of the satisfaction which flows from a secret consciousness of good actions: this secret satisfaction is truly excellent—when we have some friend to whom we may discover[14] its excellence."

He now paus'd a moment to relight his pipe, when a clock, that stood at his back, struck eleven; he started up at the sound, took his hat and his cane, and nodding good night with his head, walked out of the room. The gentleman of the house called a servant to bring the stranger's surtout.[15] "What sort of a night is it, fellow?" said he. "It rains, Sir, answered the servant, with an easterly wind."—"Easterly for ever!"—He made no other reply; but shrugging up his shoulders till they almost touched his ears, wrapped himself tight in his great coat, and disappeared.

"This is a strange creature," said his friend to Harley. "I cannot say, answered he, that his remarks are of the pleasant kind: it is curious to observe how the nature of truth may be changed by the garb it wears; softened to the admonition of friendship, or soured into the severity of reproof: yet this severity may be useful to some tempers; it somewhat resembles a file; disagreeable in its operation, but hard metals may be the brighter for it.

* * * * * * * *

[12]An echo of Shakespeare's banished King Lear, chastised by the thought of "poor naked wretches," whose "houseless heads and unfed sides" must endure "the pelting of [a] pitiless storm" (3.4.28ff).

[13]See, for example, Joseph Addison, *Spectator* No. 418 (30 June 1712): "[W]hen we read of Torments, Wounds, Deaths, and the like dismal Accidents, our Pleasure does not flow so properly from the Grief which such melancholly Descriptions give us, as from the secret Comparison which we make between ourselves and the Person who suffers."

[14]Reveal.

[15]Overcoat.

Chapter XXV

His skill in physiognomy.[1]

THE company at the baronet's removed to the playhouse accordingly, and Harley took his usual rout[e] into the Park.[2] He observed, as he entered, a fresh-looking elderly gentleman, in conversation with a beggar, who, leaning on his crutch, was recounting the hardships he had undergone, and explaining the wretchedness of his present condition. This was a very interesting dialogue to Harley; he was rude enough therefore to slacken his pace as he approached, and at last to make a full stop at the gentleman's back, who was just then expressing his compassion for the beggar, and regretting that he had not a farthing of change about him. At saying this he looked piteously on the fellow: there was something in his physiognomy which caught Harley's notice: indeed, physiognomy was one of Harley's foibles, for which he had been often rebuked by his aunt in the country; who used to tell him, that when he was come to her years and experience, he would know that all's not gold that glitters: and it must be owned that his aunt was a very sensible, harsh-looking, maiden lady of threescore and upwards. But he was too apt to forget this caution; and now, it seems, it had not occurred to him: stepping up, therefore, to the gentleman, who was lamenting the want of silver, "Your intentions, Sir, said he, are so good, that I cannot help lending you my assistance to carry them into execution," and gave the beggar a shilling. The other returned a suitable compliment, and extolled the benevolence of Harley. They kept walking together, and benevolence grew the topic of discourse.

The stranger was fluent on the subject. "There is no use of money, said he, equal to that of beneficence: with the profuse, it is lost; and even with those who lay it out according to the prudence of the world, the objects acquired by it pall on the sense, and have scarce become our own till they lose their value with the power of pleasing; but here the enjoyment grows on reflection, and our money is most truly ours when it ceases being in our possession."

---

[1]The "science" of judging character from features of the face and skull.
[2]Hyde Park.

"Yet I agree in some measure, answered Harley, with those who think, that charity to our common beggars is often misplaced; there are objects less obtrusive, whose title is a better one."

"We cannot easily distinguish, said the stranger; and even of the worthless, are there not many whose imprudence, or whose vice, may have been one dreadful consequence of misfortune?"

Harley looked again in his face, and blessed himself for his skill in physiognomy.

By this time they had reached the end of the walk: the old gentleman leaned on the rails to take breath, and in the mean time they were joined by a younger man, whose figure was much above the appearance of his dress, which was poor and shabby: Harley's former companion addressed him as an acquaintance, and they turned on the walk together.

The elder of the strangers complained of the closeness of the evening, and asked the other, if he would go with him into a house hard by, and take one draught of excellent cyder. "The man who keeps this house, said he to Harley, was once a servant of mine: I could not think of turning loose upon the world a faithful old fellow, for no other reason but that his age had incapacitated him; so I gave him an annuity of ten pounds, with the help of which he has set up this little place here, and his daughter goes and sells milk in the city, while her father manages his tap-room, as he calls it, at home. I can't well ask a gentleman of your appearance to accompany me to so paltry a place."—"Sir, replied Harley, interrupting him, I would much rather enter it than the most celebrated tavern in town: to give to the necessitous, may sometimes be a weakness in the man; to encourage industry, is a duty in the citizen." They entered the house accordingly.

On a table, at the corner of the room lay a pack of cards, loosely thrown together. The old gentleman reproved the man of the house for encouraging so idle an amusement: Harley attempted to defend him from the necessity of accommodating himself to the humour of his guests, and taking up the cards, began to shuffle them backwards and forwards in his hand. "Nay, I don't think cards so unpardonable an amusement as some do, replied the other; and now and then, about this time of the evening, when my eyes begin to fail me for my book, I divert myself with a game at piquet,[3] without finding my morals a bit relaxed by it. "Do you play piquet, Sir?" (to Harley.)

[3]Card game played with 32 cards.

Harley answered in the affirmative; upon which the other proposed playing a pool at a shilling the game, doubling the stakes: adding, that he never played higher with anybody.

Harley's good-nature could not refuse the benevolent old man; and the younger stranger, though he at first pleaded prior engagement, yet being earnestly solicited by his friend, at last yielded to solicitation.

When they began to play, the old gentleman, somewhat to the surprise of Harley, produced ten shillings to serve for markers of his score. "He had no change for the beggar, said Harley to himself; but I can easily account for it: it is curious to observe the affection that inanimate things will create in us by a long acquaintance. If I may judge from my own feelings, the old man would not part with one of these counters for ten times its intrinsic value; it even got the better of his benevolence! I myself have a pair of old brass sleeve buttons— Here he was interrupted by being told that the old gentleman had beat the younger, and that it was his turn to take up the conqueror. "Your game has been short;" said Harley. "I repiqued[4] him," answered the old man, with joy sparkling in his countenance. Harley wished to be repiqued too, but he was disappointed; for he had the same good fortune against his opponent. Indeed, never did fortune, mutable as she is, delight in mutability so much as at that moment; the victory was so quick, and so constantly alternate, that the stake, in a short time, amounted to no less a sum than 12 l. Harley's proportion of which was within half-a-guinea[5] of the money he had in his pocket. He had before proposed a division, but the old gentleman opposed it with such a pleasant warmth in his manner, that it was always over-ruled. Now, however, he told them that he had an appointment with some gentlemen, and it was within a few minutes of his hour. The young stranger had gained one game, and was engaged in the second with the other: they agreed, therefore, that the stake should be divided, if the old gentleman won that; which was more than probable, as his score was 90 to 35, and he was elder hand; but a momentous repique decided it in favour of his adversary, who seemed to enjoy his victory mingled with regret, for having won too much, while his friend, with great ebullience of passion, many praises of his own good play, and many malediction's on the power of chance, took up the cards, and threw them into the fire.

[4]Won 30 points on cards alone, before the game begins, thus starting at 90.

[5]12 shillings, 6 pence (2 weeks' wages for many a laborer).

Chapter XXVI

The Man of Feeling in a brothel.

The company he was engaged to meet were assembled in Fleet-street.[1] He had walked some time along the Strand,[2] amidst a crowd of those wretches who wait the uncertain wages of prostitution, with ideas of pity suitable to the scene around him, and the feelings he possessed, and had got as far as Somerset-house,[3] when one of them laid hold of his arm, and, with a voice tremulous and faint, asked him for a pint of wine, in a manner more supplicatory than is usual with those whom the infamy of their profession has deprived of shame: he turned round at the demand, and looked steadfastly on the person who made it.

She was above the common size, and elegantly formed; her face was thin and hollow, and showed the remains of tarnished beauty. Her eyes were black, but had little of their lustre left: her cheeks had some paint laid on without art, and productive of no advantage to her complexion, which exhibited a deadly paleness on the other parts of her face.

Harley stood in the attitude of hesitation; which she interpreting to her advantage, repeated her request, and endeavoured to force a leer of invitation into her countenance. He took her arm, and they walked on to one of those obsequious taverns in the neighbourhood, where the dearness of the wine is a discharge in full for the character of the house. From what impulse he did this, we do not mean to enquire; as it has ever been against our nature to search for motives where bad ones are to be found.—They entered, and a waiter showed them a room, and placed a bottle of claret on the table.

Harley filled the lady's glass; which she had no sooner tasted, than dropping it on the floor, and eagerly catching his arm, her eye grew fixed, her lip assumed a clayey whiteness, and she fell back lifeless in her chair.

Harley started from his seat, and, catching her in his arms, supported her from falling to the ground, looking wildly at the door, as

---

[1]Prostitution and publishing district.

[2]Site of booksellers and print shops.

[3]Home of the Royal Academy.

if he wanted to run for assistance, but durst not leave the miserable creature. It was not till some minutes after that it occurred to him to ring the bell, which at last however he thought of, and rung with repeated violence even after the waiter appeared. Luckily the waiter had his senses somewhat more about him; and snatching up a bottle of water, which stood on a buffet at the end of the room, he sprinkled it over the hands and face of the dying figure before him. She began to revive; and with the assistance of some hartshorn-drops,[4] which Harley now for the first time drew from his pocket, was able to desire the waiter to bring her a crust of bread, of which she swallowed some mouthfuls with the appearance of the keenest hunger. The waiter withdrew: when turning to Harley, sobbing at the same time, and shedding tears, "I am sorry, Sir, said she, that I should have given you so much trouble; but you will pity me when I tell you, that till now I have not tasted a morsel these two days past."—He fixed his eyes on hers—every circumstance but the last was forgotten; and he took her hand with as much respect as if she had been a duchess. It was ever the privilege of misfortune to be revered by him.—"Two days!—said he; and I have fared sumptuously every day!"—He was reaching to the bell; she understood his meaning, and prevented him. "I beg, Sir, said she, that you would give yourself no more trouble about a wretch who does not wish to live; but, at present, I could not eat a bit; my stomach even rose at the last mouthful of that crust." He offered to call a chair, saying, that he hoped a little rest would relieve her. He had one half-guinea left: "I am sorry, he said, that at present I should be able to make you an offer of no more than this paltry sum." She burst into tears! "Your generosity, Sir, is abused; to bestow it on me is to take it from the virtuous: I have no title but misery to plead; misery of my own procuring." "No more of that, answered Harley; there is virtue in these tears; let the fruit of them be virtue."—He rung, and ordered a chair.—"Though I am the vilest of beings, said she, I have not forgotten every virtue; gratitude, I hope, I shall still have left, did I but know who is my benefactor."—"My name is Harley"— "Could I ever have an opportunity?"—"You shall, and a glorious one too! your future conduct—but I do not mean to reproach you—if, I say—it will be the noblest reward—I will do myself the

[4]Ammonia.

pleasure of seeing you again."—Here the waiter entered, and told them the chair was at the door: the lady informed Harley of her lodgings, and he promised to wait on her at ten next morning.

He led her to the chair, and returned to clear with the waiter, without ever once reflecting that he had no money in his pocket. He was ashamed to make an excuse; yet an excuse must be made: he was beginning to frame one, when the waiter cut him short by telling him that he could not run scores; but that, if he would leave his watch, or any other pledge, it would be as safe as if it lay in his pocket. Harley jumped at the proposal, and pulling out his watch, delivered it into his hands immediately; and having, for once, had the precaution to take a note of the lodging he intended to visit next morning, sallied forth with a blush of triumph on his face, without taking notice of the sneer of the waiter, who, twirling the watch in his hand, made him a profound bow at the door, and whispered to a girl, who stood in the passage, something, in which the word CULLY[5] was honoured with a particular emphasis.

[5]Dupe.

Chapter XXVII

His skill in physiognomy is doubted.

After he had been some time with the company he had appointed to meet, and the last bottle was called for, he first recollected that he would be again at a loss how to discharge his share of the reckoning. He applied, therefore, to one of them, with whom he was most intimate, acknowledging that he had not a farthing of money about him; and, upon being jocularly asked the reason, acquainted them with the two adventures we have just now related. One of the company asked him if the old man in Hyde-park did not wear a brownish coat, with a narrow gold edging, and his companion an old green frock, with a buff-coloured waistcoat? Upon Harley's recollecting that they did; "Then, said he, you may be thankful you have come off so well; they are two as noted sharpers,[1] in their way, as any in town, and but t'other night took me in for a much larger sum: I had some thoughts of applying to a justice, but one does not like to be seen in those matters."

Harley answered, "That he could not but fancy the gentleman was mistaken, as he never saw a face promise more honesty than that of the old man he had met with."—"His face!" said a grave-looking man, who sat opposite to him, squirting the juice of his tobacco obliquely into the grate. There was something very emphatical in the action; for it was followed by a burst of laughter round the table. "Gentlemen, said Harley, you are disposed to be merry; it may be as you imagine, for I confess myself ignorant of the town: but there is one thing which makes me hear the loss of my money with temper; the young fellow who won it, must have been miserably poor; I observed him borrow money for the stake from his friend; he had distress and hunger in his countenance: be his character what it may, his necessities at least plead for him."—At this there was a louder laugh than before. "Gentlemen, said the lawyer, (one of whose conversations with Harley we have already recorded) here's a very pretty fellow for you: to have heard him talk some nights ago, as I did, you might have sworn he was a saint; yet now he games with sharpers, and loses

[1]Swindlers.

his money; and is bubbled[2] by a fine story invented by a whore, and pawns his watch: here are sanctified doings with a witness!"

"Young gentleman, said his friend on the other side of the table, let me advise you to be a little more cautious for the future; and as for faces—you may look into them to know, whether a man's nose be a long or a short one."

[2]Cheated.

Chapter XXVIII

He keeps his appointment.

The last night's raillery of his companions was recalled to his remembrance when he awoke, and the colder homilies of prudence began to suggest some things which were nowise favourable for a performance of his promise to the unfortunate female he had met with before. He rose uncertain of his purpose; but the torpor of such considerations was seldom prevalent over the warmth of his nature. He walked some turns backwards and forwards in his room; he recalled the languid form of the fainting wretch to his mind; he wept at the recollection of her tears. "Though I am the vilest of beings, I have not forgotten every virtue; gratitude, I hope, I shall still have left."—He took a larger stride—"Powers of mercy that surround me! cried he, do ye not smile upon deeds like these? to calculate the chances of deception is too tedious a business for the life of man!"—The clock struck ten!—When he was got down stairs, he found that he had forgot the note of her lodgings; he gnawed his lips at the delay; he was fairly on the pavement, when he recollected having left his purse; he did but just prevent himself from articulating an imprecation. He rushed a second time up into his chamber. "What a wretch I am, said he; ere this time, perhaps —" 'Twas a perhaps not to be borne:—two vibrations of a pendulum would have served him to lock his bureau; but they could not be spared.

When he reached the house, and inquired for Miss Atkins (for that was the lady's name) he was shown up three pair of stairs into a small room lighted by one narrow lattice, and patched round with shreds of different-coloured paper. In the darkest corner stood something like a bed, before which a tattered coverlet hung by way of curtain. He had not waited long when she appeared. Her face had the glister of new-washed tears on it. "I am ashamed, Sir, said she, that you should have taken this fresh piece of trouble about one so little worthy of it; but, to the humane, I know there is a pleasure in goodness for its own sake: if you have patience for the recital of my story, it may palliate, though it cannot excuse, my faults." Harley bowed, as a sign of assent; and she began as follows:

"I am the daughter of an officer, whom a service of forty years had advanced no higher than the rank of captain. I have had hints from himself, and been informed by others, that it was in some measure owing to those principles of rigid honour, which it was his boast to possess, and which he early inculcated on me, that he had been able to arrive at no better station. My mother died when I was a child; old enough to grieve for her death, but incapable of remembering her precepts. Though my father was doatingly fond of her, yet there were some sentiments in which they materially differed: She had been bred from her infancy in the strictest principles of religion, and took the morality of her conduct from the motives which an adherence to those principles suggested. My father, who had been in the army from his youth, affixed an idea of pusillanimity to that virtue, which was formed by the doctrines, excited by the rewards, or guarded by the terrors of revelation; his darling idol was the honour of a soldier; a term which he held in such reverence, that he used it for his most sacred asseveration.[1] When my mother died, I was some time suffered to continue in those sentiments which her instructions had produced; but soon after, though, from respect to her memory, my father did not absolutely ridicule them, yet he showed, in his discourse to others, so little regard to them, and, at times, suggested to me motives of action so different, that I was soon weaned from opinions, which I began to consider as the dreams of superstition, or the artful inventions of designing hypocrisy. My mother's books were left behind at the different quarters we removed to, and my reading was principally confined to plays, novels, and those poetical descriptions of the beauty of virtue and honour, which the circulating libraries easily afforded.[2]

"As I was generally reckoned handsome, and the quickness of my parts extolled by all our visitors, my father had a pride in showing me to the world. I was young, giddy, open to adulation, and vain of those talents which acquired it.

"After the last war, my father was reduced to half-pay; with which we retired to a village in the country, which the acquaintance of some genteel families who resided in it, and the cheapness of living, particularly recommended. My father rented a small house, with a piece of ground sufficient to keep a horse for him,

---

[1]Vow.

[2]Because books were expensive, one could subscribe to a circulating library, which stocked the popular genres—"junk" reading that later 18th-c. reformers criticized for inculcating false or unrealistic expectations of life.

and a cow for the benefit of his family. An old man-servant managed his ground; while a maid, who had formerly been my mother's, and had since been mine, undertook the care of our little dairy: they were assisted in each of their provinces by my father and me; and we passed our time in a state of tranquillity, which he had always talked of with delight, and my train of reading had taught me to admire.

"Though I had never seen the polite circles of the metropolis, the company my father had introduced me into had given me a degree of good-breeding, which soon discovered a superiority over the young ladies of our village. I was quoted as an example of politeness, and my company courted by most of the considerable families in the neighbourhood.

"Amongst the houses where I was frequently invited, was Sir George Winbrooke's. He had two daughters nearly of my age, with whom, though they had been bred up in those maxims of vulgar doctrine, which my superior understanding could not but despise, yet as their good-nature led them to an imitation of my manners in everything else, I cultivated a particular friendship.

"Some months after our first acquaintance, Sir George's eldest son came home from his travels. His figure, his address, and conversation, were not unlike those warm ideas of an accomplished man which my favourite novels had taught me to form; and his sentiments, on the article of religion, were as liberal as my own: when any of these happened to be the topic of our discourse, I, who before had been silent, from a fear of being single in opposition, now kindled at the fire he raised, and defended our mutual opinions with all the eloquence I was mistress of. He would be respectfully attentive all the while; and when I had ended, would raise his eyes from the ground, look at me with a gaze of admiration, and express his applause in the highest strain of encomium. This was an incense the more pleasing, as I seldom or never had met with it before; for the young gentlemen who visited Sir George were for the most part of that athletic order, the pleasure of whose lives is derived from fox-hunting: these are seldom solicitous to please the women at all; or if they were, would never think of applying their flattery to the mind.

"Mr. Winbrooke observed the weakness of my soul, and took every occasion of improving the esteem he had gained. He asked my opinion of every author, of every sentiment, with that submissive diffidence, which showed an unlimited confidence in my understanding. I saw myself revered, as a superior being, by one whose judgment my vanity told me was not likely to err; preferred by him to all the other visitors of my sex, whose fortunes and rank should have entitled them to a much higher degree of notice: I saw their little jealousies at the distinguished attention he paid me; it was gratitude, it was pride, it was love! Love which had made too fatal a progress in my heart, before any declaration on his part should have warranted a return: but I interpreted every look of attention, every expression of compliment, to the passion I imagined him inspired with, and imputed to his sensibility that silence which was the effect of art and design. At length, however, he took an opportunity of declaring his love: he now expressed himself in such ardent terms, that prudence might have suspected their sincerity; but prudence is rarely found in the situation I had been unguardedly led into; besides, that the course of reading to which I had been accustomed, did not lead me to conclude, that his expressions could be too warm to be sincere: nor was I even alarmed at the manner in which he talked of marriage, a subjection, he often hinted, to which genuine love should scorn to be confined. The woman, he would often say, who had merit like mine to fix his affection, could easily command it for ever. That honour too which I revered, was often called in to enforce his sentiments. I did not, however, absolutely assent to them; but I found my regard for their opposites diminish by degrees. If it is dangerous to be convinced, it is dangerous to listen; for our reason is so much of a machine, that it will not always be able to resist, when the ear is perpetually assailed.

"In short, Mr. Harley, (for I tire you with a relation, the catastrophe of which you will already have imagined) I fell a prey to his artifices. He had not been able so thoroughly to convert me, that my conscience was silent on the subject; but he was so assiduous to give repeated proofs of unabated affection, that I hushed its suggestions as they rose. The world, however, I knew, was not to be silenced; and therefore I took occasion to express my uneasiness to my seducer, and intreat him, as he valued the peace of one to whom he professed such attachment, to remove it by a marriage. He made excuse from his dependance on the will of his father, but quieted my fears by the promise of endeavouring to win his assent.

"My father had been some days absent on a visit to a dying relation, from whom he had considerable expectations. I was left at home, with no other company than my books: my books I found were not now such companions as they used to be: I was restless, melancholy, unsatisfied with myself. But judge my situation when I received a billet[3] from Mr. Winbrooke, informing me, that he had sounded Sir George on the subject we had talked of, and found him so averse to any match so unequal to his own rank and fortune, that he was obliged, with whatever reluctance, to bid adieu to a place, the remembrance of which should ever be dear to him.

"I read this letter a hundred times over. Alone, helpless, conscious of guilt, and abandoned by every better thought, my mind was one motley scene of terror, confusion, and remorse. A thousand expedients suggested themselves, and a thousand fears told me they would be vain: at last, in an agony of despair, I packed up a few clothes, took what money and trinkets were in the house, and set out for London, whither I understood he was gone; pretending to my maid, that I had received letters from my father requiring my immediate attendance. I had no other companion than a boy, a servant to the man from whom I hired my horses. I arrived in London within an hour of Mr. Winbrooke, and accidentally alighted at the very inn where he was.

"He started and turned pale when he saw me; but recovered himself in time enough to make many new protestations of regard, and beg me to make myself easy under a disappointment which was equally afflicting to him. He procured me lodgings, where I slept, or rather endeavoured to sleep, for that night. Next morning I saw him again; he then mildly observed on the imprudence of my precipitate flight from the country, and proposed my removing to lodgings at another end of the town, to elude the search of my father, till he should fall upon some method of excusing my conduct to him, and reconciling him to my return. We took a hackney-coach, and drove to the house he mentioned.

"It was situated in a dirty lane, furnished with a tawdry affectation of finery, with some old family-pictures hanging on walls which their own cobwebs would better have suited. I was struck with a secret dread at entering; nor was it lessened by the appear-

---

[3]Brief letter.

ance of the landlady, who had that look of selfish shrewdness, which, of all others, is the most hateful to those whose feelings are untinctured with the world. A girl, who she told us was her niece, sat by her, playing on a guitar, while herself was at work, with the assistance of spectacles, and had a prayer-book with the leaves folded down in several places, lying on the table before her. Perhaps, Sir, I tire you with my minuteness; but the place, and every circumstance about it, is so impressed on my mind, that I shall never forget it.

"I dined that day with Mr. Winbrooke alone. He lost by degrees that restraint which I perceived too well to hang about him before, and, with his former gaiety and good-humour, repeated the flattering things, which, though they had once been fatal, I durst not now distrust. At last, taking my hand and kissing it, "It is thus, said he, that love will last, while freedom is preserved; thus let us ever be blest, without the galling thought that we are tied to a condition where we may cease to be so." I answered, "That the world thought otherwise; that it had certain ideas of good fame, which it was impossible not to wish to maintain." "The world, said he, is a tyrant; they are slaves who obey it: let us be happy without the pale[4] of the world. To-morrow I shall leave this quarter of it, for one, where the talkers of the world shall be foiled, and lose us. Could not my Emily accompany me? my friend, my companion, the mistress of my soul! Nay, do not look so, Emily! Your father may grieve for a while, but your father shall be taken care of; this bank-bill I intend as the comfort for his daughter."

"I could contain myself no longer: "Wretch! I exclaimed, dost thou imagine that my father's heart could brook dependance on the destroyer of his child, and tamely accept of a base equivalent for her honour and his own?" "Honour, my Emily, said he, is the word of fools, or of those wiser men who cheat them. 'Tis a fantastic bauble that does not suit the gravity of your father's age; but, whatever it is, I am afraid it can never be perfectly restored to you: exchange the word then, and let pleasure be your object now." At these words he clasped me in his arms, and pressed his lips rudely to my bosom. I started from my seat, "Perfidious villain! said I, who dar'st insult the weakness thou hast undone; were

[4]Bounds of jurisdiction (paling is border-fencing).

that father here, thy coward soul would shrink from the vengeance of his honour! Curst be that wretch who has deprived him of it! oh! doubly curst, who has dragg'd on his hoary[5] head the infamy which should have crushed her own!" I snatched a knife which lay beside me, and would have plunged it in my breast; but the monster prevented my purpose, and smiling with a grin of barbarous insult, "Madam, said he, I confess you are rather too much in heroics for me: I am sorry we should differ about trifles; but as I seem somehow to have offended you, I would willingly remedy it by taking my leave. You have been put to some foolish expense in this journey on my account; allow me to reimburse you." So saying, he laid a bank-bill, of what amount I had no patience to see, upon the table. Shame, grief, and indignation choked my utterance; unable to speak my wrongs, and unable to bear them in silence, I fell in a swoon at his feet.

"What happened in the interval I cannot tell; but when I came to myself, I was in the arms of the landlady, with her niece chafing my temples, and doing all in her power for my recovery. She had much compassion in her countenance: the old woman assumed the softest look she was capable of, and both endeavoured to bring me comfort. They continued to show me many civilities, and even the aunt began to be less disagreeable in my sight. To the wretched, to the forlorn, as I was, small offices of kindness are endearing.

"Mean time my money was far spent, nor did I attempt to conceal my wants from their knowledge. I had frequent thoughts of returning to my father; but the dread of a life of scorn is insurmountable. I avoided therefore going abroad when I had a chance of being seen by any former acquaintance, nor indeed did my health for a great while permit it; and suffered the old woman, at her own suggestion, to call me niece at home, where we now and then saw (when they could prevail on me to leave my room) one or two other elderly women, and sometimes a grave business-like man, who showed great compassion for my indisposition, and made me very obligingly an offer of a room at his country-house for the recovery of my health. This offer I did not chuse to accept; but told my landlady, "that I should be glad to be employed in any way of business which my skill in needle-work could recommend me to; confessing,

5Gray.

at the same time, that I was afraid I should scarce be able to pay her what I already owed for board and lodging, and that for her other good offices, I had nothing but thanks to give her."

"My dear child, said she, do not talk of paying; since I lost my own sweet girl, (here she wept) your very picture she was, Miss Emily, I have no body, except my niece, to whom I should leave any little thing I have been able to save: you shall live with me, my dear; and I have sometimes a little millenery[6] work, in which, when you are inclined to it, you may assist us. By the way, here are a pair of ruffles we have just finished for that gentleman you saw here at tea; a distant relation of mine, and a worthy man he is. 'Twas pity you refused the offer of an apartment at his country house; my niece, you know, was to have accompanied you, and you might have fancied yourself at home: a most sweet place it is, and but a short mile beyond Hampstead. Who knows, Miss Emily, what effect such a visit might have had: if I had half your beauty, I should not waste it pining after e'er a worthless fellow of them all." I felt my heart swell at her words; I would have been angry if I could; but I was in that stupid state which is not easily awakened to anger: when I would have chid her the reproof stuck in my throat; I could only weep!

"Her want of respect increased, as I had not spirit to assert it; my work was now rather imposed than offered, and I became a drudge for the bread I eat: but my dependance and servility grew in proportion, and I was now in a situation which could not make any extraordinary exertions to disengage itself from either; I found myself with child.

"At last the wretch, who had thus trained me to destruction, hinted the purpose for which those means had been used. I discovered her to be an artful procuress for the pleasures of those, who are men of decency to the world in the midst of debauchery.

"I roused every spark of courage within me at the horrid proposal. She treated my passion at first somewhat mildly; but when I continued to exert it she resented it with insult, and told me plainly, That if I did not soon comply with her desires, I should pay her every farthing I owed, or rot in a jail for life. I trembled at the thought; still, however, I resisted her importunities, and she put her

[6]Hat-making.

threats in execution. I was conveyed to prison, weak from my condition, weaker from that struggle of grief and misery which for some time I had suffered. A miscarriage was the consequence.

"Amidst all the horrors of such a state, surrounded with wretches totally callous, lost alike to humanity and to shame, think, Mr. Harley, think what I endured: nor wonder that I at last yielded to the solicitations of that miscreant I had seen at her house, and sunk to the prostitution which he tempted. But that was happiness compared to what I have suffered since. He soon abandoned me to the common use of the town, and I was cast among those miserable beings in whose society I have since remained.

"Oh! did the daughters of virtue know our sufferings! did they see our hearts torn with anguish amidst the affectation of gaiety which our faces are obliged to assume; our bodies tortured by disease, our minds with that consciousness which they cannot lose! Did they know, did they think of this, Mr. Harley!—their censures are just; but their pity perhaps might spare the wretches whom their justice should condemn.

"Last night, but for an exertion of benevolence which the infection of our infamy prevents even in the humane, had I been thrust out from this miserable place which misfortune has yet left me; exposed to the brutal insults of drunkenness, or dragged by that justice which I could not bribe, to the punishment which may correct, but, alas! can never amend the abandoned objects of its terrors. From that, Mr. Harley, your goodness has relieved me."

He beckoned with his hand: he would have stopped the mention of his favours; but he could not speak, had it been to beg a diadem.

She saw his tears; her fortitude began to fail at the sight, when the voice of some stranger on the stairs awakened her attention. She listened for a moment, then starting up, exclaimed, "Merciful God! my father's voice!"

She had scarce uttered the word, when the door burst open, and a man entered in the garb of an officer. When he discovered his daughter and Harley, he started back a few paces; his look assumed a furious wildness! he laid his hand on his sword. The two objects of his wrath did not utter a syllable. "Villain, he cried, thou seest a father who had once a daughter's honour to preserve; blasted as it now is, behold him ready to avenge its loss!"

Harley had by this time some power of utterance. "Sir, said he, if you will be a moment calm"—"Infamous coward! interrupted the other, dost thou preach calmness to wrongs like mine!" He drew his sword. "Sir, said Harley, let me tell you"—The blood ran quicker to his cheek—his pulse beat one—no more—and regained the temperament of humanity!—"You are deceived, Sir, said he, you are much deceived; but I forgive suspicions which your misfortunes have justified: I would not wrong you, upon my soul I would not, for the dearest gratification of a thousand worlds: my heart bleeds for you!"

His daughter was now prostrate at his feet. "Strike, said she, strike here a wretch, whose misery cannot end but with that death she deserves." Her hair had fallen on her shoulders! her look had the horrid calmness of out-breathed despair! Her father would have spoken; his lip quivered, his cheek grew pale! his eyes lost the lightening of their fury! there was a reproach in them, but with a mingling of pity! He turned them up to heaven—then on his daughter.—He laid his left hand on his heart—the sword dropped from his right—he burst into tears.

Chapter XXIX

The distresses of a father.

Harley kneeled also at the side of the unfortunate daughter: "Allow me, Sir, said he, to intreat your pardon for one whose offences have been already so signally punished. I know, I feel, that those tears, wrung from the heart of a father, are more dreadful to her than all the punishments your sword could have inflicted: accept the contrition of a child whom heaven has restored to you." "Is she not lost, answered he, irrecoverably lost? Damnation! a common prostitute to the meanest ruffian!"—"Calmly, my dear Sir, said Harley, did you know by what complicated misfortunes she had fallen to that miserable state in which you now behold her, I should have no need of words to excite your compassion. Think, Sir, of what once she was. Would you abandon her to the insults of an unfeeling world, deny her opportunity of penitence, and cut off the little comfort that still remains for your afflictions and her own!" "Speak, said he, addressing himself to his daughter; speak; I will hear thee."— The desperation that supported her was lost; she fell to the ground, and bathed his feet with her tears!

Harley undertook her cause: he related the treacheries to which she had fallen a sacrifice, and again solicited the forgiveness of her father. He looked on her for some time in silence; the pride of a soldier's honour checked for a while the yearnings of his heart; but nature at last prevailed, he fell on her neck, and mingled his tears with hers.

Harley, who discovered from the dress of the stranger that he was just arrived from a journey, begged that they would both remove to his lodgings, till he could procure others for them. Atkins looked at him with some marks of surprise. His daughter now first recovered the power of speech. "Wretch as I am, said she, yet there is some gratitude due to the preserver of your child. See him now before you. To him I owe my life, or at least the comfort of imploring your forgiveness before I die." "Pardon me, young gentleman, said Atkins, I fear my passion wronged you."[1]

"Never, never, Sir, said Harley; if it had, your reconciliation to your daughter were an atonement a thousand fold." He then re-

---

[1] It would be more common to challenge a false accuser to a duel of honor.

peated his request that he might be allowed to conduct them to his lodgings, to which Mr. Atkins at last consented. He took his daughter's arm. "Come, my Emily, said he, we can never, never recover that happiness we have lost; but time may teach us to remember our misfortunes with patience."

When they arrived at the house where Harley lodged, he was informed that the first floor was then vacant, and that the gentleman and his daughter might be accommodated there. While he was upon his enquiry, Miss Atkins informed her father more particularly what she owed to his benevolence. When he turned into the room where they were, Atkins ran and embraced him; begged him again to forgive the offence he had given him, and made the warmest protestations of gratitude for his favours. We would attempt to describe the joy which Harley felt on this occasion, did it not occur to us, that one half of the world could not understand it though we did; and the other half will, by this time, have understood it without any description at all.

Miss Atkins now retired to her chamber, to take some rest from the violence of the emotions she had suffered. When she was gone, her father, addressing himself to Harley, said, "You have a right, Sir, to be informed of the present situation of one who owes so much to your compassion for his misfortunes. My daughter I find has informed you what that was at the fatal juncture when they began. Her distresses you have heard, you have pitied as they deserved; with mine perhaps I cannot so easily make you acquainted. You have a feeling heart, Mr. Harley; I bless it that it has saved my child; but you never were a father, a father torn by that most dreadful of calamities, the dishonour of a child he doated on! You have been already informed of some of the circumstances of her elopement. I was then from home, called by the death of a relation, who, though he would never advance me a shilling on the utmost exigency in his life-time, left me all the gleanings of his frugality at his death. I would not write this intelligence to my daughter, because I intended to be the bearer myself; and as soon as my business would allow me, I set out on my return, winged with all the haste of paternal affection. I fondly built those schemes of future happiness, which present prosperity is ever busy to suggest: my Emily was concerned in them all. As I approached our little dwelling, my heart throbbed with the anticipation of joy and welcome. I imagined the cheering fire, the blissful contentment of a frugal meal, made luxurious by a daughter's smile: I painted to myself her surprise at the tidings of our new-acquired riches, our fond disputes about the disposal of them.

"The road was shortened by the dreams of happiness I enjoyed, and it began to be dark as I reached the house: I alighted from my horse, and walked softly up stairs to the room we commonly sat in. I was somewhat disappointed at not finding my daughter there. I rung the bell; her maid appeared, and showed no small signs of wonder at the summons. She blessed herself as she entered the room: I smiled at her surprise. "Where is Miss Emily, Sir?" said she. "Emily!" "Yes, Sir; she has been gone hence some days, upon receipt of those letters you sent her." "Letters!" said I. "Yes, Sir; so she told me, and went off in all haste that very night."

"I stood aghast as she spoke; but was able so far to recollect myself, as to put on the affectation of calmness, and telling her there was certainly some mistake in the affair, desired her to leave me.

"When she was gone, I threw myself into a chair in that state of uncertainty which is of all others the most dreadful. The gay visions with which I had delighted myself, vanished in an instant: I was tortured with tracing back the same circle of doubt and disappointment. My head grew dizzy as I thought. I called the servant again, and asked her a hundred questions, to no purpose; there was not room even for conjecture.

"Something at last arose in my mind, which we call Hope, without knowing what it is. I wished myself deluded by it; but it could not prevail over my returning fears. I rose and walked through the room. My Emily's spinet[2] stood at the end of it, open, with a book of music folded down at some of my favourite lessons. I touched the keys; there was a vibration in the sound that froze my blood: I looked around, and methought the family-pictures on the walls gazed on me with compassion in their faces. I sat down again with an attempt at more composure; I started at every creaking of the door, and my ears rung with imaginary noises!

"I had not remained long in this situation, when the arrival of a friend, who had accidentally heard of my return, put an end to my doubts, by the recital of my daughter's dishonour. He told me he

---

[2]A small instrument like a harpsichord.

had his information from a young gentleman, to whom Winbrooke had boasted of having seduced her.

"I started from my seat, with broken curses on my lips, and without knowing whither I should pursue them, ordered my servant to load my pistols and saddle my horses. My friend, however, with great difficulty, persuaded me to compose myself for that night, promising to accompany me on the morrow, to Sir George Winbrooke's in quest of his son.

"The morrow came, after a night spent in a state little distant from madness. We went as early as decency would allow to Sir George's; he received me with politeness, and indeed compassion; protested his abhorrence of his son's conduct, and told me that he had set out some days before for London, on which place he had procured a draft for a large sum, on pretence of finishing his travels; but that he had not heard from him since his departure.

"I did not wait for any more, either of information or comfort; but, against the united remonstrances of Sir George and my friend, set out instantly for London, with a frantic uncertainty of purpose; but there all manner of search was in vain. I could trace neither of them any farther than the inn where they first put up on their arrival; and after some days fruitless inquiry, returned home destitute of every little hope that had hitherto supported me. The journeys I had made, the restless nights I had spent, above all, the perturbation of my mind, had the effect which naturally might be expected; a very dangerous fever was the consequence. From this, however, contrary to the expectation of my physicians, I recovered. It was now that I first felt something like calmness of mind; probably from being reduced to a state which could not produce the exertions of anguish or despair. A stupid melancholy settled on my soul: I could endure to live with an apathy of life; at times I forgot my resentment, and wept at the remembrance of my child.

"Such has been the tenor of my days since that fatal moment when these misfortunes began, till yesterday, that I received a letter from a friend in town, acquainting me of her present situation. Could such tales as mine, Mr. Harley, be sometimes suggested to the daughters of levity, did they but know with what anxiety the heart of a parent flutters round the child he loves, they would be less apt to construe into harshness that delicate concern for their conduct, which they often complain of as laying restraint upon things, to the young, the gay, and the thoughtless, seemingly harmless and indifferent. Alas! I fondly imagined that I needed not even these common cautions! my Emily was the joy of my age, and the pride of my soul!—Those things are now no more! they are lost for ever! Her death I could have born! but the death of her honour has added obloquy and shame to that sorrow which bends my grey hairs to the dust!"

As he spoke these last words, his voice trembled in his throat; it was now lost in his tears! He sat with his face half turned from Harley, as if he would have hid the sorrow which he felt. Harley was in the same attitude himself; he durst not meet his eye with a tear; but gathering his stifled breath, "Let me entreat you, Sir, said he, to hope better things. The world is ever tyrannical; it warps our sorrows to edge them with keener affliction. Let us not be slaves to the names it affixes to motive or to action. I know an ingenuous mind cannot help feeling when they sting: but there are considerations by which it may be overcome; its fantastic ideas vanish as they rise; they teach us—to look beyond it."

* * * * * * * *

A Fragment

Showing his success with the baronet.

* * * The card he received was in the politest style in which disappointment could be communicated. The baronet "was under a necessity of giving up his application for Mr. Harley, as he was informed that the lease was engaged for a gentleman who had long served his majesty in another capacity, and whose merit had entitled him to the first lucrative thing that should be vacant." Even Harley could not murmur at such a disposal.—"Perhaps, said he to himself, some war-worn officer, who, like poor Atkins, had been neglected from reasons which merited the highest advancement; whose honour could not stoop to solicit the preferment he deserved; perhaps, with a family, taught the principles of delicacy, without the means of supporting it; a wife and children—gracious heaven! whom my wishes would have deprived of bread."—

He was interrupted in his reverie by some one tapping him on the shoulder, and, on turning round, he discovered it to be the very man who had explained to him the condition of his gay companion at Hydepark-corner. "I am glad to see you, Sir," said he; I believe we are fellows in disappointment." Harley started, and said that he was at a loss to understand him. "Poh! you need not be so shy, answered the other; every one for himself is but fair, and I had much rather you had got it than the rascally gauger." Harley still protested his ignorance of what he meant. "Why, the lease of Bancroft-manor; had not you been applying for it?" "I confess I was, replied Harley; but I cannot conceive how you should be interested in the matter."—"Why, I was making interest for it myself, said he, and I think I had some title: I voted for this same baronet at the last election, and made some of my friends do so too; though I would not have you imagine that I sold my vote; no, I scorn it, let me tell you, I scorn it; but I thought as how this man was staunch and true, and I find he's but a double-faced fellow after all, and speechifies in the House for any side he hopes to make most by. Oh, how many fine speeches and squeezings by the hand we had of him on the canvas![1] "And if ever I shall be so happy as to have an opportunity of

[1] In the boxing ring.

serving you."—A murrain[2] on the smooth-tongu'd knave; and after all to get it for this pimp of a gauger." "The gauger! there must be some mistake, said Harley; he writes me, that it was engaged for one whose long services"—"Services! interrupted the other; you shall hear: Services! Yes, his sister arrived in town a few days ago, and is now sempstress[3] to the baronet. A plague on all rogues! says honest Sam Wrightson; I shall but just drink damnation to them to-night, in a crown's-worth of Ashley's, and leave London to-morrow by sun-rise."—"I shall leave it too," said Harley; and so he accordingly did.

In passing through Piccadilly, he had observed on the window of an inn a notification of the departure of a stage-coach for a place in his road homewards; in the way back to his lodgings, he took a seat in it for his return.

[2]Plague.
[3]Seamstress.

Chapter XXXIII

He leaves London.—Characters in a stage-coach.

The company in the stage-coach consisted of a grocer and his wife, who were going to pay a visit to some of their country friends; a young officer, who took this way of marching to quarters; a middle-aged gentlewoman, who had been hired as housekeeper to some family in the country; and an elderly, well-looking man, with a remarkable old-fashioned periwig.

Harley, upon entering, discovered but one vacant seat, next the grocer's wife, which, from his natural shyness of temper, he made no scruple to occupy, however aware that riding backwards always disagreed with him.

Though his inclination to physiognomy had met with some rubs in the metropolis, he had not yet lost his attachment to that science: he set himself therefore to examine, as usual, the countenances of his companions. Here indeed he was not long in doubt as to the preference; for besides that the elderly gentleman, who sat opposite to him, had features by nature more expressive of good dispositions, there was something in that periwig we mentioned, peculiarly attractive of Harley's regard.

He had not been long employed in these speculations, when he found himself attacked with that faintish sickness, which was the natural consequence of his situation in the coach. The paleness of his countenance was first observed by the housekeeper, who immediately made offer of her smelling-bottle, which Harley however declined, telling at the same time the cause of his uneasiness. The gentleman on the opposite side of the coach now first turned his eye from the side direction in which it had been fixed, and begged Harley to exchange places with him, expressing his regret that he had not made the proposal before. Harley thanked him; and, upon being assured that both seats were alike to him, was about to accept of his offer, when the young gentleman of the sword, putting on an arch look, laid hold of the other's arm, "So, my old boy, said he, I find you have still some youthful blood about you; but, with your leave, I will do myself the honour of sitting by this lady;" and took his place accordingly. The grocer stared him as full in the face as his own short neck would allow; and his wife, who was a little, round-fac'd woman, with a great deal of colour in her cheeks, drew up at the compliment that was paid her, looking first at the officer, and then at the housekeeper.

This incident was productive of some discourse; for before, though there was sometimes a cough or a hem from the grocer, and the officer now and then humm'd a few notes of a song, there had not a single word passed the lips of any of the company.

Mrs. Grocer observed, how ill-convenient it was for people, who could not be drove backwards, to travel in a stage. This brought on a dissertation on stage-coaches in general, and the pleasure of keeping a chay[1] of one's own; which led to another, on the great riches of Mr. Deputy Bearskin, who, according to her, had once been of that industrious order of youths who sweep the crossings of the streets for the conveniency of passengers, but, by various fortunate accidents, had now acquired an immense fortune, and kept his coach and a dozen livery servants. All this afforded ample fund for conversation, if conversation it might be called, that was carried on solely by the before-mentioned lady, nobody offering to interrupt her, except that the officer sometimes signified his approbation by a variety of oaths, a sort of phraseology in which he seemed extremely versant. She appealed indeed frequently to her husband for the authenticity of certain facts, of which the good man as often protested his total ignorance; but as he was always called fool, or something very like it, for his pains, he at last contrived to support the credit of his wife without prejudice to his conscience, and signified his assent by a noise not unlike the grunting of that animal which in shape and fatness he somewhat resembled.

The housekeeper, and the old gentleman who sat next to Harley, were now observed to be fast asleep; at which the lady, who had been at such pains to entertain them, muttered some words of displeasure, and, upon the officer's whispering to smoke the old put,[2] both she and her husband purs'd up their mouths into a contemptuous smile. Harley looked sternly on the grocer. "You are come, Sir, said he, to those years when you might have learned some reverence for age: as for this young man, who has so lately escaped from the nursery, he may be allowed to divert himself."

---

[1]Slang for *chaise,* a carriage.
[2]Make fun of the country-fellow.

"Dam'me, Sir! said the officer, do you call me young?" striking up the front of his hat, and stretching forward on his seat, till his face almost touched Harley's. It is probable, however, that he discovered something there which tended to pacify him, for, on the ladies entreating them not to quarrel, he very soon resumed his posture and calmness together, and was rather less profuse of his oaths during the rest of the journey.

It is possible the old gentleman had waked time enough to hear the last part of this discourse; at least (whether from that cause, or that he too was a physiognomist) he wore a look remarkably complacent[3] to Harley, who, on his part, showed a particular observance of him: indeed they had soon a better opportunity of making their acquaintance, as the coach arrived that night at the town where the officer's regiment lay, and the places of destination of their other fellow-travellers, it seems, were at no great distance; for next morning the old gentleman and Harley were the only passengers remaining.

When they left the inn in the morning, Harley, pulling out a little pocket-book, began to examine the contents, and make some corrections with a pencil. "This, said he, turning to his companion, is an amusement with which I sometimes pass idle hours at an inn: these are quotations from those humble poets, who trust their fame to the brittle tenure of windows and drinking-glasses."[4] "From our inns, returned the gentleman, a stranger might imagine that we were a nation of poets; machines at least containing poetry, which the motion of a journey emptied of their contents: it is from the vanity of being thought geniuses, or a mere mechanical imitation of the custom of others, that we are tempted to scrawl rhime upon such places?"

"Whether vanity is the cause of our becoming rhimesters or not, answered Harley, it is a pretty certain effect of it. An old man of my acquaintance, who deals in apothegms, used to say that he had known few men without envy, few wits without ill-nature, and no poet without vanity; and I believe his remark is a pretty just one: vanity has been immemorially the charter of poets. In this, the ancients were more honest than we are. The old poets frequently

---

[3]In the 18th-c. sense of pleasant, affable.
[4]Scratched-on rhyme.

make boastful predictions of the immortality their works shall acquire them; ours, in their dedications and prefatory discourses, employ much eloquence to praise their patrons, and much seeming modesty to condemn themselves, or at least to apologize for their productions to the world: but this, in my opinion, is the more assuming manner of the two; for of all the garbs I ever saw pride put on, that of her humility is to me the most disgusting."

"It is natural enough for a poet to be vain, said the stranger: the little worlds which he raises, the inspiration which he claims, may easily be productive of self-importance; though that inspiration is fabulous, it brings on egotism, which is always the parent of vanity."

"It may be supposed, answered Harley, that inspiration of old was an article of religious faith; in modern times it may be translated a propensity to compose; and I believe it is not always most readily found where the poets have fixed its residence, amidst groves and plains, and the scenes of pastoral retirement. The mind may be there unbent from the cares of the world; but it will frequently, at the same time, be unnerved from any great exertion: it will feel imperfect ideas which it cannot express, and wander without effort over the regions of reflection."

"There is at least, said the stranger, one advantage in the poetical inclination, that it is an incentive to philanthropy. There is a certain poetic ground, on which a man cannot tread without feelings that enlarge the heart: the causes of human depravity vanish before the romantic enthusiasm he professes; and many who are not able to reach the Parnassian heights,[5] may yet approach so near as to be bettered by the air of the climate."

"I have always thought so, replied Harley; but this is an argument with the prudent against it: they urge the danger of unfitness for the world."

"I allow it, returned the other; but I believe it is not always rightfully imputed to the bent for poetry: that is only one effect of the common cause.—Jack, says his father, is indeed no scholar; nor could all the drubbings from his master ever bring him one step forward in his accidence[6] or syntax: but I intend him for a mer-

---

[5]Mount Parnassus was home of the muses.
[6]Grammatical inflections.

chant.—Allow the same indulgence to Tom.—Tom reads Virgil and Horace when he should be casting accounts; and but t'other day he pawned his great-coat for an edition of Shakespeare.—But Tom would have been as he is, though Virgil and Horace had never been born, though Shakespeare had died a link-boy;[7] for his nurse will tell you, that when he was a child, he broke his rattle, to discover what it was that sounded within it; and burnt the sticks of his go-cart, because he liked to see the sparkling of timber in the fire.[8]— 'Tis a sad case; but what is to be done?—Why, Jack shall make a fortune, dine on venison, and drink claret.—Ay, but Tom—Tom shall dine with his brother, when his pride will let him; at other times, he shall bless God over a half-pint of ale and a Welsh-rabbit;[9] and both shall go to heaven as they may.—That's a poor prospect for Tom, says the father.—To go to heaven! I cannot agree with him."

"Perhaps, said Harley, we now-a-days discourage the romantic turn a little too much. Our boys are prudent too soon. Mistake me not, I do not mean to blame them for want of levity or dissipation; but their pleasures are those of hackneyed vice, blunted to every finer emotion by the repetition of debauch;[10] and their desire of pleasure is warped to the desire of wealth, as the means of procuring it. The immense riches acquired by individuals have erected a standard of ambition, destructive of private morals, and of public virtue.[11] The weaknesses of vice are left us; but the most allowable of our failings we are taught to despise. Love, the passion most natural to the sensibility of youth, has lost the plaintive dignity he once possessed, for the unmeaning simper of a dangling coxcomb; and the only serious concern, that of a dowry, is settled, even amongst

[7] Boy employed to carry a torch (link) to guide passengers along the streets.

[8] *Practical Education* (1798) by Maria and Richard Lovell Edgeworth opens by advising parents that children break toys not to be naughty but to figure out how they work.

[9] Inexpensive meal of cheese sauce poured over bread.

[10] In the preface to *Lyrical Ballads* (1800), Wordsworth blames a general "degrading thirst after outrageous stimulation" for "blunt[ing] the discriminating powers of the mind," reducing it to "a state of almost savage torpor" inimical to the appreciation of a poetry of deep feeling.

[11] A subject of debate in the 18th c. Bernard Mandeville's *The Fable of the Bees: Or, Private Vices, Publick Benefits* (1714), an early manifesto of capitalism, says the opposite: private vice leads to public virtue because spending increases the general wealth of the state.

the beardless leaders of the dancing-school. The Frivolous and the Interested (might a satirist say) are the characteristical features of the age; they are visible even in the essays of our philosophers. They laugh at the pedantry of our fathers, who complained of the times in which they lived; they are at pains to persuade us how much those were deceived; they pride themselves in defending things as they find them, and in exploring the barren sounds which had been reared into motives for action. To this their style is suited; and the manly tone of reason is exchanged for perpetual efforts at sneer and ridicule.[12] This I hold to be an alarming crisis in the corruption of a state; when not only is virtue declined, and vice prevailing, but when the praises of virtue are forgotten, and the infamy of vice unfelt."

They soon after arrived at the next inn upon the rout[e] of the stage-coach, when the stranger told Harley, that his brother's house, to which he was returning, lay at no great distance, and he must therefore unwillingly bid him adieu.

"I should like, said Harley, taking his hand, to have some word to remember so much seeming worth by: my name is Harley."—"I shall remember it, answered the old gentleman, in my prayers; mine is Silton."

And Silton indeed it was; Ben Silton himself! Once more, my honoured friend, farewell!—Born to be happy without the world, to that peaceful happiness which the world has not to bestow! Envy never scowled on thy life, nor hatred smiled on thy grave.

---

[12]By mid-century, the enthusiasm for Augustan satire was on the wane.

Chapter XXXIV

He meets an old acquaintance.

When the stage-coach arrived at the place of its destination, Harley began to consider how he should proceed the remaining part of his journey. He was very civilly accosted by the master of the inn, who offered to accommodate him either with a post-chaise or horses, to any distance he had a mind: but as he did things frequently in a way different from what other people call natural, he refused these offers, and set out immediately a-foot, having first put a spare shirt in his pocket, and given directions for the forwarding of his portmanteau. This was a method of travelling which he was accustomed to take; it saved the trouble of provision for any animal but himself, and left him at liberty to chuse his quarters, either at an inn, or at the first cottage in which he saw a face he liked: nay, when he was not peculiarly attracted by the reasonable creation, he would sometimes consort with a species of inferior rank, and lay himself down to sleep by the side of a rock, or on the banks of a rivulet. He did few things without a motive, but his motives were rather eccentric; and the useful and expedient were terms which he held to be very indefinite, and which therefore he did not always apply to the sense in which they are commonly understood.

The sun was now in his decline, and the evening remarkably serene, when he entered a hollow part of the road, which winded between the surrounding banks, and seamed the sward[1] in different lines, as the choice of travellers had directed them to tread it. It seemed to be little frequented now, for some of those had partly recovered their former verdure. The scene was such as induced Harley to stand and enjoy it; when, turning round, his notice was attracted by an object, which the fixture of his eye on the spot he walked had before prevented him from observing.

An old man, who from his dress seemed to have been a soldier, lay fast asleep on the ground; a knapsack rested on a stone at his right hand, while his staff and brass-hilted sword were crossed at his left.

Harley looked on him with the most earnest attention. He was one of those figures which Salvator[2] would have drawn; nor was the sur-

[1]Turf.

[2]17th-c. Italian painter Salvator Rosa.

rounding scenery unlike the wildness of that painter's back-grounds.[3] The banks on each side were covered with fantastic shrub-wood, and at a little distance, on the top of one of them, stood a finger-post, to mark the directions of two roads which diverged from the point where it was placed. A rock, with some dangling wild flowers, jutted out above where the soldier lay; on which grew the stump of a large tree, white with age, and a single twisted branch shaded his face as he slept. His face had the marks of manly comeliness impaired by time; his forehead was not altogether bald, but its hairs might have been

Salvator Rosa, "Landscape with Hermit" (National Museums, Liverpool [Walker Art Gallery])

[3]William Gilpin's influential *Essay . . . Upon the Principles of Picturesque Beauty* (1768) applied this aesthetic not only to painting but also to landscaping and even the appreciation of nature itself.

numbered; while a few white locks behind crossed the brown of his neck with a contrast the most venerable to a mind like Harley's. "Thou art old, said he to himself, but age has not brought thee rest for its infirmities; I fear those silver hairs have not found shelter from thy country, though that neck has been bronzed in its service." The stranger waked. He looked at Harley with the appearance of some confusion: it was a pain the latter knew too well to think of causing in another; he turned and went on. The old man re-adjusted his knapsack, and followed in one of the tracks on the opposite side of the road.

When Harley heard the tread of his feet behind him, he could not help stealing back a glance at his fellow-traveller. He seemed to bend under the weight of his knapsack; he halted on his walk, and one of his arms was supported by a sling, and lay motionless across his breast. He had that steady look of sorrow, which indicates that its owner has gazed upon his griefs till he has forgotten to lament them; yet not without those streaks of complacency which a good mind will sometimes throw into the countenance, through all the incumbent load of its depression.

He had now advanced nearer to Harley, and, with an uncertain sort of voice, begged to know what it was o'clock; "I fear, said he, sleep has beguiled me of my time, and I shall hardly have light enough left to carry me to the end of my journey." "Father! said Harley, (who by this time found the romantic enthusiasm rising within him) how far do you mean to go?" "But a little way, Sir, returned the other; and indeed it is but a little way I can manage now: 'tis just four miles from the height to the village, thither I am going." "I am going there too, said Harley; we may make the road shorter to each other. You seem to have served your country, Sir, to have served it hardly too; 'tis a character I have the highest esteem for.—I would not be impertinently inquisitive; but there is that in your appearance which excites my curiosity to know something more of you: in the mean time, suffer me to carry that knapsack."

The old man gazed on him; a tear stood in his eye! "Young gentleman, said he, you are too good: may heaven bless you for an old man's sake, who has nothing but his blessing to give! but my knapsack is so familiar to my shoulders, that I should walk the worse for wanting it; and it would be troublesome to you, who have not been used to its weight." "Far from it, answered Harley, I should tread the lighter; it would be the most honourable badge I ever wore."

"Sir, said the stranger, who had looked earnestly in Harley's face during the last part of his discourse, is not your name Harley?" "It is, replied he; I am ashamed to say I have forgotten yours." "You may well have forgotten my face, said the stranger, 'tis a long time since you saw it; but possibly you may remember something of old Edwards."—"Edwards! cried Harley, Oh! heavens! and sprung to embrace him; let me clasp those knees on which I have sat so often: Edwards!—I shall never forget that fire-side, round which I have been so happy! But where, where have you been? where is Jack? where is your daughter? How has it fared with them, when fortune, I fear, has been so unkind to you?"—"'Tis a long tale, replied Edwards; but I will try to tell it you as we walk.

"When you were at school in the neighbourhood, you remember me at South-hill: that farm had been possessed by my father, grandfather, and great-grandfather, which last was a younger brother of that very man's ancestor who is now lord of the manor. I thought I managed it, as they had done, with prudence; I paid my rent regularly as it became due, and had always as much behind as gave bread to me and my children. But my last lease was out soon after you left that part of the country; and the squire, who had lately got a London-attorney for his steward, would not renew it, because, he said, he did not chuse to have any farm under £300 a year value on his estate; but offered to give me the preference on the same terms with another, if I chose to take the one he had marked out, of which mine was a part.

"What could I do, Mr. Harley? I feared the undertaking was too great for me; yet to leave, at my age, the house I had lived in from my cradle! I could not, Mr. Harley, I could not; there was not a tree about it that I did not look on as my father, my brother, or my child: so I even ran the risk, and took the squire's offer of the whole. But had soon reason to repent of my bargain; the steward had taken care that my former farm should be the best land of the division: I was obliged to hire more servants, and I could not have my eye over them all; some unfavourable seasons followed one another, and I found my affairs entangling on my hands. To add to my distress, a considerable corn-factor[4] turned bankrupt with a

---

[4]Middle-man or sales-agent.

sum of mine in his possession: I failed paying my rent so punctually as I was wont to do, and the same steward had my stock taken in execution[5] in a few days after. So, Mr. Harley, there was an end of my prosperity. However, there was as much produced from the sale of my effects as paid my debts and saved me from a jail: I thank God I wronged no man, and the world could never charge me with dishonesty.

"Had you seen us, Mr. Harley, when we were turned out of South-hill, I am sure you would have wept at the sight. You remember old Trusty, my shag house-dog; I shall never forget it while I live; the poor creature was blind with age, and could scarce crawl after us to the door; he went however as far as the gooseberry-bush; that you may remember stood on the left side of the yard; he was wont to bask in the sun there: when he had reached that spot, he stopped; we went on: I called to him; he wagged his tail, but did not stir: I called again; he lay down: I whistled, and cried Trusty; he gave a short howl, and died! I could have lain down and died too; but God gave me strength to live for my children."

The old man now paused a moment to take breath. He eyed Harley's face; it was bathed with tears: the story was grown familiar to himself; he dropped one tear, and no more.

"Though I was poor, continued he, I was not altogether without credit. A gentleman in the neighbourhood, who had a small farm unoccupied at the time, offered to let me have it, on giving security[6] for the rent, which I made shift to procure. It was a piece of ground which required management to make anything of; but it was nearly within the compass of my son's labour and my own. We exerted all our industry to bring it into some heart.[7] We began to succeed tolerably, and lived contented on its produce, when an unlucky accident brought us under the displeasure of a neighbouring justice of the peace, and broke all our family-happiness again.

"My son was a remarkable good shooter; he had always kept a pointer on our former farm, and thought no harm in doing so now; when one day, having sprung a covey[8] in our own ground, the dog,

---

[5]Possessions seized in lieu of payment.

[6]Collateral, or a guarantor.

[7]Fertility.

[8]A brood of partridges.

of his own accord, followed them into the justice's.[9] My son laid down his gun, and went after his dog to bring him back: the game-keeper, who had marked the birds, came up, and seeing the pointer, shot him just as my son approached. The creature fell; my son ran up to him: he died with a complaining sort of cry at his master's feet. Jack could bear it no longer; but flying at the game-keeper, wrenched his gun out of his hand, and with the butt end of it, felled him to the ground.

"He had scarce got home, when a constable came with a warrant, and dragged him to prison; there he lay, for the justices would not take bail, till he was tried at the quarter-sessions for the assault and battery. His fine was hard upon us to pay; we contrived however to live the worse for it, and make up the loss by our frugality: but the justice was not content with that punishment, and soon after had an opportunity of punishing us indeed.

"An officer with press-orders[10] came down to our county, and having met with the justices, agreed that they should pitch on a certain number, who could most easily be spared from the county, of whom he would take care to clear it: my son's name was in the justices' list.

"'Twas on a Christmas eve, and the birth-day too of my son's little boy. The night was piercing cold, and it blew a storm, with showers of hail and snow. We had made up a cheering fire in an inner room; I sat before it in my wicker-chair, blessing providence, that had still left a shelter for me and my children. My son's two little ones were holding their gambols around us; my heart warmed at the sight; I brought a bottle of my best ale, and all our misfortunes were forgotten.

"It had long been our custom to play a game at blind-man's-buff on that night, and it was not omitted now; so to it we fell, I, and my son, and his wife, the daughter of a neighbouring farmer, who happened to be with us at the time, the two children, and an old maid-servant, who had lived with me from a child. The lot fell on my son to be blindfolded: we had continued some time in our game, when he groped his way into an outer room in pursuit of

---

[9]The notorious Black Act (1723–1823) made illegal hunting on private lands a capital offense, and the estate's gamekeeper was within his rights in killing Jack's dog.

[10]Impressments; compelled military service.

some of us, who, he imagined, had taken shelter there; we kept snug in our places, and enjoyed his mistake. He had not been long there, when he was suddenly seized from behind; "I shall have you now," said he, and turned about. "Shall you so, master, answered the ruffian, who had laid hold of him; we shall make you play at another sort of game by and by."—At these words Harley started with a convulsive sort of motion, and grasping Edwardses sword, drew it half out of the scabbard, with a look of the most frantic wildness. Edwards gently replaced it in its sheath, and went on with his relation.

"On hearing these words in a strange voice, we all rushed out to discover the cause; the room by this time was almost full of the gang. My daughter-in-law fainted at the sight; the maid and I ran to assist her, while my poor son remained motionless, gazing by turns on his children and their mother. We soon recovered her to life, and begged her to retire and wait the issue of the affair; but she flew to her husband, and clung round him in an agony of terror and grief.

"In the gang was one of a smoother aspect, whom, by his dress, we discovered to be a serjeant of foot: he came up to me, and told me, that my son had his choice of the sea or land service, whispering at the same time that, if he chose the land, he might get off, on procuring him another man, and paying a certain sum for his freedom. The money we could just muster up in the house, by the assistance of the maid, who produced, in a green bag, all the little savings of her service; but the man we could not expect to find. My daughter-in-law gazed upon her children with a look of the wildest despair: "My poor infants! said she, your father is forced from you; who shall now labour for your bread; or must your mother beg for herself and you?" I prayed her to be patient; but comfort I had none to give her. At last, calling the serjeant aside, I asked him, "If I was too old to be accepted in place of my son?" "Why, I don't know, said he; you are rather old to be sure, but yet the money may do much." "I put the money in his hand; and coming back to my children, "Jack, said I, you are free; live to give your wife and these little ones bread; I will go, my child, in your stead: I have but little life to lose, and if I staid, I should add one to the wretches you left behind." "No, replied my son, I am not that coward you imagine me; heaven forbid, that my father's grey hairs should be so exposed, while I sat idle at home; I am young and able to endure much, and God will take care of you and my family." "Jack, said I, I will put an end to this matter; you have never hitherto disobeyed me; I will not be contradicted in this; stay at home, I charge you, and, for my sake, be kind to my children."

"Our parting, Mr. Harley, I cannot describe to you; it was the first time we ever had parted: the very press-gang could scarce keep from tears; but the serjeant, who had seemed the softest before, was now the least moved of them all. He conducted me to a party of new-raised recruits, who lay at a village in the neighbourhood; and we soon after joined the regiment. I had not been long with it, when we were ordered to the East Indies,[11] where I was soon made a serjeant, and might have picked up some money, if my heart had been as hard as some others were; but my nature was never of that kind, that could think of getting rich at the expense of my conscience.

"Amongst our prisoners was an old Indian, whom some of our officers supposed to have a treasure hidden somewhere; which is no uncommon practice in that country. They pressed him to discover it. He declared he had none, but that would not satisfy them: so they ordered him to be tied to a stake, and suffer fifty lashes every morning, till he should learn to speak out, as they said. Oh! Mr. Harley, had you seen him, as I did, with his hands bound behind him, suffering in silence, while the big drops trickled down his shrivelled cheeks, and wet his grey beard, which some of the inhuman soldiers plucked in scorn! I could not bear it, I could not for my soul, and one morning, when the rest of the guard were out of the way, I found means to let him escape. I was tried by a courtmartial for negligence of my post, and ordered, in compassion of my age, and having got this wound in my arm and that in my leg in the service, only to suffer three hundred lashes and be turned out of the regiment; but my sentence was mitigated as to the lashes, and I had only two hundred. When I had suffered these, I was turned out of the camp, and had betwixt three and four hundred miles to travel before I could reach a sea-port, without guide to conduct me, or money to buy me provisions by the way. I set out, however, resolved to walk as far as I could, and then to lay myself down and die. But I had scarce gone a mile when I was met by the Indian

[11]Present-day India and China.

whom I had delivered. He pressed me in his arms, and kissed the marks of the lashes on my back a thousand times: he led me to a little hut, where some friend of his dwelt; and after I was recovered of my wounds, conducted me so far on my journey himself, and sent another Indian to guide me through the rest. When we parted he pulled out a purse with two hundred pieces of gold in it. "Take this, said he, my dear preserver, it is all I have been able to procure." "I begged him not to bring himself to poverty for my sake, who should probably have no need of it long;" but he insisted on my accepting it. He embraced me:—"You are an Englishman, said he, but the Great Spirit has given you an Indian heart; may he bear up the weight of your old age, and blunt the arrow that brings it rest!" We parted; and not long after I made shift to get my passage to England. 'Tis but about a week since I landed, and I am going to end my days in the arms of my son. This sum may be of use to him and his children; 'tis all the value I put upon it. I thank heaven I never was covetous of wealth; I never had much, but was always so happy as to be content with my little."

When Edwards had ended his relation, Harley stood a while looking at him in silence; at last he pressed him in his arms, and when he had given vent to the fulness of his heart by a shower of tears, "Edwards, said he, let me hold thee to my bosom; let me imprint the virtue of thy sufferings on my soul. Come, my honoured veteran! let me endeavour to soften the last days of a life, worn out in the service of humanity: call me also thy son, and let me cherish thee as a father." Edwards, from whom the recollection of his own suffering had scarce forced a tear, now blubbered like a boy; he could not speak his gratitude, but by some short exclamations of blessings upon Harley.

Chapter XXXV

He misses an old acquaintance.—
An adventure consequent upon it.

When they had arrived within a little way of the village they journeyed to, Harley stopped short, and looked steadfastly on the mouldering walls of a ruined house that stood on the road side: "Oh heavens! he cried, what do I see: silent, unroofed, and desolate! Are all thy gay tenants gone? do I hear their hum no more? Edwards, look there, look there! the scene of my infant joys, my earliest friendships, laid waste and ruinous! That was the very school where I was boarded when you were at Southhill; 'tis but a twelve-month since I saw it standing, and its benches filled with cherubs: that opposite side of the road was the green on which they sported; see it now ploughed up! I would have given fifty times its value to have saved it from the sacrilege of that plough."

"Dear Sir, replied Edwards, perhaps they have left it from choice, and may have got another spot as good." "They cannot, said Harley, they cannot! I shall never see the sward covered with its daisies, nor pressed by the dance of the dear innocents: I shall never see that stump decked with the garlands which their little hands had gathered. These two long stones, which now lie at the foot of it, were once the supports of a hut I myself assisted to rear: I have sat on the sods within it, when we had spread our banquet of apples before us, and been more blessed—Oh! Edwards! infinitely more blessed, than ever I shall be again."

Just then a woman passed them on the road, and discovered some signs of wonder at the attitude of Harley, who stood, with his hands folded together, looking with a moistened eye on the fallen pillars of the hut. He was too much entranced in thought to observe her at all; but Edwards civilly accosting her, desired to know, if that had not been the school-house, and how it came into the condition in which they now saw it? "Alack a day! said she, it was the school-house indeed; but to be sure, Sir, the squire has pulled it down, because it stood in the way of his prospects."—"What! how! prospects! pulled down!" cried Harley.—"Yes, to be sure, Sir; and the green, where the children used to play, he has ploughed up, because, he said, they hurt his fence on the other side of it."—

"Curses on his narrow heart, cried Harley, that could violate a right so sacred! Heaven blast the wretch!

"And from his derogate body never spring
"A babe to honour him!"[1]—

But I need not, Edwards, I need not, (recovering himself a little) he is cursed enough already: to him the noblest source of happiness is denied; and the cares of his sordid soul shall gnaw it, while thou sittest over a brown crust, smiling on those mangled limbs that have saved thy son and his children!" "If you want any thing with the school-mistress, Sir, said the woman, I can show you the way to her house." He followed her without knowing whither he went.

They stopped at the door of a snug habitation, where sat an elderly woman with a boy and a girl before her, each of whom held a supper of bread and milk in their hands. "There, Sir, is the school-mistress."—"Madam, said Harley, was not an old venerable man school-master here some time ago?" "Yes, Sir, he was; poor man! the loss of his former school-house, I believe, broke his heart, for he died soon after it was taken down; and as another has not yet been found, I have that charge in the mean time."—"And this boy and girl, I presume, are your pupils?"—"Ay, Sir, they are poor orphans, put under my care by the parish; and more promising children I never saw." "Orphans! said Harley. "Yes, Sir, of honest creditable parents as any in the parish; and it is a shame for some folks to forget their relations, at a time when they have most need to remember them."—"Madam, said Harley, let us never forget that we are all relations." He kissed the children.

"Their father, Sir, continued she, was a farmer here in the neighbourhood, and a sober industrious man he was; but nobody can help misfortunes: what with bad crops, and bad debts, which are worse, his affairs went to wreck, and both he and his wife died of broken hearts. And a sweet couple they were, Sir; there was not a properer man to look on in the county than John Edwards, and so indeed were all the Edwardses." "What Edwardses? cried the old soldier hastily. "The Edwardses of South-hill;

---

[1]Echoing Lear's curse on his daughter, who has refused his demands for accommodation (*King Lear* 1.4.280–81); derogate: debased.

and a worthy family they were."—"South-hill! said he, in a languid voice, and fell back into the arms of the astonished Harley. The school-mistress ran for some water, and a smelling-bottle, with the assistance of which they soon recovered the unfortunate Edwards. He stared wildly for some time, then folding his orphan grandchildren in his arms, "Oh! my children, my children! he cried, have I found you thus? My poor Jack! art thou gone? I thought thou shouldst have carried thy father's grey hairs to the grave! and these little ones"—his tears choked his utterance, and he fell again on the necks of the children.

"My dear old man! said Harley, Providence has sent you to relieve them; it will bless me, if I can be the means of assisting you."—"Yes, indeed, Sir, answered the boy; father, when he was a-dying, bade God bless us; and prayed, that if grandfather lived, he might send him to support us."—"Where did they lay my boy?" said Edwards. "In the Old Church-yard, replied the woman, hard by his mother."—"I will show it you, answered the boy; for I have wept over it many a time when first I came amongst strange folks." He took the old man's hand, Harley laid hold of his sister's, and they walked in silence to the church-yard.

There was an old stone, with the corner broken off, and some letters, half covered with moss, to denote the names of the dead: there was a cyphered R. E. plainer than the rest: it was the tomb they sought. "Here it is, grandfather, said the boy. Edwards gazed upon it without uttering a word: the girl, who had only sighed before, now wept outright; her brother sobbed, but he stifled his sobbing. "I have told sister, said he, that she should not take it so to heart; she can knit already, and I shall soon be able to dig: we shall not starve, sister, indeed we shall not, nor shall grandfather neither." The girl cried afresh; Harley kissed off her tears as they flowed, and wept between every kiss.

Chapter XXXVI

He returns home.—A description of his retinue.

It was with some difficulty that Harley prevailed on the old man to leave the spot where the remains of his son were laid. At last, with the assistance of the school-mistress, he prevailed; and she accommodated Edwards and him with beds in her house, there being nothing like an inn nearer than the distance of some miles.

In the morning Harley persuaded Edwards to come, with the children, to his house, which was distant but a short day's journey. The boy walked in his grandfather's hand; and the name of Edwards procured him a neighbouring farmer's horse, on which a servant mounted, with the girl on a pillow before him.

With this train Harley returned to the abode of his fathers: and we cannot but think, that his enjoyment was as great as if he had arrived from the tour of Europe with a Swiss valet for his companion, and half a dozen snuff-boxes, with invisible hinges, in his pocket. But we take our ideas from sounds which folly has invented; Fashion, Bon-ton and Virtu,[1] are the names of certain idols, to which we sacrifice the genuine pleasures of the soul: in this world of semblance, we are contented with personating happiness; to feel it, is an art beyond us.

It was otherwise with Harley: he ran upstairs to his aunt with the history of his fellow-travellers glowing on his lips. His aunt was an economist;[2] but she knew the pleasure of doing charitable things, and withal was fond of her nephew, and solicitous to oblige him. She received old Edwards therefore with a look of more complacency than is perhaps natural to maiden-ladies of threescore, and was remarkably attentive to his grandchildren: she roasted apples with her own hands for their supper, and made up a little bed beside her own for the girl. Edwards made some attempts towards an acknowledgment for these favours; but his young friend stopped them in their beginnings. "Whosoever receiveth any of these children"[3]—said his aunt; for her acquaintance with her bible was habitual.

[1] Polite behavior and a taste for works of art.

[2] Thrifty.

[3] Jesus takes a child, turns to his disciples, and says, "Whosoever shall receive one of such children in my name, receiveth me" (Mark 9.36–37; see also Luke 9.48).

Early next morning, Harley stole into the room where Edwards lay: he expected to have found him a-bed; but in this he was mistaken: the old man had risen, and was leaning over his sleeping grandson, with the tears flowing down his cheeks. At first he did not perceive Harley; when he did, he endeavoured to hide his grief, and crossing his eyes with his hand, expressed his surprise at seeing him so early astir. "I was thinking of you, said Harley, and your children: I learned last night that a small farm of mine in the neighbourhood is now vacant: if you will occupy it I shall gain a good neighbour and be able in some measure to repay the notice you took of me when a boy; and as the furniture of the house is mine, it will be so much trouble saved." Edwardses tears gushed afresh, and Harley led him to see the place he intended for him.

The house upon this farm was indeed little better than a hut; its situation, however, was pleasant, and Edwards, assisted by the beneficence of Harley, set about improving its neatness and convenience. He staked out a piece of the green before for a garden, and Peter, who acted in Harley's family as valet, butler, and gardener, had orders to furnish him with parcels of the different seeds he chose to sow in it. I have seen his master at work in this little spot, with his coat off, and his dibble[4] in his hand: it was a scene of tranquil virtue to have stopped an angel on his errands of mercy! Harley had contrived to lead a little bubbling brook through a green walk in the middle of the ground, upon which he had erected a mill in miniature for the diversion of Edwardses infant-grandson, and made shift in its construction to introduce a pliant bit of wood, that answered with its fairy clack to the murmuring of the rill that turned it. I have seen him stand, listening to these mingled sounds, with his eye fixed on the boy, and the smile of conscious satisfaction on his cheek; while the old man, with a look half-turned to Harley, and half to Heaven, breathed an ejaculation of gratitude and piety.

Father of mercies! I also would thank thee! that not only hast thou assigned eternal rewards to virtue, but that, even in this bad world, the lines of our duty, and our happiness, are so frequently woven together.

---

[4]Seeder.

A Fragment

The Man of Feeling talks of what he does not understand.—
An incident.

* * * * "Edwards, said he, I have a proper regard for the prosperity of my country: every native of it appropriates to himself some share of the power, or the fame, which, as a nation, it acquires; but I cannot throw off the man so much, as to rejoice at our conquests in India.[1] You tell me of immense territories subject to the English: I cannot think of their possessions, without being led to enquire, by what right they possess them. They came there as traders, bartering the commodities they brought for others which their purchasers could spare; and however great their profits were, they were then equitable. But what title have the subjects of another kingdom to establish an empire in India? to give laws to a country where the inhabitants received them on the terms of friendly commerce? You say they are happier under our regulations than the tyranny of their own petty princes. I must doubt it, from the conduct of those by whom these regulations have been made. They have drained the treasuries of Nabobs, who must fill them by oppressing the industry of their subjects. Nor is this to be wondered at, when we consider the motive upon which those gentlemen do not deny their going to India. The fame of conquest, barbarous as that motive is, is but a secondary consideration: there are certain stations in wealth to which the warriors of the East aspire. It is there indeed where the wishes of their friends assign them eminence, where the question of their country is pointed at their return. When shall I see a commander return from India in the pride of honourable poverty?—You describe the victories they have gained; they are sullied by the cause in which they fought: you enumerate the spoils of those victories; they are covered with the blood of the vanquished!

"Could you tell me of some conqueror giving peace and happiness to the conquered? did he accept the gifts of their princes to use them for the comfort of those whose fathers, sons, or husbands, fell in battle? did he use his power to gain security and freedom to the regions of oppression and slavery? did he endear the British name

---

[1] The man: humanity. By the 1780s, British abuses in India were a scandal, leading to the trial of its governor, Warren Hastings.

by examples of generosity, which the most barbarous or most depraved are rarely able to resist? did he return with the consciousness of duty discharged to his country, and humanity to his fellow-creatures? did he return with no lace on his coat, no slaves in his retinue, no chariot at his door, and no Burgundy at his table?—these were laurels[2] which princes might envy—which an honest man would not condemn!"

"Your maxims, Mr. Harley, are certainly right, said Edwards. I am not capable of arguing with you; but I imagine there are great temptations in a great degree of riches, which it is no easy matter to resist: those a poor man like me cannot describe, because he never knew them; and perhaps I have reason to bless God that I never did; for then, it is likely, I should have withstood them no better than my neighbours. For you know, Sir, that it is not the fashion now, as it was in former times, that I have read of in books, when your great generals died so poor, that they did not leave wherewithal to buy them a coffin; and people thought the better of their memories for it: if they did so now-a-days, I question if any body, except yourself, and some few like you, would thank them."

"I am sorry, replied Harley, that there is so much truth in what you say; but however the general current of opinion may point, the feelings are not yet lost that applaud benevolence, and censure inhumanity. Let us endeavour to strengthen them in ourselves; and we, who live sequestered from the noise of the multitude, have better opportunities of listening undisturbed to their voice."

They now approached the little dwelling of Edwards. A maid-servant, whom he had hired to assist him in the care of his grandchildren, met them a little way from the house: "There is a young lady within with the children," said she. Edwards expressed his surprise at the visit: it was however not the less true; and we mean to account for it.

This young lady then was no other than Miss Walton. She had heard the old man's history from Harley, as we have already related it. Curiosity, or some other motive, made her desirous to see his grandchildren: this she had an opportunity of gratifying soon, the children, in some of their walks, having strolled as far as her father's avenue. She put several questions to both; she was delighted

---

[2]Accolades.

with the simplicity of their answers, and promised, that if they continued to be good children, and do as their grandfather bid them, she would soon see them again, and bring some present or other for their reward. This promise she had performed now: she came attended only by her maid, and brought with her a complete suit of green for the boy, and a chintz gown, a cap, and a suit[3] of ribbands, for his sister. She had time enough, with her maid's assistance, to equip them in their new habiliments before Harley and Edwards returned. The boy heard his grandfather's voice, and, with that silent joy which his present finery inspired, ran to the door to meet him: putting one hand in his, with the other pointed to his sister, "See, said he, what Miss Walton has brought us!"—Edwards gazed on them. Harley fixed his eyes on Miss Walton: her's were turned to the ground;—in Edwardses was a beamy moisture.—He folded his hands together—"I cannot speak, young lady, said he, to thank you." Neither could Harley. There were a thousand sentiments;—but they gushed so impetuously on his heart, that he could not utter a syllable. * * * *

[3]Cluster.

Chapter XL

The Man of Feeling jealous.

The desire of communicating knowledge or intelligence, is an argument with those who hold that man is naturally a social animal. It is indeed one of the earliest propensities we discover; but it may be doubted whether the pleasure (for pleasure there certainly is) arising from it be not often more selfish than social: for we frequently observe the tidings of Ill communicated as eagerly as the annunciation of Good. Is it that we delight in observing the effects of the stronger passions? for we are all philosophers in this respect; and it is perhaps amongst the spectators at Tyburn that the most genuine are to be found.[1]

Was it from this motive that Peter came one morning into his master's room with a meaning face of recital?[2] His master indeed did not at first observe it; for he was sitting, with one shoe buckled, delineating portraits in the fire. "I have brushed those clothes, Sir, as you ordered me."—Harley nodded his head; but Peter observed that his hat wanted brushing too: his master nodded again. At last Peter bethought him, that the fire needed stirring; and, taking up the poker, demolished the turban'd-head of a Saracen,[3] while his master was seeking out a body for it. "The morning is main cold, Sir," said Peter. "Is it?" said Harley. "Yes, Sir; I have been as far as Tom Dowson's to fetch some barberries he had picked for Mrs. Margery. There was a rare junketting[4] last night at Thomas's among Sir Harry Benson's servants: he lay at Squire Walton's, but he would not suffer his servants to trouble the family; so, to be sure, they were all at Tom's, and had a fiddle and a hot supper in the big room where the justices meet about the destroying of hares and partridges, and them things; and Tom's eyes looked so red and so bleared when I called him to get the barberries:—And I hear as how Sir Harry is going to be married to Miss

---

[1]Felons were executed at Tyburn gallows, west of London. In his essay on the sublime (p. 209), Edmund Burke remarks that people will leave a performance of tragedy to witness a real execution.

[2]Eager to talk.

[3]Harley is still dreaming. A Saracen is a near-Eastern character, frequent in tales such as *Arabian Nights*.

[4]Feasting.

Walton."—"How! Miss Walton married!" said Harley. "Why, it mayn't be true, Sir, for all that; but Tom's wife told it me, and to be sure the servants told her, and their master told them, as I guess, Sir; but it mayn't be true for all that, as I said before."—"Have done with your idle information, said Harley:—Is my aunt come down into the parlour to breakfast?"—"Yes, Sir."—"Tell her I'll be with her immediately."—

When Peter was gone, he stood with his eyes fixed on the ground, and the last words of his intelligence vibrating in his ears. "Miss Walton married!" he sighed—and walked down stairs, with his shoe as it was, and the buckle in his hand. His aunt, however, was pretty well accustomed to those appearances of absence; besides, that the natural gravity of her temper, which was commonly called into exertion by the care of her household concerns, was such as not easily to be discomposed by any circumstance of accidental impropriety. She too had been informed of the intended match between Sir Harry Benson and Miss Walton. "I have been thinking, said she, that they are distant relations; for the great-grandfather of this Sir Harry Benson, who was knight of the shire in the reign of Charles the First and one of the cavaliers of those times, was married to a daughter of the Walton family." Harley answered drily, that it might be so; but that he never troubled himself about those matters. "Indeed, said she, you are to blame, nephew, for not knowing a little more of them: before I was near your age, I had sewed the pedigree of our family in a set of chair-bottoms, that were made a present of to my grandmother, who was a very notable woman, and had a proper regard for gentility, I'll assure you; but now-a-days it is money, not birth, that makes people respected; the more shame for the times."[5]

Harley was in no very good humour for entering into a discussion of this question; but he always entertained so much filial respect for his aunt, as to attend to her discourse.

"We blame the pride of the rich, said he; but are not we ashamed of our poverty?"

"Why, one would not choose, replied his aunt, to make a much worse figure than one's neighbours; but, as I was saying before, the times (as my friend Mrs. Dorothy Walton, observes) are shamefully

[5]An accurate report of the social transformations across the 18th c., welcome by many aspirants, if not Harley's aunt.

degenerated in this respect. There was but t'other day at Mr. Walton's, that fat fellow's daughter, the London merchant, as he calls himself, though I have heard that he was little better than the keeper of a chandler's[6] shop:—We were leaving the gentlemen to go to tea. She had a hoop, forsooth, as large and as stiff—and it showed a pair of bandy legs,[7] as thick as two—I was nearer the door by an apron's length, and the pert hussy brushed by me, as who should say, Make way for your betters, and with one of her London-bobs[8]—but Mrs. Dorothy did not let her pass with it; for all the time of drinking tea, she spoke of the precedency of family, and the disparity there is between people who are come of something and your mushroom-gentry[9] who wear their coats of arms in their purses."

Her indignation was interrupted by the arrival of her maid with a damask table-cloth, and a set of napkins, from the loom, which had been spun by her mistresses own hand. There was the family-crest in each corner, and in the middle a view of the battle of Worcester, where one of her ancestors had been a captain in the king's forces; and, with a sort of poetical licence in perspective, there was seen the Royal Oak, with more wig than leaves upon it.[10]

On all this the good lady was very copious, and took up the remaining intervals of filling tea, to describe its excellencies to Harley; adding, that she intended this as a present for his wife, when he should get one. He sighed and looked foolish, and commending the serenity of the day, walked out into the garden.

He sat down on a little seat which commanded an extensive prospect round the house. He leaned on his hand, and scored the ground with his stick: "Miss Walton married! said he; but what is that to me? May she be happy! her virtues deserve it; to me her marriage is otherwise indifferent:—I had romantic dreams! they are fled!—it is perfectly indifferent."

---

[6]Candle-maker's.

[7]Bow-legged.

[8]Hair in a bun.

[9]Mushrooms grow suddenly and rapidly.

[10]The battle of Worcester in 1650 ended the Civil Wars, putting Oliver Cromwell in power. Defeated King Charles II wandered the countryside, hiding at one point in an oak, later called "the Royal Oak," until he could escape to France. Charles II was restored to the throne in 1660.

Just at that moment he saw a servant, with a knot of ribbands in his hat, go into the house. His cheeks grew flushed at the sight! He kept his eye fixed for some time on the door by which he had entered, then starting to his feet, hastily followed him.

When he approached the door of the kitchen where he supposed the man had entered, his heart throbbed so violently, that when he would have called Peter, his voice failed in the attempt. He stood a moment listening in this breathless state of palpitation: Peter came out by chance. "Did your honour want any thing?"—"Where is the servant that came just now from Mr. Walton's?" "From Mr. Walton's, Sir! there is none of his servants here that I know of."—"Nor of Sir Harry Benson's?"—He did not wait for an answer; but having by this time observed the hat with its particoloured ornament hanging on a peg near the door, he pressed forwards into the kitchen, and addressing himself to a stranger whom he saw there, asked him, with no small tremor in his voice, If he had any commands for him? The man looked silly, and said, That he had nothing to trouble his honour with. "Are not you a servant of Sir Harry Benson's?"—"No, sir."—"You'll pardon me, young man; I judged by the favour in your hat."—"Sir, I'm his majesty's servant, God bless him! and these favours we always wear when we are recruiting."—"Recruiting!" his eyes glistened at the word: he seized the soldier's hand, and shaking it violently, ordered Peter to fetch a bottle of his aunt's best dram.[11] The bottle was brought: "You shall drink the king's health, said Harley, in a bumper."[12]— "The king and your honour."—"Nay, you shall drink the king's health by itself; you may drink mine in another."[13] Peter looked in his master's face, and filled with some little reluctance. "Now to your mistress, said Harley; every soldier has a mistress." The man excused himself—"to your mistress! you cannot refuse it." 'Twas Mrs. Margery's best dram! Peter stood with the bottle a little inclined, but not so as to discharge a drop of its contents: "Fill it, Peter, said his master, fill it to the brim." Peter filled it; and the soldier having named Suky Simpson, dispatched it in a twinkling. "Thou art an honest fellow, said Harley, and I love thee;" and shaking his

---

[11]A cordial or liquor.

[12]A cup (of wine or other spirits).

[13]Harley is wildly relieved that he has *not* been summoned with news of an engagement.

hand again, desired Peter to make him his guest at dinner, and walked up into his room with a pace much quicker and more springy than usual.

This agreeable disappointment however he was not long suffered to enjoy. The curate happened that day to dine with him: his visits indeed were more properly to the aunt than the nephew; and many of the intelligent ladies in the parish, who, like some very great philosophers, have the happy knack at accounting for every thing, gave out that there was a particular attachment between them, which wanted only to be matured by some more years of courtship to end in the tenderest connection. In this conclusion indeed, supposing the premises to have been true, they were somewhat justified by the known opinion of the lady, who frequently declared herself a friend to the ceremonial of former times, when a lover might have sighed seven years at his mistresses feet, before he was allowed the liberty of kissing her hand. 'Tis true Mrs. Margery was now about her grand climacteric;[14] no matter: that is just the age when we expect to grow younger. But I verily believe there was nothing in the report; the curate's connection was only that of a genealogist; for in that character he was no way inferior to Mrs. Margery herself. He dealt also in the present times; for he was a politician and a news-monger.

He had hardly said grace after dinner, when he told Mrs. Margery, that she might soon expect a pair of white gloves, as Sir Harry Benson, he was very well informed, was just going to be married to Miss Walton. Harley spilt the wine he was carrying to his mouth: he had time however to recollect himself before the curate had finished the different particulars of his intelligence, and summing up all the heroism he was master of, filled a bumper and drank to Miss Walton. "With all my heart, said the curate, the bride that is to be." Harley would have said bride too; but the word Bride stuck in his throat. His confusion indeed was manifest: but the curate began to enter on some point of descent with Mrs. Margery, and Harley had very soon after an opportunity of leaving them, while they were deeply engaged in a question, whether the name of some great man in the time of Henry the Seventh was Richard or Humphrey.

[14]63rd year.

He did not see his aunt again till supper; the time between he spent in walking, like some troubled ghost, round the place where his treasure lay. He went as far as a little gate, that led into a copse near Mr. Walton's house, to which that gentleman had been so obliging as to let him have a key. He had just begun to open it when he saw, on a terrass below, Miss Walton walking with a gentleman in a riding-dress, whom he immediately guessed to be Sir Harry Benson. He stopped of a sudden; his hand shook so much that he could hardly turn the key; he opened the gate however, and advanced a few paces. The lady's lap-dog pricked up its ears, and barked: he stopped again. —

—"The little dogs and all,
Tray, Blanch, and Sweetheart, see they bark at me!"[15]

His resolution failed; he slunk back, and, locking the gate as softly as he could, stood on tiptoe looking over the wall till they were gone. At that instant a shepherd blew his horn: the romantic melancholy of the sound quite overcame him!—it was the very note that wanted to be touched—he sighed! he dropped a tear!—and returned.

At supper his aunt observed that he was graver than usual; but she did not suspect the cause: indeed it may seem odd that she was the only person in the family who had no suspicion of his attachment to Miss Walton. It was frequently matter of discourse amongst the servants: perhaps her maiden coldness—but for those things we need not account.

In a day or two he was so much master of himself as to be able to rhime upon the subject. The following pastoral he left, some time after, on the handle of a tea-kettle, at a neighbouring house where we were visiting; and as I filled the tea-pot after him, I happened to put it in my pocket by a similar act of forgetfulness. It is such as might be expected from a man who makes verses for amusement. I am pleased with somewhat of good-nature that runs through it, because I have commonly observed the writers of those complaints to bestow epithets on their lost mistresses rather too harsh for the mere liberty of choice, which led them to prefer another to the poet himself: I do not doubt the vehemence of their

[15]A bathetic echo of mad King Lear (3.6.62–63).

passion; but, alas! the sensations of love are something more than
the returns of gratitude.

LAVINIA. A PASTORAL.

Why steals from my bosom the sigh?
    Why fix'd is my gaze on the ground?
Come, give me my pipe,° and I'll try   *flute*
    To banish my cares with the sound.

Erewhile were its notes of accord   5
    With the smile of the flow'r-footed muse;
Ah! why by its master implor'd
    Shou'd it now the gay carrol refuse?

'Twas taught by LAVINIA'S sweet smile
    In the mirth-loving chorus to join;   10
Ah me! how unweeting° the while!   *unknowing*
    LAVINIA—can never be mine!

Another, more happy, the maid
    By fortune is destin'd to bless —
Tho' the hope has forsook that betray'd,   15
    Yet why should I love her the less?

Her beauties are bright as the morn,
    With rapture I counted them o'er;
Such virtues these beauties adorn,
    I knew her, and prais'd them no more.   20

I term'd her no goddess of love,
    I call'd not her beauty divine:
These far other passions may prove,
    But they could not be figures of mine.

It ne'er was apparell'd with art,   25
    On words it could never rely;
It reign'd in the throb of my heart,
    It gleam'd in the glance of my eye.

Oh fool! in the circle to shine
    That fashion's gay daughters approve,   30
You must speak as the fashions incline; —
    Alas! are there fashions in love?

Yet sure they are simple who prize
    The tongue that is smooth to deceive;
Yet sure she had sense to despise,   35
    The tinsel that folly may weave.

When I talk'd, I have seen her recline,
    With an aspect so pensively sweet, —
Tho' I spoke what the shepherds opine,
    A fop were ashamed to repeat.   40

She is soft as the dew-drops that fall
    From the lip of the sweet-scented pea;
Perhaps, when she smil'd upon all,
    I have thought that she smil'd upon me.

But why of her charms should I tell?   45
    Ah me! whom her charms have undone
Yet I love the reflection too well,
    The painful reflection to shun.

Ye souls of more delicate kind,
    Who feast not on pleasure alone,   50
Who wear the soft sense of the mind,
    To the sons of the world still unknown;

Ye know, tho' I cannot express,
    Why I foolishly doat on my pain;
Nor will ye believe it the less   55
    That I have not the skill to complain.

I lean on my hand with a sigh,
    My friends the soft sadness condemn;
Yet, methinks, tho' I cannot tell why,
    I should hate to be merry like them.   60

When I walk'd in the pride of the dawn,
    Methought all the region look'd bright:
Has sweetness forsaken the lawn?
    For, methinks, I grow sad at the sight.

When I stood by the stream, I have thought   65
    There was mirth in the gurgling soft sound;
But now 'tis a sorrowful note,
    And the banks are all gloomy around!

I have laugh'd at the jest of a friend;
    Now they laugh and I know not the cause,   70
Tho' I seem with my looks to attend,
    How silly! I ask what it was!

They sing the sweet song of the May,
    They sing it with mirth and with glee;
Sure I once thought the sonnet was gay,   75
    But now 'tis all sadness to me.

Oh! give me the dubious light
    That gleams thro' the quivering shade;
Oh! give me the horrors of night
    By gloom and by silence array'd!   80

Let me walk where the soft-rising wave
    Has pictur'd the moon on its breast:
Let me walk where the new cover'd grave
    Allows the pale lover to rest!

When shall I in its peaceable womb   85
    Be laid with my sorrows asleep!
Should LAVINIA but chance on my tomb —
    I could die if I thought she would weep.

Perhaps, if the souls of the just
    Revisit these mansions of care,   90
It may be my favourite trust
    To watch o'er the fate of the fair.

Perhaps the soft thought of her breast
 With rapture more favour'd to warm;
Perhaps, if with sorrow oppress'd,   95
 Her sorrow with patience to arm.

Then! then! in the tenderest part
 May I whisper, "Poor COLIN was true;"
And mark if a heave of her heart
 The thought of her COLIN pursue.   100

The Pupil. A Fragment.

* * * * "BUT as to the higher part of education, Mr. Harley, the culture of the Mind;—let the feelings be awakened, let the heart be brought forth to its object, placed in the light in which nature would have it stand, and its decisions will ever be just. The world

Will smile, and smile, and be a villain;[1]

and the youth, who does not suspect its deceit, will be content to smile with it.—Men will put on the most forbidding aspect in nature, and tell him of the beauty of virtue.

"I have not, under these grey hairs, forgotten that I was once a young man, warm in the pursuit of pleasure, but meaning to be honest as well as happy. I had ideas of virtue, of honour, of benevolence, which I had never been at the pains to define; but I felt my bosom heave at the thoughts of them, and I made the most delightful soliloquies—It is impossible, said I, that there can be half so many rogues as are imagined.

"I travelled, because it is the fashion for young men of my fortune to travel: I had a travelling tutor, which is the fashion too; but my tutor was a gentleman, which it is not always the fashion for tutors to be. His gentility indeed was all he had from his father, whose prodigality had not left him a shilling to support it.

"I have a favour to ask of you, my dear Mountford, said my father, which I will not be refused: You have travelled as became a man; neither France nor Italy have made anything of Mountford, which Mountford before he left England would have been ashamed of: my son Edward goes abroad, would you take him under your protection?"—He blushed—my father's face was scarlet—he pressed his hand to his bosom, as if he had said,—my heart does not mean to offend you. Mountford sighed twice—"I am a proud fool, said he, and you will pardon it;—there! (he sighed again) I can hear of dependance, since it is dependance on my Sedley."—"Dependance! answered my father; there can be no such word between us: what is there in £9000 a year that should make me un-

---

[1]Learning from the ghost of his father's murder by Claudius, Hamlet vows to "set it down" in the "tables" of his brain, "That one may smile, and smile, and be a villain!" (1.5.108).

worthy of Mountford's friendship?"—They embraced; and soon after I set out on my travels, with Mountford for my guardian.

"We were at Milan, where my father happened to have an Italian friend, to whom he had been of some service in England. The count, for he was of quality, was solicitous to return the obligation by a particular attention to his son: We lived in his palace, visited with his family, were caressed by his friends, and I began to be so well pleased with my entertainment, that I thought of England as of some foreign country.

"The count had a son not much older than myself. At that age a friend is an easy acquisition: we were friends the first night of our acquaintance.

"He introduced me into the company of a set of young gentlemen, whose fortunes gave them the command of pleasure, and whose inclinations incited them to the purchase. After having spent some joyous evenings in their society, it became a sort of habit which I could not miss without uneasiness; and our meetings, which before were frequent, were now stated and regular.

"Sometimes, in the pauses of our mirth, gaming was introduced as an amusement: it was an art in which I was a novice; I received instruction, as other novices do, by losing pretty largely to my teachers. Nor was this the only evil which Mountford foresaw would arise from the connection I had formed; but a lecture of sour injunctions was not his method of reclaiming. He sometimes asked me questions about the company; but they were such as the curiosity of any indifferent man might have prompted: I told him of their wit, their eloquence, their warmth of friendship, and their sensibility of heart; "And their honour, said I, laying my hand on my breast, is unquestionable." Mountford seemed to rejoice at my good fortune, and begged that I would introduce him to their acquaintance. At the next meeting I introduced him accordingly.

"The conversation was as animated as usual; they displayed all that sprightliness and good-humour which my praises had led Mountford to expect; subjects too of sentiment occurred, and their speeches, particularly those of our friend the son of Count Respino, glowed with the warmth of honour, and softened into the tenderness of feeling. Mountford was charmed with his companions; when we parted he made the highest eulogiums upon them: "When shall we see them again?" said he. I was delighted with the demand, and promised to reconduct him on the morrow.

"In going to their place of rendezvous, he took me a little out of the road, to see, as he told me, the performances of a young statuary.[2] When we were near the house in which Mountford said he lived, a boy of about seven years old crossed us in the street. At sight of Mountford he stopped, and grasping his hand, "My dearest Sir, said he, my father is likely to do well; he will live to pray for you, and to bless you: yes, he will bless you, though you are an Englishman, and some other hard word that the monk talked of this morning which I have forgot, but it meant that you should not go to heaven;[3] but he shall go to heaven, said I, for he has saved my father: come and see him, Sir, that we may be happy."—"My dear, I am engaged at present with this gentleman."—"But he shall come along with you; he is an Englishman too, I fancy; he shall come and learn how an Englishman may go to heaven."—Mountford smiled, and we followed the boy together.

"After crossing the next street, we arrived at the gate of a prison. I seemed surprised at the sight; our little conductor observed it. "Are you afraid, Sir? said he; I was afraid once too, but my father and mother are here, and I am never afraid when I am with them." He took my hand, and led me through a dark passage that fronted the gate. When we came to a little door at the end, he tapped; a boy, still younger than himself, opened it to receive us. Mountford entered with a look in which was pictured the benign assurance of a superior being. I followed in silence and amazement.

"On something like a bed lay a man, with a face seemingly emaciated with sickness, and a look of patient dejection; a bundle of dirty shreds served him for a pillow; but he had a better support—the arm of a female who kneeled beside him, beautiful as an angel, but with a fading languor in her countenance, the still life of melancholy, that seemed to borrow its shade from the object on which she gazed. There was a tear in her eye! the sick man kissed it off in its bud, smiling through the dimness of his own!—when she saw Mountford, she crawled forward on the ground and clasped his knees; he raised her from the floor; she threw her arms round

---

[2]The statues of a sculptor.

[3]The Catholic monk has probably called him a "heretic" for being of the Church of England (Anglican).

his neck, and sobbed out a speech of thankfulness, eloquent beyond the power of language.

"Compose yourself, my love, said the man on the bed; but he,
whose goodness has caused that emotion, will pardon its effects."—
"How is this, Mountford? said I; what do I see? what must I do?"—
"You see, replied the stranger, a wretch, sunk in poverty, starving in
prison, stretched on a sick bed! but that is little:—there are his wife
and children, wanting the bread which he has not to give them! Yet
you cannot easily imagine the conscious serenity of his mind; in the
gripe of affliction, his heart swells with the pride of virtue! it can even
look down with pity on the man whose cruelty has wrung it almost
to bursting. You are, I fancy, a friend of Mr. Mountford's; come
nearer, and I will tell you; for, short as my story is, I can hardly command breath enough for a recital. The son of count Respino (I
started as if I had trod on a viper) has long had a criminal passion for
my wife: this her prudence had concealed from me; but he had lately
the boldness to declare it to myself. He promised me affluence in exchange for honour; and threatened misery, as its attendant, if I kept
it. I treated him with the contempt he deserved: the consequence was,
that he hired a couple of bravoes[4] (for I am persuaded they acted under his direction) who attempted to assassinate me in the street; but I
made such a defence as obliged them to fly, after having given me
two or three stabs, none of which however were mortal. But his revenge was not thus to be disappointed: in the little dealings of my
trade I had contracted some debts, of which he had made himself
master for my ruin; I was confined here at his suit, when not yet recovered from the wounds I had received; the dear woman, and these
two boys, followed me, that we might starve together; but Providence interposed, and sent Mr. Mountford to our support: he has relieved my family from the gnawings of hunger, and rescued me from
death, to which a fever, consequent on my wounds, and increased by
the want of every necessary, had almost reduced me."

"Inhuman villain!" I exclaimed, lifting up my eyes to heaven. "Inhuman indeed! said the lovely woman who stood at my side: Alas! Sir,
what had we done to offend him? what had these little ones done,
that they should perish in the toils of his vengeance?"—I reached a
pen which stood in the inkstand dish at the bed-side—"May I ask
what is the amount of the sum for which you are imprisoned?"—"I

---

[4]Paid assassins.

was able, he replied, to pay all but five hundred crowns."—I wrote a draught on the banker with whom I had a credit from my father for 2500, and presenting it to the stranger's wife, "You will receive, Madam, on presenting this note, a sum more than sufficient for your husband's discharge; the remainder I leave for his industry to improve." I would have left the room: each of them laid hold of one of my hands; the children clung to my coat:—Oh! Mr. Harley, methinks I feel their gentle violence at this moment; it beats here with delight inexpressible!—"Stay, Sir, said he, I do not mean attempting to thank you (he took a pocket-book from under his pillow) let me but know what name I shall place here next to Mr. Mountford's?"—Sedley—he writ it down—"An Englishman too I presume."—"He shall go to heaven notwithstanding," said the boy who had been our guide. It began to be too much for me; I squeezed his hand that was clasped in mine; his wife's I pressed to my lips, and burst from the place to give vent to the feelings that laboured within me.

"Oh! Mountford!" said I, when he had overtaken me at the door: "It is time, replied he, that we should think of our appointment; young Respino and his friends are waiting us."—"Damn him, damn him! said I; let us leave Milan instantly; but soft—I will be calm; Mountford, your pencil." I wrote on a slip of paper,

To Signor RESPINO,

"When you receive this I am at a distance from Milan. Accept of my thanks for the civilities I have received from you and your family. As to the friendship with which you were pleased to honour me, the prison, which I have just left, has exhibited a scene to cancel it for ever. You may possibly be merry with your companions at my weakness, as I suppose you will term it. I give you leave for derision: you may affect a triumph; I shall feel it.

EDWARD SEDLEY."

"You may send this if you will, said Mountford coolly; but still Respino is *a man of honour;* the world will continue to call him so."— "It is probable, I answered, they may; I envy not the appellation.[5] If this is the world's honour, if these men are the guides of its manners" —"Tut! said Mountford, do you eat macaroni?"[6]—

---

[5]Name, title.
[6]A fashionable thing to do, but not done by every gentleman.

* * * * * * * *

[At this place had the greatest depredations of the curate begun. There were so very few connected passages of the subsequent chapters remaining, that even the partiality of an editor could not offer them to the public. I discovered, from some scattered sentences, that they were of much the same tenor with the preceding; recitals of little adventures, in which the dispositions of a man, sensible[7] to judge, and still more warm to feel, had room to unfold[8] themselves. Some instruction, and some example, I make no doubt they contained; but it is likely that many of those, whom chance has led to a perusal of what I have already presented, may have read it with little pleasure, and will feel no disappointment from the want of those parts which I have been unable to procure: to such as may have expected the intricacies of a novel, a few incidents in a life undistinguished, except by some features of the heart, cannot have afforded much entertainment.

Harley's own story, from the mutilated passages I have mentioned, as well as from some inquiries I was at the trouble of making in the country, I found to have been simple to excess. His mistress I could perceive was not married to Sir Harry Benson: but it would seem, by one of the following chapters, which is still entire, that Harley had not profited on the occasion by making any declaration of his own passion, after those of the other had been unsuccessful. The state of his health for some part of this period, appears to have been such as to forbid any thoughts of that kind: he had been seized with a very dangerous fever, caught by attending old Edwards in one of an infectious kind. From this he had recovered but imperfectly, and though he had no formed complaint, his health was manifestly on the decline.

It appears that the sagacity of some friend had at length pointed out to his aunt a cause from which this might be supposed to proceed, to wit, his hopeless love for Miss Walton; for according to the conceptions of the world, the love of a man of Harley's fortune for the heiress of £4000 a-year is indeed desperate. Whether it was so in this case may be gathered from the next chapter, which, with the two subsequent, concluding the performance, have escaped those accidents that proved fatal to the rest.]

[7]Rational.
[8]Explain.

Chapter LV

He sees Miss Walton, and is happy.

Harley was one of those few friends whom the malevolence of fortune had yet left me: I could not therefore but be sensibly concerned for his present indisposition; there seldom passed a day on which I did not make inquiry about him.

The physician who attended him had informed me the evening before, that he thought him considerably better than he had been for some time past. I called next morning to be confirmed in a piece of intelligence so welcome to me.

When I entered his apartment, I found him sitting on a couch, leaning on his hand, with his eye turned upwards in the attitude of thoughtful inspiration. His look had always an open benignity, which commanded esteem; there was now something more—a gentle triumph in it.

He rose, and met me with his usual kindness. When I gave him the good accounts I had had from his physician, "I am foolish enough, said he, to rely but little, in this instance, upon physic: my presentiment may be false; but I think I feel myself approaching to my end, by steps so easy, that they woo me to approach it.

"There is a certain dignity in retiring from life at a time, when the infirmities of age have not sapped our faculties. This world, my dear Charles, was a scene in which I never much delighted. I was not formed for the bustle of the busy, nor the dissipation of the gay: a thousand things occurred where I blushed for the impropriety of my conduct when I thought on the world, though my reason told me I should have blushed to have done otherwise.—It was a scene of dissimulation, of restraint, of disappointment. I leave it to enter on that state, which I have learned to believe, is replete with the genuine happiness attendant upon virtue. I look back on the tenor[1] of my life, with the consciousness of few great offences to account for. There are blemishes, I confess, which deform in some degree the picture. But I know the benignity of the Supreme Being, and rejoice at the thoughts of its exertion in my favour. My mind expands at the thought I shall enter into the society of the blessed, wise as angels, with the simplicity of children." He had by this time clasped

[1]Continuous movement and underlying, persistent meaning.

my hand, and found it wet by a tear which had just fallen upon it.—His eye began to moisten too—we sat for some time silent—At last, with an attempt to a look of more composure, "There are some remembrances (said Harley) which rise involuntary on my heart, and make me almost wish to live. I have been blessed with a few friends, who redeem my opinion of mankind. I recollect, with the tenderest emotion, the scenes of pleasure I have passed among them; but we shall meet again, my friend, never to be separated. There are some feelings which perhaps are too tender to be suffered by the world. The world is in general selfish, interested, and unthinking, and throws the imputation of romance or melancholy on every temper more susceptible than its own. I cannot think but in those regions which I contemplate, if there is any thing of mortality left about us, that these feelings will subsist;—they are called,—perhaps they are—weaknesses here;—but there may be some better modifications of them in heaven, which may deserve the name of virtues." He sighed as he spoke these last words. He had scarcely finished them, when the door opened, and his aunt appeared, leading in Miss Walton. "My dear, says she, here is Miss Walton, who has been so kind as to come and inquire for you herself." I could observe a transient glow upon his face. He rose from his seat—"If to know Miss Walton's goodness, said he, be a title to deserve it, I have some claim." She begged him to resume his seat, and placed herself on the sofa beside him. I took my leave. Mrs. Margery accompanied me to the door. He was left with Miss Walton alone. She inquired anxiously about his health. "I believe, said he, from the accounts which my physicians unwillingly give me, that they have no great hopes of my recovery."—She started as he spoke; but recollecting herself immediately, endeavoured to flatter him into a belief that his apprehensions were groundless. "I know, said he, that it is usual with persons at my time of life to have these hopes which your kindness suggests; but I would not wish to be deceived. To meet death as becomes a man, is a privilege bestowed on few.—I would endeavour to make it mine;—nor do I think that I can ever be better prepared for it than now:—It is that chiefly which determines the fitness of its approach."—"Those sentiments, answered Miss Walton, are just: but your good sense, Mr. Harley, will own, that life has its proper value.—As the province of virtue, life is ennobled; as such, it is to be desired.—To virtue has the Supreme Director of all things assigned rewards enough even here to fix its attachment."

The subject began to overpower her.—Harley lifted his eyes from the ground—"There are, said he, in a very low voice, there are attachments, Miss Walton"—His glance met hers—They both betrayed a confusion, and were both instantly withdrawn.—He paused some moments—"I am in such a state as calls for sincerity, let that also excuse it—It is perhaps the last time we shall ever meet. I feel something particularly solemn in the acknowledgment, yet my heart swells to make it, awed as it is by a sense of my presumption, by a sense of your perfections"—He paused again—"Let it not offend you to know their power over one so unworthy—It will, I believe, soon cease to beat, even with that feeling which it shall lose the latest.[2]—To love Miss Walton could not be a crime;—if to declare it is one—the expiation will be made."—Her tears were now flowing without control.—"Let me intreat you, said she, to have better hopes—Let not life be so indifferent to you; if my wishes can put any value on it—I will not pretend to misunderstand you—I know your worth—I have known it long—I have esteemed it—What would you have me say?—I have loved it as it deserved."—He seized her hand—a languid colour reddened his cheek—a smile brightened faintly in his eye. As he gazed on her, it grew dim, it fixed, it closed—He sighed and fell back on his seat.— Miss Walton screamed at the sight—His aunt and the servants rushed into the room—They found them lying motionless together.—His physician happened to call at that instant. Every art was tried to recover them—With Miss Walton they succeeded—But Harley was gone for ever!

[2]Hold onto until the last.

Chapter LVI

The emotions of the heart.

I entered the room where his body lay; I approached it with reverence, not fear: I looked; the recollection of the past crowded upon me. I saw that form which, but a little before, was animated with a soul which did honour to humanity, stretched without sense or feeling before me. 'Tis a connection we cannot easily forget:—I took his hand in mine; I repeated his name involuntarily:—I felt a pulse in every vein at the sound. I looked earnestly in his face; his eye was closed, his lip pale and motionless. There is an enthusiasm in sorrow that forgets impossibility; I wondered that it was so. The sight drew a prayer from my heart; it was the voice of frailty and of man! the confusion of my mind began to subside into thought; I had time to weep!

I turned, with the last farewell upon my lips, when I observed old Edwards standing behind me. I looked him full in the face; but his eye was fixed on another object: he pressed between me and the bed, and stood gazing on the breathless remains of his benefactor. I spoke to him I know not what; but he took no notice of what I said, and remained in the same attitude as before. He stood some minutes in that posture, then turned and walked towards the door. He paused as he went;—he returned a second time: I could observe his lips move as he looked: but the voice they would have uttered was lost. He attempted going again; and a third time he returned as before.—I saw him wipe his cheek; then covering his face with his hands, his breast heaving with the most convulsive throbs, he flung out of the room.

The Conclusion

He had hinted that he should like to be buried in a certain spot near the grave of his mother. This is a weakness; but it is universally incident to humanity: 'tis at least a memorial for those who survive; for some indeed a slender memorial will serve; and the soft affections, when they are busy that way, will build their structures, were it but on the paring of a nail.

He was buried in the place he had desired. It was shaded by an old tree, the only one in the church-yard, in which was a cavity worn by time. I have sat with him in it, and counted the tombs. The last time we passed there, methought he looked wistfully on the tree: there was a branch of it, that bent towards us, waving in the wind; he waved his hand, as if he mimicked its motion. There was something predictive in his look! perhaps it is foolish to remark it; but there are times and places when I am a child at those things.

I sometimes visit his grave; I sit in the hollow of the tree. It is worth a thousand homilies! every nobler feeling rises within me! every beat of my heart awakens a virtue!—but it will make you hate the world—No: there is such an air of gentleness around, that I can hate nothing; but, as to the world—I pity the men of it.

FINIS.

CONTEXTS

Sublimity, the Supernatural, the Real

In his first preface (see p. 3) and his letter to Mme. Du Deffand (see p. 267), Walpole cheered *The Castle of Otranto* for refusing neo-classical rules of art, rules upheld by writers such as Samuel Johnson and Clara Reeve, who feared that wayward novels would corrupt youthful minds. Walpole's example not only inspired Reeve (who still wanted a more realistic mode of gothic) but also encouraged other writers to attempt a Burkean sublime and to theorize a new supernatural mode for the imagination.

Edmund Burke (1729–1797)

*Born in Ireland but spending most of his life in London, Edmund Burke was a prominent Whig in the House of Commons. His influential treatise on aesthetics encouraged Uvedale Price (*An Essay on the Picturesque, *1794) and John Milner (*Essays on Gothic Architecture, *1800) to judge gothic architecture, in its obscure effects, more sublime than the Greek. The campy tone of Walpole's* Otranto *makes it difficult to decide whether it is presenting or parodying the aesthetics of the sublime.*

from *A Philosophical Enquiry into the Origin of Our Ideas of the Sublime and the Beautiful* (1757)[1]

from PART I. SECTION VII. Of the Sublime

Whatever is fitted in any sort to excite the ideas of pain and danger; that is to say, whatever is in any sort terrible, or is conversant about terrible objects, or operates in a manner analogous to terror, is a source of the *sublime*; that is, it is productive of the strongest emotion which the mind is capable of feeling. When danger or pain press too nearly, they are incapable of giving any delight, and are simply terrible; but at certain distances, and with certain modifications, they may be, and they are, delightful, as we every day experience. The cause of this I shall endeavour to investigate hereafter.

from PART II. SECTION I. Of the passion caused by the Sublime

The passion caused by the great and sublime in *nature*, when those causes operate most powerfully, is astonishment; and astonishment is that state of the soul in which all its motions are suspended with some degree of horror. In this case the mind is so entirely filled with its object, that it cannot entertain any other, nor by consequence reason on that object which employs it. Hence arises the great power of the sublime, that, far from being produced by them, it anticipates our reasonings; and hurries us on by an irresistible force.

from SECTION II. Terror

No passion so effectually robs the mind of all its powers of acting and reasoning as fear; for fear being an apprehension of pain or death, it operates in a manner that resembles actual pain. Whatever therefore is terrible, with regard to sight, is sublime too, whether the cause of terror, be endued with greatness of dimensions or not; for it is impossible to look on any thing as trifling, or contemptible, that may be dangerous.

from SECTION III. Obscurity

To make any thing very terrible, obscurity seems in general to be necessary. When we know the full extent of any danger, when we can accustom our eyes to it, a great deal of the apprehension vanishes. Every one

[1]London, 1759 ed., 58–59, 95–97, 99–100, 101, 105, 107–108, 110.

will be sensible of this, who considers how greatly night adds to our dread in all cases of danger, and how much the notions of ghosts and goblins, of which none can form clear ideas, affect minds which give credit to the popular tales concerning such sorts of beings. [. . .]

from SECTION IV: Of the difference between Clearness and Obscurity with regard to the passions

It is our ignorance of things that causes all our admiration, and chiefly excites our passions. Knowledge and acquaintance make the most striking causes affect but little. It is thus with the vulgar; and all men are as the vulgar in what they do not understand. [. . .] Hardly any thing can strike the mind with its greatness which does not make some sort of approach towards infinity; which nothing can do whilst we are able to perceive its bounds: but to see distinctly, and to perceive its bounds, is one and the same thing. A clear idea is therefore another name for a little idea.

from SECTION V. Power

I know of nothing sublime which is not some modification of power. And this branch rises [. . .] naturally [. . .] from terror, the common stock of every thing that is sublime.

Anna Letitia Aikin [Barbauld] (1743–1825) and John Aikin (1747–1822)

Walpole believed this essay was a defense of Otranto *against his critics.*[1]

from "On the Pleasure Derived from Objects of Terror; with Sir Bertrand, A Fragment," *Miscellaneous Pieces in Prose* (1773)[2]

The old Gothic romance and the Eastern tale with their genii, giants, enchantments, and transformations, however a refined critic may censure them as absurd and extravagant, will ever retain a

---

[1]Letter to Mason, April 8, 1778, *Yale Edition of Walpole's Correspondence*, vol. 28, 382. On attribution to Barbauld alone, see Mandell, http://www.muohio.edu/womenpoets/barbauld/aboutsirbert.html.

[2]From *Miscellaneous Pieces in Prose*, 119, 122, 123–27.

most powerful influence on the mind, and interest the reader independently of all peculiarity[3] of taste. [. . .]

How are we then to account for the pleasure derived from such objects? I have often been led to imagine that there is a deception in these cases; and that the avidity with which we attend is not a proof of our receiving real pleasure. The pain of suspense, and the irresistible desire of satisfying curiosity, when once raised, will account for our eagerness to go quite through an adventure, though we suffer actual pain during the whole course of it. We rather chuse to suffer the smart pang of a violent emotion than the uneasy craving of an unsatisfied desire. That this principle, in many instances, may involuntarily carry us through what we dislike, I am convinced from experience. This is the impulse which renders the poorest and most insipid narrative interesting when once we get fairly into it; and I have frequently felt it with regard to our modern novels, which, if lying on my table, and taken up in an idle hour, have led me through the most tedious and disgusting pages, while, like the Pistol eating his leek,[4] I have swallowed and execrated to the end. And it will not only force us through dullness, but through actual torture—through the relation of a Damien's execution, or an inquisitor's act of faith.[5] When children, therefore, listen with pale and mute attention to the frightful stories of apparitions, we are not, perhaps, to imagine that they are in a state of enjoyment, any more than the poor bird which is dropping into the mouth of the rattlesnake—they are chained by the ears, and fascinated by curiosity. This solution, however, does not satisfy me with respect to the well-wrought scenes of artificial terror which are formed by a sublime and vigorous imagination. Here, though we know beforehand what to expect, we enter into them with eagerness, in quest of a pleasure already experienced. This is the pleasure constantly attached to the excitement of surprise from new and wonderful objects. A strange and unexpected event awakens the mind, and keeps it on the stretch; and where the agency of invisible beings is introduced, of "forms unseen, and mightier far than we,"[6] our imagination, darting

[3]Individuality.
[4]Forced to eat a rotten leek, Pistol swears revenge in Shakespeare's *Henry the Fifth* (5.1.1–79).
[5]Henry Brooke, *The Fool of Quality* (1765).
[6]Alexander Pope, *An Essay on Man* (1733–34): Nature "taught the weak to bend, the proud to pray / To Pow'r unseen, and mighter far than they" (3.251–52).

forth, explores with rapture the new world which is laid open to view, and rejoices in the expansion of its powers. Passion and fancy co-operating elevate the soul to its highest pitch; and the pain of terror is lost in amazement.

Hence, the more wild, fanciful, and extraordinary are the circumstances of a scene of horror, the more pleasure we receive from it; and where they are too near common nature, though violently borne by curiosity through the adventure, we cannot repeat it or reflect on it, without an over-balance of pain. In the *Arabian Nights*[7] are many most striking examples of the terrible joined with the marvellous: the story of Aladdin and the travels of Sinbad are particularly excellent. The *Castle of Otranto* is a very spirited modern attempt upon the same plan of mixed terror, adapted to the model of Gothic romance. The best conceived, and most strongly worked-up scene of mere natural horror that I recollect, is in Smollet's *Ferdinand Count Fathom* [1753]; where the hero, entertained in a lone house in a forest, finds a corpse just slaughtered in the room where he is sent to sleep, and the door of which is locked upon him. It may be amusing for the reader to compare his feelings upon these, and from thence form his opinion of the justness of my theory.

David Hume (1711–1776)

> *Scottish empiricist philosopher David Hume wrote this essay ca. 1737 and published it in 1748. Skeptical of testimonies to miracles (by priests, say, or by the Bible), Hume went so far as to argue that a miracle violates natural law, being logically impossible on an experiential basis. Clara Reeve's criticism of* The Castle of Otranto, *particularly its supernatural devices, reflects this scruple.*

from "Of Miracles" (new ed., 1777)[1]

A miracle is a violation of the laws of nature; and as a firm and unalterable experience has established these laws, the proof against

---

[7]A group of Persian stories translated into French by Antoine Galland (1704) and then into English (1706–17).

[1]From *Essays and Treatises on Several Subjects*, 2.10.1.117, 122–23; 2.10.2.127–28.

a miracle, from the very nature of the fact, is as entire as any argument from experience can possibly be imagined. Why is it more than probable,[2] that all men must die; that lead cannot, of itself, remain suspended in the air; that fire consumes wood, and is extinguished by water; unless it be, that these events are found agreeable to the laws of nature, and there is required a violation of these laws, or in other words, a miracle to prevent them? Nothing is esteemed a miracle, if it ever happen in the common course of nature. It is no miracle that a man, seemingly in good health, should die on a sudden: because such a kind of death, though more unusual than any other, has yet been frequently observed to happen. But it is a miracle, that a dead man should come to life; because that has never been observed in any age or country. There must, therefore, be a uniform experience against every miraculous event, otherwise the event would not merit that appellation. [. . .]

The plain consequence is (and it is a general maxim worthy of our attention), "That no testimony is sufficient to establish a miracle, unless the testimony be of such a kind, that its falsehood would be more miraculous, than the fact, which it endeavours to establish. [. . .]"

It forms a strong presumption against all supernatural and miraculous relations,[3] that they are observed chiefly to abound among ignorant and barbarous nations; or if a civilized people has ever given admission to any of them, that people will be found to have received them from ignorant and barbarous ancestors, who transmitted them with that inviolable sanction and authority, which always attend to received opinions. When we peruse the first histories of all nations, we are apt to imagine ourselves transported into some new world; where the whole frame of nature is disjointed, and every element performs its operations in a different manner, from what it does at present. Battles, revolutions, pestilence, famine, and death, are never the effect of those natural causes, which we experience. Prodigies, omens, oracles, judgments, quite obscure the few natural events, that are intermingled with them. But as the former grow thinner every page, in proportion as we advance nearer the enlightened ages, we soon learn, that there is nothing mysterious, and that, though this inclina-

[2]Earlier in this essay, Hume defines "probability" as the degree to which one set of "experiments and observations" "overbalances" those indicating the opposite (2.10.1.119).

[3]Tales.

tion may at intervals receive a check from sense and learning, it can never be thoroughly extirpated from human nature.

It is strange, a judicious reader is apt to say, upon the perusal of these wonderful historians, *that such prodigious events never happen in our days*. But it is nothing strange, I hope, that men should lie in all ages. You must surely have seen instances enow of that frailty. You have yourself heard many such marvellous relations started, which, being treated with scorn by all the wise and judicious, have at last been abandoned even by the vulgar. Be assured, that those renowned lies, which have spread and flourished to such a monstrous height, arose from like beginnings; but being sown in a more proper soil, shot up at last into prodigies almost equal to those which they relate.[4]

Samuel Johnson (1709–1784)

A prolific essayist whose work appeared in his own journals The Rambler *and* The Idler *as well as in other mid-century periodicals such as* Gentleman's Magazine *and* The Adventurer, *Samuel Johnson also directed the first major dictionary of the English language (1755) and wrote* Lives of the English Poets *(1781). His conversational wit was immortalized by James Boswell's* The Life of Samuel Johnson *(1791). In this* Rambler *essay, and again in his Preface to Shakespeare, Johnson worries about the power of imagination to disorder usual senses of reality, and so advocates a moralistic, didactic, and realistic literature formed on the rules that Walpole wished to escape and that later Romantics ignored.*

The Rambler No. 4 (March 31, 1750)

> *Simul et jucunda et idonea dicere vitae.*
> HORACE, *Ars Poetica*, 334
> And join both profit and delight in one. CREECH[1]

The works of fiction, with which the present generation seems more particularly delighted, are such as exhibit life in its true state, diversified

---

[4]A professed atheist, Hume will go on to doubt the miracles described by early Christians, hinting that Christianity itself is one of those "renowned lies."

[1]Horace's phrase, translated by 17th-c. scholar Thomas Creech, on poetic excellence.

only by accidents that daily happen in the world, and influenced by passions and qualities which are really to be found in conversing with mankind.

This kind of writing may be termed not improperly the comedy of romance,[2] and is to be conducted nearly by the rules of comic poetry. Its province is to bring about natural events by easy means, and to keep up curiosity without the help of wonder: it is therefore precluded from the machines and expedients of the heroic romance, and can neither employ giants to snatch away a lady from the nuptial rites, nor knights to bring her back from captivity; it can neither bewilder its personages in deserts, nor lodge them in imaginary castles. [. . .] Almost all the fictions of the last age will vanish, if you deprive them of a hermit and a wood, a battle, and a shipwreck.

Why this wild strain of imagination found reception so long in polite and learned ages, it is not easy to conceive; but we cannot wonder that while readers could be procured, the authors were willing to continue it; for when a man had by practice gained some fluency of language, he had no further care than to retire to his closet,[3] let loose his invention, and heat his mind with incredibilities; a book was thus produced without fear of criticism, without the toil of study, without knowledge of nature, or acquaintance with life.

The task of our present writers is very different; it requires together with that learning which is to be gained from books, that experience which can never be attained by solitary diligence, but must arise from general converse[4] and accurate observation of the living world. Their performances have, as Horace expresses it, *plus oneris quantum veniae minus*, little indulgence, and therefore more difficulty.[5] They are engaged in portraits of which every one knows the original, and can detect any deviation from exactness of resemblance. [. . .]

But the fear of not being approved as just copiers of human manners, is not the most important concern that an author of this sort ought to have before him. These books are written chiefly to

---

[2]Johnson's term for the realistic novel; "comedy" means common daily life, as opposed to the heroic feats of knights and kings.

[3]Private room.

[4]Sociable interchange.

[5]Translating Horace's *Epistles* Book II, Epistle 1: *To Augustus* 324; the performances are the novels.

the young, the ignorant, and the idle. [. . .] They are the entertainment of minds unfurnished with ideas, and therefore easily susceptible of impressions. [. . .] In the romances formerly written, every transaction and sentiment was so remote from all that passes among men, that the reader was in very little danger of making any applications to himself. [. . .] But when an adventurer is levelled with the rest of the world [. . .]; young spectators [. . .] hope, by observing his behaviour and success, to regulate their own practices. [. . .] If the power of example is so great as to take possession of the memory by a kind of violence, and produce effects almost without the intervention of the will, care ought to be taken, that, when the choice is unrestrained, the best examples only should be exhibited. [. . .] If the world be promiscuously described, I cannot see of what use it can be to read the account; or why it may not be as safe to turn the eye immediately upon mankind as upon a mirror which shows all that presents itself without discrimination.

from Preface to *The Plays of William Shakespeare* (1765)[6]

Nothing can please many, and please long, but just representations of general nature. [. . .] Fanciful invention may delight awhile, [. . .] but the pleasures of sudden wonder are soon exhausted, and the mind can only repose on the stability of truth.

Shakespeare is, above all writers, at least above all modern writers, the poet of nature; the poet that holds up to his readers a faithful mirror of manners and of life. [. . .] Other dramatists can only gain attention by hyperbolical or aggravated characters, by fabulous and unexampled excellence or depravity, as the writers of barbarous romances invigorated the reader by giant or a dwarf; and he that should form his expectations of human affairs from the play, or from the tale, would be equally deceived. Shakespeare has no heroes; his scenes are occupied only by men, who act and speak as the reader thinks that he should himself have spoken or acted on the same occasion. Even where the agency is supernatural the dialogue is level with life. Other writers disguise the most natural passions and most frequent incidents; so that he who contemplates them in the book will not know them in the world:

[6]*Lives of the Most Eminent English Poets* (New York, 1870), 508–9.

Shakespeare approximates the remote, and familiarizes the wonderful; the event which he represents will not happen, but if it were possible, its effects would probably be such as he has assigned; and it may be said, that he has not only shown human nature as it acts in real exigencies, but as it would be found in trials, to which it cannot be exposed.

This therefore is the praise of Shakespeare, that his drama is the mirror of life; that he who has mazed his imagination, in following the phantoms which other writers raise up before him, may here be cured of his delirious ecstasies, by reading human sentiment in human language; by scenes from which a hermit may estimate the transactions of the world, and a confessor predict the progress of the passions.

Clara Reeve (1729–1807)

In The Progress of Romance, *Clara Reeve means to distinguish Romances from novels. In her staged dialogue, Hortensius (like most critics) ranks both as low, even bad art, in contrast to high epic poetry. While Euphrasia (her name means "beautiful phrasing") thinks he is illogical, she agrees about the pernicious effect of some novels. In her Preface to* The Old English Baron, *introducing a work that came to be regarded as the second gothic novel, Reeve explains her desire to keep her tale within the realm of the probable.*

from *The Progress of Romance* (1785)

from Preface[1]

Romances may not improperly be called the polite literature of early ages, and they have been the favourite amusements of later times. [. . .] It is remarkable, that among the many learned and ingenious writers who have treated this subject, few have taken proper notice of the Greek Romances, which may justly be deemed the parents of all the rest.[2] The learned men of our own country, have in

---

[1] 1:iii, xi, xv–xvi.

[2] Calling Homer's epics "Romances," Reeve tweaks contemporary debates about "the ancients versus the moderns" by discerning modern modes in ancient Homer.

general affected a contempt for this kind of writing,[3] and looked upon Romances, as proper furniture only for a lady's Library. [. . .]

Romances are of universal growth, and not confined to any particular period or countries. They were the delight of barbarous ages, and they have always kept their ground amongst the multiplied amusements of more refined and cultivated periods, containing like every other branch of human literature, both good and evil things. They are not to be put into the hands of young persons without distinction and reserve, but under proper restrictions and regulations they will afford much useful instruction, as well as rational and elegant amusement. In this view therefore they are equally entitled to our attention and respect, as any other works of Genius and literature.

from EVENING VII.

Euphrasia. The Romance is an heroic fable, which treats of fabulous persons and things.—The Novel is a picture of real life and manners, and of the times in which it is written. The Romance in lofty and elevated language, describes what never happened nor is likely to happen.—The Novel gives a familiar relation of such things, as pass every day before our eyes, such as may happen to our friend, or to ourselves; and the perfection of it, is to represent every scene, in so easy and natural a manner, and to make them appear so probable, as to deceive us into a persuasion (at least while we are reading) that all is real, until we are affected by the joys or distresses, of the persons in the story, as if they were our own.

from EVENING XI.

Euphrasia. Eastern Tales [. . .] are all wild and extravagant to the highest degree; they are indeed so far out of the bounds of Nature and probability, that it is difficult to judge of them by rules drawn from these sources. [. . .]

Hortensius. They are certainly dangerous books for youth,— they create and encourage the wildest excursions of imagination, which it is, or ought to be, the care of parents and preceptors to restrain, and to give them a just and true representation of human nature, and of the duties and practice of common life. [. . .]

[3]See, for example, John Langhorne's review of *The Castle of Otranto*, p. 266.

from EVENING XII.[4]

Euphrasia. A Circulating Library[5] is indeed a great evil,—young people are allowed to subscribe to them, and to read indiscriminately all they contain; and thus both food and poison are conveyed to the young mind together.

Hortensius. I should suppose that if books of the worst kind were excluded; still there would be enough to lay a foundation of idleness and folly. [. . .] There are yet more and greater evils behind.—The seeds of vice and folly are sown in the heart,—the passions are awakened,—false expectations are raised.—A young woman is taught to expect adventures and intrigues,—she expects to be addressed in the style of these books, with the language of flattery and adulation.—If a plain man addresses her in rational terms and pays her the greatest of compliments,—that of desiring to spend his life with her,—that is not sufficient, her vanity is disappointed, she expects to meet a Hero in Romance.[6] [. . .]

From this kind of reading, young people fancy themselves capable of judging men and manners, and that they are knowing, while involved in the profoundest ignorance. They believe themselves wiser than their parents and guardians, whom they treat with contempt and ridicule:—Thus armed with ignorance, conceit, and folly, they plunge into the world and its dissipations, and who can wonder if they become its victims?—For such as the foundation is, such will be the superstructure.

Preface to *The Old English Baron* (2nd ed., 1778)[7]

This Story is the literary offspring of the CASTLE OF OTRANTO, written upon the same plan, with a design to unite the most attractive and interesting circumstances of the ancient Romance and modern Novel, at the same time it assumes a character and manner of its own that differs from both; it is distinguished by the appellation of

---

[4]1.111; 2.58–59, 77–79.

[5]From which, in the era before public libraries, one could borrow for a fee; three-volume novels were much in demand.

[6]In Charlotte Lennox's *The Female Quixote* (1752), the romance-infected heroine imagines a servant and her cousin out to ravish her, and a passerby as a knight sent by providence to save her.

[7]*Ballantyne's Novelist's Library* (Edingburgh, 1823), 5.604–5.

a Gothic Story, being a picture of Gothic times and manners. [. . .] *The Castle of Otranto* [. . .] is an attempt to unite the various merits and graces of the ancient Romance and modern Novel. To attain this end, there is required a sufficient degree of the marvellous, to excite attention; enough of the manners of real life, to give an air of probability to the work; and enough of the pathetic to engage the heart in its behalf.

The book we have mentioned is excellent in the last two points, but has a redundancy in the first. The opening excites the attention very strongly; the conduct of the story is artful and judicious; the characters are admirably drawn and supported; the diction polished and elegant; yet, with all these brilliant advantages, it palls upon the mind (though it does not upon the ear;) and the reason is obvious, the machinery is so violent, that it destroys the effect it is intended to excite. Had the story been kept within the utmost verge of probability, the effect had been preserved, without losing the least circumstance that excites or detains the attention.

For instance; we can conceive, and allow of, the appearance of a ghost; we can even dispense with an enchanted sword and helmet; but then they must keep within certain limits of credibility. A sword so large as to require an hundred men to lift it; a helmet that by its own weight forces a passage through a court-yard, into an arched vault, big enough for a man to go through; a picture that walks out of its frame; a skeleton ghost in a hermit's cowl:—When your expectation is wound up to the highest pitch, these circumstances take it down with a witness, destroy the work of imagination, and instead of attention, excite laughter. I was both surprised and vexed to find the enchantment dissolved, which I wished might continue to the end of the book; and several of its readers have confessed the same disappointment to me. The beauties are so numerous, that we cannot bear the defects, but want it to be perfect in all respects.

Samuel Taylor Coleridge (1772–1834)

In his second preface, Walpole explains his plan of combining ancient and modern romance so as to leave "the powers of fancy at liberty to expatiate through the boundless realms of invention," while conduct-

ing his "mortal agents" in accord with "rules of probability; in short, to make them think, speak, and act, as it might be supposed mere men and women would do in extraordinary positions" (pp. 7–8). In a famous phrase, Coleridge described this aesthetics as "the willing suspension of disbelief." The context is his collaboration with poet William Wordsworth on Lyrical Ballads.

from *Biographia Literaria* (1817)[1]

Our conversations turned frequently on the two cardinal points of poetry, the power of exciting the sympathy of the reader by a faithful adherence to the truth of nature, and the power of giving the interest of novelty by the modifying colours of imagination. [. . .] a series of poems might be composed of two sorts. In the one, the incidents and agents were to be, in part at least, supernatural; and the excellence aimed at was to consist in the interesting of the affections by the dramatic truth of such emotions, as would naturally accompany such situations, supposing them real. [. . .] It was agreed, that my endeavours should be directed to persons and characters supernatural, or at least romantic;[2] yet so as to transfer from our inward nature a human interest and a semblance of truth sufficient to procure for these shadows of imagination that willing suspension of disbelief for the moment, which constitutes poetic faith. [. . .] With this view I wrote the "Ancient Mariner."

[1]2.1–3.
[2]Fantastic, wild.

The Gothic Revival and Chivalry

In 1872, C. L. Eastlake proclaimed Horace Walpole the "inventor" of the gothic revival in architecture—the renewed use of all those parapets, towers, and pointed arches that embellish gothic castles and cathedrals. It is no surprise so many revival architects were close friends of Walpole (William Kent, Richard Bentley) or helped develop his own gothic confabulation, Strawberry Hill (Robert Adam, James Essex, and John Carter).[1] The gothic revival extended to antiquarian literary endeavors: Bishop Thomas Percy, George Ellis, and Walter Scott all published collections of medieval songs and ballads,[2] others produced work on medieval culture and customs, and still others followed Walpole and set their novels in a fantasy of medieval times.

William Chambers (1726–1796)

In the first edition of Civil Architecture, *published in 1759 (six years before* The Castle of Otranto), *Sir William Chambers, Surveyor General of His Majesty's Buildings, shows no love of the gothic vogue. But a later edition, published in 1791 (by which time* Otranto *was in its sixth edition and saw an expensive Italian edition),[1] manages two paragraphs extolling gothic architecture.*

[1]J. Mordaunt Crook, "Walpole's 'little Gothic castle,'" *Times Literary Supplement* (February 28, 1997): 15.

[2]Percy, *Reliques of Ancient English Poetry*, 1765; Ellis, *Specimens of the Early English Poets*, 1790; Scott, *Minstrelsy of the Scottish Border*, 1802.

[1]See Hazen 56.

from *A Treatise on Civil Architecture* (1759)[2]

from "Of Persians and Caryatides"[3]

If they are employed to support the covering of a Throne, they may be represented under the figures and symbols of Heroic Virtues; if to adorn a Sacred Building, they must have an affinity to Religion; and when they are placed in Banqueting-Rooms, they must be of kinds proper to inspire Mirth and Jollity.

In composing them particular care must be taken to avoid indecent attitudes, distorted features, and all kinds of monstrous and horrid productions, of which there are such frequent instances in the works of the Goths.

from *A Treatise on the Decorative Part of Civil Architecture* (1791)[4]

from the new Introduction: "Of the ORIGIN and PROGRESS of BUILDING"

To those usually called Gothick architects, we are indebted for the first considerable improvements in construction; there is a lightness in their works, an art and boldness of execution; to which the ancients never arrived: and which the moderns comprehend and imitate with difficulty. England contains many magnificent examples of this species of architecture, equally admirable for the art with which they are built, the taste and ingenuity with which they are composed.

One cannot refrain from wishing, that the Gothick structures were more considered; better understood; and in higher estimation; than they hitherto seem to have been. Would our dilettanti instead of importing the gleanings of Greece; or our antiquaries, instead of publishing loose incoherent prints; encourage persons duly qualified to undertake a correct elegant of our own cathedrals, and other buildings called Gothick, before they totally fall to ruin;[5] it would be of real service to the arts of design; preserve the remembrance of

---

[2]London, 37.

[3]Columns formed of male (Persians) and female (Caryatids) figures.

[4]3rd augmented edition, 24, 72.

[5]In *Gothic Ornaments in the Cathedral Church of York* (York, 1800), Joseph Halfpenny addresses this call, quoting Chambers' remarks.

an extraordinary stile of building now sinking fast into oblivion; and at the same time publish to the world the riches of Britain, in the splendor of her ancient structures.

from "Of Persians and Caryatides"

In composing them, particular care must be taken to avoid indecent attitudes, distorted features, and all kinds of monstrous and horrid productions, of which there are such frequent instances in the works of our northern predecessors.

John Carter (1748–1817)

It was to Walpole *that John Carter dedicated* Specimens of Ancient Sculpture and Painting *(1786). Also author of* The Ancient Architecture of England, *Carter contributed essays, by "An Architect," about British buildings to* The Gentleman's Magazine.

from *The Gentleman's Magazine* 85 (1799): 189–91[1]

Has it not been the general opinion, that our charming ancient structures were barbarous Gothic works; that our ancestors were savage, and without any taste for what is called the fine arts. [. . .] I have lived to see part of the veil torn from the dark mind of prejudice, which had so long overshadowed the native beauties of our ancient structures; and I may yet live to see the time when our ancestors may be allowed to have had the same refined taste to bring to perfection all the elegancies of life as is presumed to be the case at the present day. [. . .]

Of the meaning of Gothic age and Gothic architecture I am entirely ignorant. I believe the word "Gothic" was invented as an ungrateful term of reproach and disgrace towards our beautiful ancient structures by the introducers of the Roman and Grecian styles in the reign of Henry VIII.

[1]*Sacred and Medieval Architecture*, ed. G. L. Gomme (1891), 1.19–20, 22.

from *The Gentleman's Magazine* 89 (1801): 413[2]

A term of reproach, a barbarous appellation, an invidious designation, a vulgar epithet, an ignorant by-word, a low nickname, given to hold up to shame and ignominy our ancient English architecture, the pride of human art, and the excellence of all earthly and scientific labours.

At length the opportunity is arrived to tear down this rag of prejudice, this scum of innovation, this word "Gothic," which for a century has branded with ignominy all our national works. [His work exposing the source of the denigration will provide] a beacon to warn all antiquity-followers to shun the hidden rocks and savage shores of innovating taste and Gothic defamation!

Horace Walpole (1717–1797)

From 1753 to 1776 Walpole transformed Strawberry Hill, a simple cottage when he purchased it in 1748, into a gothic castle. When the preface by "William Marshal" to the first edition of The Castle of Otranto *indicates the scene as "some real castle," readers might well suspect Strawberry Hill, a real castle so famous that, Walpole complained, it was constantly besieged by tourists. He published this* Description *as a guide.*

from *A Description of the Villa of Mr. Horace Walpole, at Strawberry-Hill near Twickham* (1774 [1786])[1]

Preface

It will look, I fear, a little like arrogance in a private Man to give a printed Description of his Villa and Collection, in which almost every thing is diminutive. It is not, however, intended for public sale, and originally was meant only to assist those who should visit the place. A farther view succeeded; that of exhibiting specimens of Gothic architecture, as collected from standards in cathedrals and

---

[2]Gomme 1.118.

[1]*The Works of Horatio Walpole*, ed. Mary Berry (London, 1798), 2.395, 398–400, 442, 453.

chapel-tombs, and shewing how they may be applied to chimney-pieces, ceilings, windows, ballustrades, loggias, &c. The general disuse of Gothic architecture, and the decay and alterations so frequently made in churches, give prints a chance of being the sole preservatives of that style. [. . .]

—But I do not mean to defend by argument a small capricious house. It was built to please my own taste, and in some degree to realize my own visions. I have specified what it contains: could I describe the gay but tranquil scene where it stands, and add the beauty of the landscape to the romantic cast of the mansion, it would raise more pleasing sensations than a dry list of curiosities can excite: at least the prospect would recall the good humour of those who might be disposed to condemn the fantastic fabric, and think it a very proper habitation of, as it was the scene that inspired, the author of Otranto.

A Description of the Villa of Mr. Horace Walpole at Strawberry-Hill near Twickenham.

Where the Gothic Castle now stands, was originally a small tenement,[2] built in 1698, and let as a lodging-house: Cibber once took it and wrote one of his plays here, *The Refusal, or the Lady's Philosophy.*[3] [. . .] When Mr. Walpole bought Strawberry-hill, there were but five acres belonging to the house: the rest have been purchased since. The castle now existing was not entirely built from the ground, but formed at different times, by alterations of and additions to the old small house. The library, and refectory[4] or great parlour, were entirely new built in 1753; the gallery, round tower, great cloyster, and cabinet, in 1760 and 1761; the great north bed-chamber in 1770; and the Beauclerc tower with the hexagon closet in 1776.

---

[2]It was built by the earl of Bradford's coachman, and was called by the common people, *Chopp'd-Straw-Hall*, they supposing, that by feeding his lord's horses with chopped straw, he had saved money enough to build his house; but the piece of ground on which it stands is called in all the old leases, *Strawberry-Hill-Shot*, from whence it takes its name [Walpole's note]. Chopped straw is leftover from other animals' chomping, cheaper to gather up than to purchase bound bales.

[3]Colley Cibber (1671–1757), major playwright, actor, producer, and manager.

[4]Dining hall.

The embattled[5] wall to the road is taken from a print of Ashton-house in Warwickeshire, in Dugdale's history of that county.[6]

Entering by the great north gate, the first object that presents itself is a small oratory inclosed with iron rails; in front, an altar, on which stands a saint in bronze; open niches, and stone basons for holy water. [. . .] Passing on the left, by a small cloyster,[7] is the entrance of the house.

The Library

The books are ranged within Gothic arches of pierced work, taken from a side-dore case to the choir in Dugdale's St. Paul's. The doors themselves were designed by Mr. Chute. The chimney-piece[8] is imitated from the tomb of John of Eltham earl of Cornwall, in Westminster-abbey; the stone-work from that of Thomas duke of Clarence, at Canterbury. [. . .] The ceiling was painted by Clermont, from Mr. Walpole's design drawn out by Mr. Bentley.[9] In the middle is the shield of Walpole surrounded with the quarters borne by the family. At each end in a round is a knight on horseback, in the manner of ancient seals. [. . .]

At the four corners are shields, helmets, and mantles;[10] on one shield [. . .] is the Saracen's head, the crest of the family. [. . .] On either side is the motto of the family, *Fari quae sentiat*;[11] and at the

[5]Shaped like a battlement, scalloped with loopholes (crenellated).

[6]William Dugdale wrote *Antiquities of Warwickshire* (1656; rpt. 1730, 1765). In designing Strawberry Hill, Walpole took inspiration from illustrations in Dugdale's *History of St. Paul's Cathedral* (1658; rpt. 1716), John Dart's *History and Antiquities of the Cathedral church of Canterbury* (1726), and his drawings of Westminster Abbey in *Westmonasterium* (1742).

[7]In this cloyster are two blue and white Delft flower-pots. [. . .] On a pedestal, stands the large blue and white china tub in which Mr. Walpole's cat was drowned; on a label of the pedestal is written the first stanza of Mr. Gray's beautiful ode on that occasion [Walpole's note, referring to Thomas Gray's *Ode on the Death of a Favourite Cat, Drowned in a Tub of Goldfishes* (1747), written at Walpole's request].

[8]An elaborate construction including the fireplace, hearth, mantelpiece, and chimney wall.

[9]Richard Bentley and John Chute, among the original designers of Strawberry Hill, made many drawings and watercolors of it, which Walpole put in his *Description* (see the illustrations on pp. 15, 21, 24, 42, 85, and 229).

[10]Robes of estate.

[11]Latin: To speak what one feels. This is an elaborate description of the Walpole family coat of arms. Walpole's father, Robert Walpole (1676–1745), not born of nobility, was knighted after a controversial ministry (1721–42), incurring the hatred of many, including Alexander Pope and Jonathan Swift.

The Library at Strawberry Hill (King Library, Miami University)

ends, M.DCC.LIV. the year in which this room was finished, expressed in Gothic letters: the whole on mosaic ground. [. . .]

In the PLAID BEDCHAMBER, in the South Tower, is the portrait of Henry Walpole the jesuit, who was executed for attempting to poison queen Elizabeth. He is crowned with glory and holds a palm-branch, the emblem of martyrdom; the arms of the family in one corner. This picture came from Mr. Walpole's of Lincolnshire, the last of the Roman catholic branch of the family, who died about the year 1748. [. . .]

Horace Walpole (1717–1797) and George Vertue (1684–1756)

For a history of English art, George Vertue collected materials, which Walpole purchased for the first history (claims the Preface) of English painting: To Vertue, "the antiquarian world" of historians and collectors owes "singular obligations." The selections presented here concern the emergence of the gothic revival.

from *Anecdotes of Painting* (1762–71)[1]

Architects in the Reign of George II. [1727–60]

It was in this reign that architecture resumed all her rights. Noble publications of Palladio, Jones, and the antique,[2] recalled her to true principles and correct taste; she found men of genius to execute her rules, and patrons to countenance their labours. She found more, and what Rome could not boast, men of the first rank who contributed to embellish their country by buildings of their own design in the purest style of antique composition. [. . .]

I must mention a more barbarous architect before I come to the luminaries of the science. This was

Batty Langley[3]

who endeavoured to adapt Gothic architecture to Roman measures. [. . .] All that his books achieved, has been to teach carpenters to massacre that venerable species, and to give occasion to those who know nothing of the matter, and who mistake his clumsy efforts for real imitations. [. . .]

William Kent[4]

[. . .] a painter, an architect, and the father of modern gardening. In the first character, he was below mediocrity; in the second, he was a restorer of the science; in the last, an original, and the inventor of an art that realizes painting, and improves nature. Mohamet imagined an Elysium, but Kent created many. [. . .] As Kent's genius was not universal, he has succeeded [. . .] ill in Gothic. The King's-bench

---

[1] *Works* 3.483, 485, 488, 490.

[2] Italian architect Andrea Palladio (1518–80) developed the classical style ("Palladianism"). His *Architecture* was translated and republished throughout the early 18th c. A 1742 edition contained "notes and remarks by Inigo Jones," the great late Renaissance British architect, famous for the banqueting house in London's Whitehall Palace (built 1619–22). "The grotesque antique" is another name for gothic.

[3] Batty Langley (1696–1751) published widely on gothic architecture, including a book of prints for builders, *Gothick Architecture, Improved by Rules and Proportions* (1747).

[4] William Kent (1685–1748) was also famous for furniture design and other art. He sculpted the bust of William Shakespeare for the poet's corner in Westminster Abbey.

at Westminster, and Mr. Pelham's house at Esher,[5] are proofs how little he conceived either the principles or graces of that architecture. Yet he was sometimes sensible of its beauties.

Alexander Pope (1688–1744)

Alexander Pope found gothic architecture an apt comparison for Shakespeare's English manner.

from Preface to *The Works of Shakespear* (1725)[1]

I will conclude by saying of Shakespear, that with all his faults, and with all the irregularity of his *drama*, one may look upon his works, in comparison of those that are more finished and regular, as upon an ancient majestick piece of Gothic architecture, compared with a neat modern building: The latter is more elegant and glaring, but the former is more strong and solemn. It must be allowed, that in one of these there are materials enough to make many of the other. It has much the greater variety, and much the nobler apartments; tho' we are often conducted to them by dark, odd, and uncouth passages. Nor does the whole fail to strike us with greater reverence, tho' many of the parts are childish, ill-placed, and unequal to its grandeur.

Richard Hurd (1720–1808)

Revising a view of the middle ages as merely barbarous, Richard Hurd discerned an age of gothic chivalry and romance.

---

[5]King's Bench, the highest court of law, resided at Westminster Hall, the oldest building of Parliament (11th c.). Since 1735, Kent had been applying "the natural style" to the parks of Claremont House, home of Thomas Pelham-Holles, Duke of Newcastle.

---

[1]*Works of Pope*, ed. William Warburton (London, 1751), 6.346–47.

from *Letters on Chivalry and Romance* (1762)[1]

from LETTER I.

The ages, we call barbarous, present us with many a subject of curious speculation. What, for instance, is more remarkable than the Gothic CHIVALRY? or than the spirit of ROMANCE, which took its rise from that singular institution? [. . .] The spirit of Chivalry, was a fire which soon spent itself: But that of *Romance*, which was kindled at it, burnt long, and continued its light and heat even to the politer ages.

The greatest geniuses of our own and foreign countries, such as Ariosto and Tasso in Italy, and Spenser and Milton in England, were seduced by these barbarities of their forefathers; were even charmed by the Gothic Romances. Was this caprice and absurdity in them? Or, may there not be something in the Gothic Romance peculiarly suited to the views of a genius, and to the ends of poetry? And may not the philosophic moderns have gone too far, in their perpetual ridicule and contempt of it?

from LETTER II.

The old inhabitants of North-West parts of Europe were extremely given to the love and exercise of arms. The feats of Charlemagne and our Arthur, in particular, were so famous as in later times, when books of Chivalry were composed, to afford a principal subject to the writers of them.

But CHIVALRY, properly so called, and under the idea "of a distinct military order, conferred in the way of investiture, and accompanied with the solemnity of an oath and other ceremonies, as described in the old historians and romancers," was of later date, and seems to have sprung immediately out of the FEUDAL CONSTITUTION.

The FIRST and most sensible effect of this constitution [. . .] was the erection of a prodigious number of petty tyrannies. For, though the great barons were closely tied to the service of their Prince by the conditions of their tenure, yet the power which was given them by it over their own numerous vassals[2] was so great, that, in effect, they all set up for themselves; affected an independency; and were,

---

[1]London, 1, 3–4, 6–8, 11–20.

[2]Peasants who depend on the baron's or prince's protection from marauders.

in truth, a sort of absolute Sovereigns, at least with regard to one another. Hence, their mutual aims and interests often interfering, the feudal state was, in a good degree, a state of war: the feudal chiefs were in frequent enmity with each other: the several combinations of feudal tenants were so many separate armies under their head or chief: and their castles were so many fortresses, as well as palaces, of these puny princes.

In this state of things one sees, that all imaginable encouragement was to be given to the use of arms. [. . .] And this condition of the times, I suppose, gave rise to that military institution, which we know by the name of CHIVALRY.

from LETTER III.

If the conjecture, I advanced, of the rise of Chivalry, from the circumstances of the feudal government, be thought reasonable, it will now be easy to account for the several CHARACTERISTICS of this singular profession.

I. "The passion for arms; the spirit of enterprize; the honour of knighthood; the rewards of valour; the splendour of equipages;" in short, every thing that raises our ideas of the prowess, gallantry, and magnificence of these sons of Mars,[3] is naturally and easily explained on this supposition.

Ambition, interest, glory, all concurred, under such circumstances, to produce these effects. The feudal principles could terminate in nothing else. And when, by the necessary operations of policy, this turn was given to the thoughts and passions of men, use and fashion would do the rest; and carry them to all the excesses of military fanaticism, which are painted so strongly, but scarcely exaggerated in the old Romances. [. . .]

II. "Their romantic ideas of justice; their passion for adventures; their eagerness to run to the succour of the distressed; the pride they took in redressing wrongs, and removing grievances;" All these distinguishing characters of genuine Chivalry are explained on the same principle. For, the feudal state being a state of war, or rather of almost perpetual violence, rapine, and plunder, it was unavoidable that, in their constant skirmishes, stratagems, and surprizes, numbers of the tenants or followers of one Baron

---

[3]Roman god of war.

should be seized upon and carried away by the followers of another: And the interest, each had to protect his own, would of course introduce the point of honour in attempting by all means not only to retaliate on the enemy, but to rescue the captive sufferers out of the hands of their oppressors.

It would be meritorious, in the highest degree, to fly to their assistance, when they knew where they were to be come at; or to seek them out with diligence, when they did not. This last service they called, *Going in quest of adventures*; which at first, no doubt, was confined to those of their own party, but afterwards, by the habit of acting on this principle, would be extended much father. So that, in process of time, we find the Knights errant, as they were now properly styled, wandering the world over in search of occasions on which to exercise their generous and disinterested valour. [. . .]

III. "The courtesy, affability, and gallantry, for which these adventurers were so famous, are but the natural effects and consequences of their situation."

For the castles of the Barons were, as I said, the courts of these little sovereigns, as well as their fortresses; and the resort of their vassals thither, in honour of their chiefs, and for their own proper security, would make that civility and politeness, which is seen in courts and insensibly prevails there, a predominant part in the character of these assemblies. [. . .]

Further, The free commerce of the ladies, in those knots and circles of the great, would operate so far on the sturdiest knights as to give birth to the attentions of gallantry.[4] But this gallantry would take a refined turn, not only from the necessity there was of maintaining the strict forms of decorum, amidst a promiscuous conversation under the eye of the Prince and in his own family; but also from the inflamed sense they must needs have of the frequent outrages committed, by their neighbouring clans of adversaries, on the honour of the Sex,[5] when by chance of war they had fallen into their hands. Violations of chastity being the most atrocious crimes they had to charge on their enemies, they would pride themselves in the glory of being its protectors: And as this virtue was, of all others, the fairest and strongest claim of the sex itself to such protec-

[4]Flirtation.
[5]Women.

tion, it is no wonder that the notions of it were, in time, carried to so platonic[6] an elevation.

IV. It only remains to account for that "character of Religion," which was so deeply imprinted on the minds of all the knights and was essential to their institution. We are even told, that *the love of God and of the Ladies* went hand in hand, in the duties and ritual of Chivalry.

[One reason] that may be assigned for this singularity: [. . .] the superstition of the Times,[7] in which Chivalry arose; which was so great that no institution of a public nature could have found credit in the world, that was not consecrated by the Church-men, and closely interwoven with religion.

Walter Scott (1771–1832)

In his encyclopedia entry, Walter Scott traces the etymology of the word "chivalry," delineating its historical context and conventions.

from "Essay on Chivalry, Romance, and the Drama" (1824)[1]

The primitive sense of this well-known word, derived from the French *Chevalier*, signifies merely cavalry, or a body of soldiers serving on horseback; and has been used in that general acceptation by the best of our poets, ancient and modern, from Milton to Thomas Campbell.

But the present article respects the peculiar meaning given to the word in modern Europe, as applied to the order of knighthood, established in almost all her kingdoms during the middle ages, and the laws, rules, and customs, by which it was governed. Those laws and customs have been long antiquated, but their effects may still be traced in European manners; and, excepting only the change which flowed from the introduction of the Christian religion, we know no cause which has produced such general and permanent

---

[6]Ideal, purified of sexual interest.

[7]Protestant term for Roman Catholicism.

---

[1]*Encyclopedia Britannica*, 4th ed., 1824; text here: *Essays on Chivalry, Romance, and The Drama* (London: Frederick Warne, 1887), 1–2, 4–5.

difference betwixt the ancients[2] and the moderns, as that which has arisen out of the institution of chivalry. [. . .]

From the time that cavalry becomes used in war, the horseman who furnishes and supports a charger arises, in all countries, into a person of superior importance to the mere foot-soldier. [. . .] But, in the middle ages, the distinction ascribed to soldiers serving on horseback, assumed a very peculiar and imposing character. They were not merely respected on account of their wealth or military skill, but were bound together by a union of a very peculiar character, which monarchs were ambitious to share with the poorest of their subjects, and governed by laws directed to enhance, into enthusiasm, the military spirit and sense of personal honour associated with it. The aspirants to this dignity were not permitted to assume the sacred character of knighthood until after a long and severe probation, during which they practised, as acolytes, the virtues necessary to the order of Chivalry. Knighthood was the goal to which the ambition of every noble youth turned; and to support its honours, which (in theory at least) could only be conferred on the gallant, the modest, and the virtuous, it was necessary he should spend a certain time in a subordinate situation, attendant upon some knight of eminence, observing the conduct of his master, as what must in future be the model of his own, and practising the virtues of humility, modesty, and temperance, until called upon to display those of a higher order. [. . .]

The original institution of Chivalry has been often traced to the custom of the German tribes. [. . .] Instances might be pointed out, in which the ancient customs of the Gothic tribes may be traced in the history of Chivalry, [. . .] enough to prove that the seeds of that singular institution existed in German forests, though they did not come to maturity until the destruction of the Roman empire, and the establishment of the modern states of Europe upon its ruins. [. . .]

In every age and country valour is held in esteem, and the more rude the period and the place, the greater respect is paid to boldness of enterprise and success in battle. But it was peculiar to the institution of chivalry, to blend military valour with the strongest passions which actuate the human mind, the feelings of devotion and those of love. The Greeks and Romans fought for liberty or for conquest,

[2]Greeks and Romans.

and the knights of the middle ages for God and for their ladies. Loyalty to their sovereigns was a duty also incumbent upon these warriors; but although a powerful motive, and by which they often appear to have been strongly actuated, it entered less warmly into the composition of the chivalrous principle than the two preceding causes. Of patriotism, [. . .] we find comparatively few traces in the institutions of knighthood. But the love of personal freedom, and the obligation to maintain and defend it in the persons of others as in their own, was a duty particularly incumbent on those who attained the honour of chivalry. Generosity, gallantry, and an unblemished reputation, were no less necessary ingredients in the character of a perfect knight. He was not called upon simply to practise these virtues when opportunity offered, but to be sedulous and unwearied in searching for the means of exercising them, and to push them without hesitation to the brink of extravagance, or even beyond it. Founded on principles so pure, the order of chivalry could not, in the abstract at least, but occasion a pleasing, though a romantic development of the energies of human nature.

Marriage, Obedience, Sentiment

Debating the Hardwicke Act

In 1753, Parliament passed the Earl of Hardwicke's bill "for the Better preventing of Clandestine Marriages." Sometimes performed by clergymen of questionable authority, these marriages could be contracted "without witnesses, banns, license or record," without parental consent, and between parties under the age of 21, and long had status under common law.[1] The debate in the House of Commons was quite contentious. Although there had been legislation transforming marriage from a church-regulated sacrament into a state-sanctioned contract, this was the first act, effective January 1, 1754, to invalidate clandestine marriage. Both Charles Townsend and *The Man of Feeling* reflect the peril for women. Under ecclesiastical jurisdiction, a man could be compelled to keep a promise of marriage, even if verbal, without witnesses, or without words (Howard 1.338–39). In the world of civil marriage, Emily has no recourse with the faithless Mr. Winbrooke: The state had rendered any promise to marry, no matter how public, how written and sworn to, invalid if made by a minor without a father's approval.

The Marriage Act not only withdrew protection for the Emilys of the world but also shored up the waning authority of parents. No small concern was securing the legitimate succession of the family estate, by protecting impressionable daughters from fortune

---

[1]George Elliott Howard, *A History of Matrimonial Institutions*, 2 vols. (Univ. of Chicago Press, 1904), 1.449–50, n. 3, cited hereafter in the text.

hunters or naïve sons from designing women. If Matilda and Isabella in *The Castle of Otranto* honor the conservative order, the eighteenth century at large was witnessing the rise of "affective individualism" (so historian Lawrence Stone[2] terms it): "the dying away of the siege mentality" of medieval times, with less pressure on obedience and conformity within the family and society. This relaxation, argues Stone, spurred a "new confidence that the pursuit of happiness, best achieved by domestic affection, was the prime legitimate goal in life" and supported the culture of sentiment. Young people were ready to marry for love, whatever their parents may have in mind. The Marriage Act's strictures found support in the conduct literature for young men and women, though the trend was clearly in the modern direction.

William Cobbett (1763–1835)

In his last speech in the House of Commons, 62-year-old Attorney General Dudley Ryder spoke for the bill. So did 28-year-old Charles Townsend, winning wide acclaim, with Walpole in the chorus (Memoires, 1.340–41; see p. 242). In William Cobbett's retelling of their speeches, Ryder presents an old-fashioned view of parental authority, while Townsend, urging parental responsibility for their children's happiness, gives the view of the modern novels. Townsend also manages to expose the degree to which sentimental romance defies the class boundaries that seem so immutable in the patriarchal world of gothic romance.

from *The Parliamentary History of England, from the Earliest Period to the Year 1803* (1806–20)[1]

Debates in the Commons on the
Clandestine Marriage Bill, May 14, 1753

Mr. Attorney General *Ryder*: Sir; the Bill which has been now read a second time, is designed for putting an end to an evil which has been

---

[2]*The Family, Sex, and Marriage in England 1500–1800* (abridged ed.; New York: Harper & Row, 1979), 176, 180.

---

[1]London, T. C. Hansard, vol. 15, col. 1–3, 6, 10, 51–52, 58, 61.

long and grievously complained of, an evil by which many of our best families have often suffered, and which our laws have often endeavoured to prevent, but always hitherto without success; and yet, it is an evil which, one would think, should rarely happen, if we consider that duty and respect which children ought to show towards their parents, and that indulgence and affection parents ought to have for their children, especially in that affair of their marriage, which is generally the first step that people of all ranks make into the world, and a step upon which their future happiness, prosperity and success almost entirely depends. In this step the happiness both of the parents and children is so intimately concerned, that children ought never to make it without the approbation of their parents, nor ought the parent to refuse his approbation, when the match proposed is not such as apparently tends to the dishonour of the family, or may probably bring the ruin of his child. Yet we often find the passion called love triumphing over the duty of children to their parents, and on the other hand we sometime find the passion of pride or avarice triumphing over the duty of parents to their children. And when a young gentleman or lady happens to be born to a good fortune, they are so beset with selfish designing people, and so many arts made use of for engaging their affection, that their innocence often becomes a prey to the lowest and vilest seducer. How often have we known the heir of a good family seduced, and engaged in a clandestine marriage, perhaps with a common strumpet? How often have we known a rich heiress carried off by a man of low birth, or perhaps by an infamous sharper? What distress some of our best families have been brought into, what ruin some of their sons or daughters have been involved in, by such means, every gentleman may from his own knowledge recollect. [. . .]

Nothing can, in my opinion, Sir, be effectual for the preventing clandestine marriages of every kind, but that of declaring all such marriages null and void to all intents and purposes. This, I am persuaded, our ancestors were sensible of, but a superstitious opinion then prevailed, that when a marriage between two persons come to the age of consent[2] was once solemnized by a man in holy orders, it was so firmly established by divine law, that it could not be

---

[2]Ryder later specifies that girls at age 12 and boys at age 14 have arrived at "the age of consent" (15.7). The "superstitious opinion" is Roman Catholic law.

annulled and made void by any human law whatever. Thank God! we have in this age got the better of this, as well as we have of a great many other superstitious opinions; [. . .] Nothing can be more inconsistent with common sense than to say, that the supreme legislature of a society cannot put contracts of marriage, as well as every other contract, under what regulations they think most conducive to the good of that society.

Mr. *Charles Townsend*: As to those who are unequal with respect to fortune, they are so far from being a public evil, that they are a public benefit, because they serve to disperse the wealth of the kingdom through the whole body of the people, and to prevent the accumulating and monopolizing it into a few hands; which is an advantage to every society, especially a free and trading society. The same may be said of clandestine marriages that are unequal both as to rank and fortune; for if a lord of a good estate should marry a taylor's or a shoe-maker's daughter of good character, though not worth a groat, or if a lady of quality, entitled to a good estate, should marry such a man's son, who was of a good character, but had no fortune, it would be no disadvantage, but rather a benefit to the public, nor would there be any thing really scandalous or infamous in the marriage; because if such a daughter or son were by the industry of the father, or the gift of any relation, possessed of a plentiful fortune, neither parents nor relations would think the match dishonourable; and surely riches can never make that honourable which would otherwise be infamous, nor can poverty make that infamous, which would otherwise be no way dishonourable. Nay, I will go farther, I will say, that such marriages seldom, if ever, bring shame or misery upon the contracting parties. [. . .]

The only kind of clandestine marriages, therefore, Sir, that can be said to be a public evil, are those I have called scandalous and infamous; and those alone I think such, that are entered into between a gentleman of character and an abandoned prostitute, or a lady of character and a notorious rogue or common sharper; I mean, Sir, a sharper of low rank; for we may perhaps, have sharpers amongst us, whose addresses would be approved of even by the parents of most ladies of quality in the kingdom. [. . .]

But with regard to [women] this Bill will be a most cruel law. It is impossible to prevent an innocent credulous young creature from trusting to the solemn promises of the man she loves, and every man may find twenty reasons for convincing a young woman who loves him, of the danger of their marrying at that time. It would therefore be vain to imagine that such promises will not hereafter be made, and still more vain to imagine that they will not be too often trusted to. [. . .] As the law now stands, if a treacherous young fellow should refuse to perform such a promise, the young woman who trusted to it may sue him in the ecclesiastical court, where she may put him to his oath, and if he confesses the promise, or she can otherwise prove it, he must either marry her, or be imprisoned upon the writ *de excommunicato capiendo*.[3] But if this Bill passes into a law, she can have no relief: the statute of frauds and perjuries will be a bar to her action at common law, unless she has been so cautious as to take a promise in writing. [. . .]

I hope no gentleman will from any thing I have said suppose, that I am for encouraging children to be undutiful to their parents. I think children are in duty bound to consult their parents upon all occasions of importance, especially in that of their marriage, and even to curb their inclinations, if possible, when they find them disagreeable to their parents. But the duty is reciprocal: there is a duty owing by parents to their children, as well as by children to their parents; and an exact and affectionate performance of that duty on the side of the parent is the best way to secure it on the part of the child. If you establish a tyrannical power in the father, as you propose to do by this Bill, you will make many fathers forget that duty they owe to their children, and the consequence will be a neglect of duty on the other side, as soon as it is in their power.

Horace Walpole (1717–1797)

It is not surprising that Mackenzie would share Townsend's view that character matters more than status in a happy marriage, but it might be surprising to find Walpole in agreement. His own niece had contracted a clandestine marriage with George III's brother in 1766 but, fortunately for her, the Hardwicke Act made exceptions for the royal family

---

[3]In church law, a promise was as good as a betrothal, and a cad could be excommunicated. Such law was abrogated by Hardwicke's Act (Howard 1.385).

(Howard 449–50, n. 3). Walpole's remarks (published many years after his death, by his instruction) bitterly oppose any system of tyrannical power and unquestioning obedience, whether in the private relationship between parents and children or in the political arena.

from *Memoires of the Last Ten Years of the Reign of George the Second* (1822)[1]

Whether from mere partiality to an ordinance thus become his own, or whether in shaping a law, new views of power opened to a mind, fond of power, fond of dictating; so it was that the Chancellor [Hardwicke] gave all his attention to a statute in which he had breathed the very spirit of aristocracy and insolent nobility. It was amazing, in a country where liberty gives choice, where trade and money confer equality, and where facility of marriage had always been supposed to produce populousness, it was amazing to see a law promulged, that cramped inclination, that discountenanced matrimony, and that seemed to annex as sacred privileges to birth, as could be devised in the proudest poorest little Italian principality.[2]

Tobias Smollett (1721–1771)

Novelist Tobias Smollett echoes Townsend's sentiment about "good character" mattering more than class or fortune (Mackenzie's Harley, for instance, is a worthy, though penniless, suitor to Miss Walton). He also has the modern view of the value of money and land circulating more freely across class lines as a preventative of the sort of revolution against entrenched aristocracy that ruptured France in 1789. Moreover, as Smollett points out, Hardwicke's Act couldn't keep lovers from finding loopholes, eloping to Scotland where the Act was not in effect, or marrying without all the mandated protocols of banns (that is, public proclamation of marriage in church during several Sunday services before the event), licenses, and parental permission. By 1800, with nearly 50% of first children

---

[1]London, John Murray, vol. 1, 336–38; also in Cobbett's *History*, vol. 15, col. 13.

[2]Recall that the Castle of Otranto is in Italy.

conceived out of wedlock as officially defined by the Act,[1] lower-class communities were managing their own rituals for marriage, in defiance of the Hardwicke strictures.[2]

from Nicolas Tindal, *Continuation of The Complete History of England* (1762)[3]

The bill, when first considered in the lower-house, gave rise to a variety of debates; in which the members appeared to be divided rather according to their real sentiments, than by the rules of any political distinction. [. . .] The principal objections imported, that such restrictions on marriage would damp the spirit of love and propagation; promote mercenary matches, to the ruin of domestic happiness, as well as to the prejudice of posterity and population; impede the circulation of property, by preserving the wealth of the kingdom among a kind of aristocracy of opulent families, who would always intermarry within their own pale; subject the poor to many inconveniencies, and extraordinary expence, from the nature of the forms to be observed; and throw an additional power into the hands of the chancellor. They affirmed, that no human power had a right to dissolve a vow solemnly made in the sight of heaven; and that, in proportion as the bill prevented clandestine marriages it would encourage fornication and debauchery, insomuch as the parties, restrained from indulging their mutual passions in an honourable manner, would be tempted to gratify them by stealth, at the hazard of their reputation. [. . .] Certain it is, the abuse of clandestine marriage might have been removed upon much easier terms than those imposed upon the subject by this bill, which, after all, hath been found ineffectual.

---

[1]See Lawrence Stone, "The New Eighteenth Century," *New York Review of Books* 31.5 (March 29, 1984): 46; review essay of E. A. Wrigley, "Marriage, Fertility and Population Growth in Eighteenth-Century England," in *Marriage and Society*, ed. R. B. Outhwaite (New York: St. Martin's Press, 1981).

[2]See Douglas Hay and Nicholas Rogers, *Eighteenth-Century English Society* (New York: Oxford Univ. Press, 1997), 49.

[3]New ed., London, vol. 1, 147–49.

Fleet Marriage

Another version of clandestine marriage was the Fleet marriage, so named for the district populated by the overflow from London's too-crowded Fleet prison. Denizens were married by ministers of dubious reputation, one of whom seems to have done this 36,000 times in 30 years (Howard 1.440).

Thomas Pennant (1726–1798)

> *The carnivalesque character of Fleet marriages is captured in the selection from Thomas Penant's guidebook to London. It is a far cry from the solemn ideas of love and marriage in* The Castle of Otranto *and* The Man of Feeling.

from *Of London* (1790)[1]

In walking along the street, in my youth, on the side next to the prison, I have often been tempted by the question, *Sir, will you be pleased to walk in and be married?* Along this most lawless space was hung up the frequent sign of a male and female hand conjoined, with, *Marriages performed within*, written beneath. A dirty fellow invited you in. The parson was seen walking before his shop; a squalid profligate figure, clad in a tattered plaid night-gown, with a fiery face, and ready to couple you for a dram of gin, or roll of tobacco. Our great chancellor, lord HARDWICK, put these *demons* to flight, and saved thousands from the misery and disgrace which would be entailed by these extemporary[2] thoughtless unions.

Alexander Keith (d. 1758)

> *Many pamphlets debating the question of clandestine marriage appeared during the Parliamentary debates. Alexander Keith's offered a particularly vivid description of the moral corruption these marriages caused.*

[1]London, 208–9.
[2]Spur of the moment.

from *Observations on the Act for Preventing Clandestine Marriages* (1753)[1]

I remember once on a time, I was at a public-house in Radcliff, which was then full of sailors and their girls, there was fiddling, piping, jigging, and eating; at length, one of the tars starts up, and says, D—n ye Jack, I will be married just now; I will have my partner; and B—d we will get a boy that shall kill the French King.[2] The joke took, and in less than two hours ten couples set out for the Flete. I staid their return. They returned in coaches; five women in each coach; the tars some running before, others riding on the coach-box, and others behind. The cavalcade being over, the couples went up into an upper room, where they concluded the evening with great jollity. The next time I went that way, I called on my landlord, and asked him concerning this marriage-adventure; he at first stared at me, but recollecting he said, those things were so frequent, that he hardly took any notice of them; for added he, it is common thing, when a fleet comes in, to have two or three hundred marriages in a week's time, among the sailors.

Conduct Literature

The conduct manuals written by sober fathers (domestic and ecclesiastical) for young women exhorted obedience to husbands and parents. Although the sentimental novel was widely censured for stuffing young ladies' heads with dangerous sentimental nonsense, there was also a hope that its virtuous characters could set an example and its foolish or villainous characters convey a warning.

George Savile, Lord Halifax (1633–1695)

In this popular treatise (reprinted throughout the eighteenth century), Lord Halifax means to save any daughter from embarrassing her father by making "an ill Figure."

---

[1]London, 24.

[2]Having just contended with France in America (1744–48), England was about to embark on another war with France.

from *The Lady's New-Years Gift: or,*
Advice to a Daughter (1688)[1]

Husband

It is one of the Disadvantages belonging to your *Sex*, that young Women are seldom permitted to make their own *Choice*; their Friends Care and Experience are thought safer Guides to them, than their own *Fancies*; and their *Modesty* often forbiddeth them to refuse when their Parents recommend, though their *inward Consent* may not entirely go along with it: In this case there remaineth nothing for them to do, but to endeavour to make that easie which falleth to their *Lot*, and by a wise use of every thing they may dislike in a *Husband*, turn that by degrees to be very supportable[2] which, if neglected, might in time beget an *Aversion*.

You must first lay it down for a Foundation in general That there is *Inequality* in the *Sexes*, and that for the better Oecomony of the World, the *Men*, who are to be the Law-givers, had the largest share of *Reason* bestowed upon them; by which means your Sex is better prepar'd for the *Compliance* that is necessary for the better performance of those *Duties* which seem'd to be most properly assign'd to it. This looks a little uncourtly at the first appearance; but upon examination it will be found that *Nature* is so far from being unjust to you, that she is partial on your side. [. . .] You have more strength in your *Looks* than we have in our *Laws*; and more power by your *Tears*, than we have by our *Arguments*.

It is true, that the *Laws* of *Marriage*, run in a harsher stile towards your *Sex*. *Obey* is an ungentle word. [. . .] It appeareth reasonable, that there might be an *Exemption* for extraordinary Women, from ordinary Rules. [. . .] Some Wives might [. . .] plead, [. . .] where Nature is so kind, as to raise them above the *level* of their own Sex, that they might have *Relief*, and obtain a *Mitigation* in their own particular, of a Sentence which was given generally against *Woman-kind*. [. . .] But the Answer is, in short, That the *Institution* of *Marriage* is too sacred to admit of a *Liberty of Objection* to it; that the Supposition of your being the weaker Sex, having without all doubt a good Foundation, maketh it reasonable to subject it to the *Masculine Dominion*.

[1]London, 5, 24–30.
[2]Bearable.

James Fordyce (1720–1796)

James Fordyce's Sermon reveals anxiety about the moral propriety and influence of novels on the young woman: firing her imagination, they might corrupt her virtue.

from "Sermon IV: On Female Virtue" (1765)[1]

Avoid Dangerous Connexions. If that be not done, what is there on earth, or in heaven, that can save you? Of miraculous interposition I think not at present. She can have no right to expect it, who throws herself into the broad way of temptation. What those dangerous connexions are, it may not be always easy to explain, when it becomes a question in real life. [. . .] The man that behaves with open rudeness, the man that avowedly laughs at virtue, the man that impudently pleads for vice; such a man is to be shunned like a rattle-snake. [. . .]

The fatal poison to virtue, which is conveyed by Profligate and by Improper Books. When entertainment is made the vehicle of instruction, nothing surely can be more harmless, agreeable, or useful. To prohibit young minds the perusal of any writings, where Wisdom addresses the affections in the language of the imagination, may be sometimes well meant, but must be always injudicious. [. . .] Happy indeed, beyond the vulgar storytelling tribe, and highly to be praised, is he who, to fine sensibilities and a lively fancy superadding clear and comprehensive views of men and manners, writes to the heart with simplicity and chasteness, through a series of adventures well conducted, and relating chiefly to scenes in ordinary life; where the solid joys of Virtue, and her sacred sorrows, are strongly contrasted with the hollowness and the horrors of vice; where, by little unexpected yet natural incidents of the tender and domestic kind, so peculiarly fitted to touch the soul, the most important lessons are impressed, and the most generous sentiments awakened. [. . .]

Amongst the few works of this kind which I have seen, I cannot but look on those of Mr. Richardson as well entitled to the first rank; [. . .] an author, to whom your sex are under singular obligations for his uncommon attention to their best interests; but

[1]From *Sermons to Young Women*, 2 vols., 3rd corrected ed. (London, 1776), 128–29, 137, 144–53, 155–57.

particularly for presenting, in a character sustained throughout with inexpressible pathos and delicacy, the most exalted standard of female excellence that was ever held up to their imitation.[2] [. . .] Beside the beautiful productions of that incomparable pen, there seem to me to be very few, in the style of Novel, that you can read with safety, and yet fewer that you can read with advantage. [. . .] A sweet sensibility, a charming tenderness, a delightful anguish, exalted generosity, heroic worth, and refinement of thought; how seldom are these best ingredients of virtuous love mixed with any judgment or care in the composition of their principal characters!

In the old Romance[3] the passion appeared with all its enthusiasm. But then it was the enthusiasm of honour; for love and honour were the same. The men were sincere, magnanimous, and noble; the women were patterns of chastity, dignity, and affection. They were only to be won by real heroes; and this title was founded in protecting, not in betraying, the sex. The proper merit with them consisted in the display of disinterested goodness, undaunted fortitude, and unalterable fidelity. [. . .] The times in which we live are in no danger of adopting a system of romantic virtue. [. . .] What has a modish[4] young gentleman to do with those antiquated notions of gallantry, that were connected with veneration for female excellence, invincible honour, and unspotted fame? [. . .]

To come back to the species of writing which so many young women are apt to doat upon, the offspring of our present Novelists, [. . .]—Is this a kind of reading calculated to improve the principles, or preserve the Sobriety, of female minds? How much are those women to be pitied, that have no wise parents or faithful tutors to direct them in relation to the books which are, or which are not, fit for them to read! How much are those parents and tutors to be commended, who with particular solicitude watch over them in so important a concern!

[2]Throughout vol. 1 of Samuel Richardson's *Pamela; or, Virtue Rewarded* (1741), heroine Pamela resists a Lord's attempt first to prostitute and then to rape her. Her virtue is rewarded with his hand in marriage.

[3]The comparison of medieval Romances (stories often in verse) to modern "romance" is also made by Clara Reeve in *The Progress of Romance* (see p. 218) and Walpole's second preface to *Otranto* (see p. 7).

[4]Fashionable.

Cultures of Feeling

Often called "The Age of Reason," the eighteenth century was also an era of sensibility: of being exquisitely alive to sensation and exquisitely sensitive to the feelings of others. The "cult of sensibility" was given a philosophical foundation by the writings of Francis Hutcheson; by Adam Smith, whose *Theory of Moral Sentiments* was just as influential as his treatise on economy, *The Wealth of Nations*; and by a wealth of novelists who took their patterns of character from these philosophers: not only Mackenzie but also his comrades in sentiment, Samuel Richardson, Jean-Jacques Rousseau, and Laurence Sterne. This new "aristocracy of feeling" (so Herman Melville termed it[1]) set new standards for developing and discerning moral character, standards of particular consequence for the evaluation of women, traditionally viewed, but not always admired, for their susceptibility of tender feeling.

Francis Hutcheson (1694–1746)

Francis Hutcheson argues that humans have a natural "moral sense" and that benevolence toward others is completely natural and only need be exhibited, not taught, to be compelling. The excerpt presented here shows the grounds for Harley's interest in phrenology (the determination of moral character from the shape of a skull). Mackenzie may mock this pseudo-science in order to credit the more moderate argument that goodness can be seen in face, figure, and demeanor, especially of women.

[1]To Nathaniel Hawthorne, June 1851, *The Letters of Herman Melville* (Yale Univ. Press, 1960), 126.

from *An Inquiry Concerning the Original of Our Ideas of Virtue or Moral Good* (1725)[1]

from Introduction.

Some Actions have to Men an *immediate Goodness*; or, that by a *superior Sense*, which I call a *Moral one*, we *approve* the Actions of others, and perceive them to be their Perfection and Dignity, and are determin'd to love the Agent; a like Perception we have in reflecting on such Actions of our own, without any View of *natural Advantage* from them.

I.viii. "That as the AUTHOR of *Nature*[2] has determin'd us to receive, by our *external Senses*, pleasant or disagreeable Ideas of Objects, according as they are useful or hurtful to our Bodys; and to receive from *uniform Objects* the Pleasures of *Beauty* and *Harmony* [. . .]; in the same manner he has given us a MORAL SENSE, to direct our Actions, and to give us still *nobler Pleasures*. [. . .]"

We are not to imagine, that this *moral Sense*, more than the other Senses, supposes any *innate Ideas,*[3] *Knowledge*, or *practical Proposition*: We mean by it only a *Determination of our Minds to receive the simple Ideas of Approbation or Condemnation, from Actions observ'd, antecedent to any Opinions of Advantage or Loss to redound to our selves from them.* [. . .] Virtue is then called *amiable* or *lovely*, from raising the *Good-will* or *Love* in Spectators toward the Agent; and not from the Agent's perceiving the virtuous Temper to be advantageous to him, or desiring to obtain it under that View. [. . .]

II.x. Having remov'd these *false Springs of virtuous Actions*, let us next establish the *true ones*, viz. *some Determination of our Nature to study the Good of others; or some Instinct, antecedent to all Reason from Interest, which influences us to the Love of others*; even as the *moral Sense*, above explain'd, determines us to *approve* the Actions which flow from *this Love* in ourselves or others. [. . .]

V.viii. Let us next consider another determination of our *Mind*, which strongly proves *Benevolence* to be *natural* to us,

---

[1]4th corr. ed., 1738, London, 109–10, 128–29, 145, 159–60, 239, 251–52.

[2]In the Deist notion, God does not actively intervene in human affairs, but rather creates the world and then sets it into motion according to rational laws.

[3]Hutcheson agrees with John Locke (1632–1704) that the mind at birth has no innate ideas but is a *tabula rasa*, a blank slate on which experience gets inscribed. This was an important notion for contesting the aristocratic view that those born of noble blood had innate intellectual and spiritual superiority.

and that is COMPASSION; by which we are dispos'd to study the *Interest* of others, without any Views of *private Advantage*. This needs little Illustration. Every Mortal is made uneasy by any grievous Misery he sees another involv'd in, unless the Person be imagin'd *evil* in a *moral Sense*: Nay, it is almost impossible for us to be unmov'd, even in that Case. *Advantage* may make us do a cruel Action, or may overcome *Pity*; but it scarce ever extinguishes it. A sudden Passion of *Hatred* or *Anger* may represent a person as absolutely evil, and so extinguish pity; but when the Passion is over, it often returns. Another *disinterested* View may even in cold blood overcome *Pity*; such as *Love* to our *Country*, or *Zeal* for *Religion*. *Persecution* is generally occasioned by *Love* of *Virtue*, and a *Desire* of the *eternal Happiness* of *Mankind*, altho' our *Folly* makes us choose absurd Means to promote it. [. . .]

VI.iii. There is a farther Consideration which must not be pass'd over, concerning the EXTERNAL BEAUTY of Persons, which all allow to have a great Power over human Minds. Now it is some apprehended *Morality*, some natural or imagin'd Indication of *concomitant Virtue*, which gives it this powerful Charm above all other kinds of *Beauty*. Let us consider the Characters of *Beauty*, which are commonly admir'd in Countenances, and we shall find them to be *Sweetness, Mildness, Majesty, Dignity, Vivacity, Humility, Tenderness, Good-nature*; that is, that certain *Airs, Proportions, je ne sais quoy's*,[4] are natural Indications of such Virtues, or of abilitys or Dispositions toward them. As we observ'd above, of *Misery* or *Distress*, appearing in Countenances; so it is certain, almost all *habitual Dispositions* of *Mind* form the Countenance in such a manner, as to give some Indications of them to the Spectator. Our *violent* Passions are obvious at first View in the Countenance; so that sometimes no Art can conceal them: and smaller Degrees of them give some less obvious Turns to the Face, which an accurate Eye will observe. Now, when the *natural Air* of a Face approaches to that which any Passion would form it unto, we make a Conjecture from this concerning the *leading Disposition* of a Person's *Mind*. [. . .]

---

[4]*I know not what*; a French phrase for that quality toward which language can merely gesture.

Samuel Richardson (1689–1761)

This Preface to the first, anonymous edition of Pamela *was reprinted immediately in the* Weekly Miscellany, *setting the didactic paradigm for the literature of sensibility—one against which not only the characters but also the readers of* The Man *of* Feeling *may be measured. In the Preface, Samuel Richardson pretends to be the editor of the letters that comprise* Pamela.

Preface to *Pamela or, Virtue Rewarded* (1740)[1]

IF to *Divert* and *Entertain,* and at the same time to *Instruct,*[2] and *Improve* the Minds of the YOUTH of both *Sexes*:

IF to inculcate *Religion* and *Morality* in so easy and agreeable a manner, as shall render them equally *delightful* and *profitable* to the *younger Class* of Readers, as well as worthy of the Attention of Persons of *maturer* Years and Understandings:

IF to set forth in the most exemplary Lights, the *Parental,* the *Filial,* and the *Social* Duties, and that from *low* to *high* Life:

IF to paint VICE in its proper Colours, to make it *deservedly Odious*; and to set VIRTUE in its own amiable Light, to make it *truly Lovely*:

IF to draw Characters *justly,* and to support them *equally*:

IF to raise a Distress from *natural* Causes, and to excite Compassion from *proper* Motives:

IF to teach the Man of *Fortune* how to use it; the Man of *Passion* how to subdue it; and the Man of *Intrigue,* how, gracefully, and with Honour to himself, to *reclaim*:[3]

IF to give *practical* Examples, worthy to be followed in the most *critical* and *affecting* Cases, by the modest *Virgin,* the chaste *Bride,* and the obliging *Wife*:

IF to effect all these good Ends, in so probable,[4] so natural, so lively a manner, as shall engage the Passions of every sensible Reader, and strongly interest them in the edifying Story:

---

[1]London, iii–vi.

[2]Horace's injunction in *Ars Poetica* (1st c. B.C.E.) is that poets are those who mix profit with pleasure ("qui miscuit utile dulci," 343), instruction with delight.

[3]Reform.

[4]Realistic.

AND all without raising a *single Idea* throughout the Whole, that shall shock the exactest Purity, even in those tender Instances where the exactest Purity would be most apprehensive:

IF these, (embellished with a great Variety of entertaining Incidents) be laudable or worthy Recommendations of any Work, the Editor of the following Letters, which have their Foundation in *Truth* and *Nature*, ventures to assert, that all these desirable Ends are obtained in these Sheets: And as he is therefore confident of the favourable Reception which he boldly bespeaks for this little Work; he thinks any further *Preface* or *Apology* for[5] it, unnecessary: And the rather for two Reasons, 1st. Because he can Appeal from his own Passions, (which have been uncommonly moved in persuing these engaging Scenes) to the Passions of *Every one* who shall read them with the least Attention: And, in the next place, because an *Editor* may reasonably be supposed to judge with an Impartiality which is rarely to be met with in an *Author* towards his own Works.

Adam Smith (1723–1790)

Preceding his influential Wealth of Nations *by 17 years, Adam Smith's* Theory of Moral Sentiments *describes the dynamics of sympathetic identification with the suffering of others. Thus Mackenzie's Harley, hearing the story about the invasion of a press-gang into the Edwards's home, attempts to draw Edwards's sword, as if combating a present enemy (see p. 175).*

from *Theory of Moral Sentiments* (1759)[1]

I.i.1 *Of Sympathy.* How selfish soever man may be supposed, there are evidently some principles in his nature, which interest him in the fortune of others, and render their happiness necessary to him, though he derives nothing from it except the pleasure of feeling it. Of this kind is pity or compassion, the emotion which we feel for the misery of others, when we either see it, or are made to conceive it in a very lively manner. That we often derive sorrow from the sor-

---

[5]Defense of.

---

[1]London, 1–3.

row of others is too obvious to require any instances to prove it; for this sentiment, like all other original passions of human nature, is by no means confined to the virtuous and humane, though they perhaps may feel it with the most exquisite sensibility. The greatest ruffian, the most hardened violator of the laws of society, is not altogether without it.

As we have no immediate experience of what other men feel, we can form no idea of the manner in which they are affected, but by conceiving what we ourselves should feel in the like situation. Though our brother is upon the rack, as long as we are at our ease, our senses will never inform us of what he suffers. They never did and never can carry us beyond our own persons, and it is by the imagination only that we can form any conception of what are his sensations. Neither can that faculty help us to this any other way, than by representing to us what would be our own, if we were in his case. It is the impressions of our own senses only, not those of his, which our imaginations copy. By the imagination we place ourselves in his situation, we conceive ourselves enduring all the same torments, we enter as it were into his body, and become in some measure him, and thence form some idea of his sensations, and even feel something which, though weaker in degree, is not altogether unlike them. His agonies, when they are thus brought home to ourselves, when we have thus adopted and made them our own, begin at last to affect us, and we then tremble and shudder at the thought of what he feels. For as to be in pain or distress of any kind excites the most excessive sorrow, so to conceive or imagine that we are in it, excites some degree of the same emotion, in proportion to the vivacity or dullness of the conception.

Jean-Jacques Rousseau (1712–1778)

In Rousseau and the Republic of Virtue *(1986), Carol Blum proposes that Rousseau's sensibility of "pleasurable weeping" was less an exercise of moral sympathy than a "sensual outlet" that substituted for sexual desire (48). In the passage presented here, Rousseau describes his feelings as he sits with women in an audience viewing his opera* Le Devin du Village *(The Cunning-Man). Such complexities of sympathy seem to surround Mackenzie's Harley as well.*

Frontispiece to "Elegy Written in a Country Church Yard." Richard Bentley described his drawing: "A Gothic gateway in ruins with the emblems of nobility on one side; on the other, the implements and employments of the Poor. Thro' the arch appears a church-yard, and village-church built out of the remains of an abbey. A countryman showing an epitaph to a passenger" (*Designs by Mr. R. Bentley, for Six Poems by Mr. T. Gray*, London, 1775).

from *Confessions* (w. 1764–70; p. 1782–89)[1]

I heard about me a whispering of women, who seemed to me as beautiful as angels. They said to each other in a low voice: This is charming: That is ravishing: There is not a sound which does not go to the heart. The pleasure of giving this emotion to so many amiable persons, moved me to tears; and these I could not contain in the first duo, when I remarked that I was not the only person who wept. [. . .] However, I am certain the voluptuousness of the sex[2] was more predominant than the vanity of the author, and had none but men been present, I certainly should not have had the incessant desire I felt of catching on my lips the delicious tears I had caused to flow.

Henry Mackenzie (1745–1831)

As editor and main contributor of two journals, The Mirror *(1779–80) and* The Lounger *(1785–87), Mackenzie was called "the Scottish Addison," an epithet repeated by Robert Burns in 1787 and by Walter Scott in his dedication of* Waverley *to Mackenzie in 1814 (Thompson 178). Mackenzie shares the concerns of Samuel Johnson and Clara Reeve about the moral impact of novels (see pp. 215 and 218), even worrying about the effects of such virtuously sentimental novels as* The Man of Feeling.

from *The Lounger* 20 (June 18, 1785)[1]

The principal danger of novels, as forming a mistaken and pernicious system of morality, seems to me to arise from that contrast between one virtue or excellence and another, that war of duties which is to be found in many of them, particularly in that species called the sentimental. [. . .] In the enthusiasm of sentiment there is much the same danger as in the enthusiasm of religion, of substituting certain impulses and feelings of what may be called a visionary kind, in the place of real practical duties, which in morals, as in the-

---

[1]Translation here: *The Confessions of J. J. Rousseau, Citizen of Geneva,* trans. [anonymous] (Dublin: P. Byrne, et. al., 1791), 1.156–57.

[2]Of women; a modern translation replaces "the voluptuousness of the sex" with "sexual sensuality.".

---

[1]Rpt. *Works* (1808), 5.181–83.

ology, we might not improperly denominate good works. In morals, as in religion, there are not wanting instances of refined sentimentalists, who are contented with talking of virtues which they never practise, who pay in words what they owe in actions; or, perhaps, what is fully as dangerous, who open their minds to impressions which never have any effect upon their conduct, but are considered as something foreign to and distinct from it.

Alexander Bicknell (d. 1796)

> *Not all people in the eighteenth century took sensibility seriously, nor everyone all the time. Himself a novelist in the sentimental vein, Alexander Bicknell here comments on a caricature, "Evening; or, the Man of Feeling," drawn by Henry William Bunbury.*

from *Painting Personified: or, the Caricatures and Sentimental Pictures, of the Principal Artists of the Present Times, Fancifully Explained* (London, 1790)[1]

From the humorous Print referred to, we learn, that what we term *Feeling*, does not always mean, according to its common Acceptation, a tender, sympathizing Attention to the Misfortunes of others; but that it is a *fundamental* Principle in ourselves, which confines our Attention to *ourselves only*; and instead of requiring an Exertion of the humane and charitable Propensities to give Ease to the painful Excitations occasioned by it, needs only the Aid of a little *white Diachylon*,[2] spread on a convenient Quantity of Linen or Leather.

So that according to the Painter's *nouvelle* depictured Syllogism, he who from the continual Friction created by a jolting Horse, finds, after a long Ride, the cutaneous Covering of the Part which has been in Contact with the Saddle displaced, and a troublesome Irritation brought on thereby, may as well lay Claim to the enviable Title of a *Man of Feeling*, as he who, when he hears a Tale of Woe, sees an Instance of it, perceives the pearly Drop, impregnated with Compassion, starting from his Eye, and is not at Ease till he has contributed all in his Power towards the Relief of the Sufferer.

---

[1]London, 1.151–53.

[2]Salve for saddle sores.

The Novelty of the Thought, and Humour of the Design, compensate for the Oddity of the Tenet. It would, however, require the acutest Argument of that acute Arguer, *Mr. Shandy*, to prove that a *chaffed Backside* constitutes *the Man of Feeling*.

Laurence Sterne (1713–1768)

Writer and Anglican clergyman Laurence Sterne was largely unknown until the publication, in 1759, of the first parts of Tristram Shandy, *a rambling, digressive mixture of satire and sentiment. Published in installments until 1767, its later volumes revised into Sterne's A Sentimental Journey (1768),* Tristram Shandy *often parodies the very emotions it extols. The thin plot line involves the birth and growth of the hero, but, by volume 4, Sterne has recounted only one day. In volume 6, Walter Shandy, Tristram's father, talks about how to educate Tristram with his military brother Toby and parson Yorick. You can see from the following excerpt why Alexander Bicknell (see the previous selection) invokes Walter Shandy, Tristram's father, for having those reasoning powers most capable of satirizing the sensibility according to which his brother Toby lives.*

from *The Life and Opinions of Tristram Shandy, Gentleman* (1762)[1]

from Chapter V

You see 'tis high time, said my father, addressing himself equally to my uncle Toby and Yorick, to take this young creature out of these women's hands, and put him into those of a private governor.[2] [. . .] Now as I consider the person who is to be about my son, as the mirror in which he is to view himself from morning to night, and by which he is to adjust his looks, his carriage, and perhaps the inmost sentiments of his heart—I would have one, *Yorick*, if possible, polished at all points, fit for my child to look into.—This is very good sense, quoth my uncle *Toby* to himself. [. . .]

The governor that I make choice of shall neither lisp, or squint, or wink, or talk loud, or look fierce, or foolish;—or bite his lips, or

[1]London, 6.11–16, 37, 39–46.
[2]Tutor.

grind his teeth, or speak through his nose, or pick it, or blow it with his fingers.—

He shall neither walk fast,—or slow, or fold his arms,—for that is laziness;—or hang them down,—for that is folly; or hide them in his pocket, for that is nonsense.—

He shall neither strike, nor pinch, or tickle,—or bite, or cut his nails, or hawk, or spit, or snift, or drum with his feet or fingers in company;—nor (according to *Erasmus*) shall he speak to any one in making water,—nor shall he point to carrion or excrement.—Now this is all nonsense again, quoth my uncle *Toby* to himself.

I will have [my son's tutor], continued my father, cheerful, faceté,[3] jovial; at the same time, prudent, attentive to business, vigilant, acute, argute,[4] inventive, quick in resolving doubts and speculative questions;—he shall be wise and judicious, and learned:—And why not humble, and moderate, and gentle tempered, and good? said *Yorick*:—And why not, cried my uncle *Toby*, free, and generous, and bountiful, and brave?—He shall, my dear *Toby*, replied my father, getting up and shaking him by his hand.—Then, brother *Shandy*, answered my uncle *Toby*, raising himself off the chair, and laying down his pipe to take hold of my father's other hand,—I humbly beg I may recommend poor *Le Fever*'s son to you;—a tear of joy of the first water sparkled in my uncle *Toby*'s eye,—and another, the fellow to it, in the corporal's, as the proposition was made;—you will see why when you read *Le Fever*'s story. [*A soldier traveling from Ireland to join his regiment in Flanders, accompanied by his son, Le Fever falls ill while staying at an inn near uncle Toby's house; the landlord comes to beg for a glass of sack to help the man—Toby sends him away with bottles and asks his servant corporal Trim to investigate.*]

from Chapter VIII. *The story of* Le Fever *continued*.

It was to my uncle *Toby*'s eternal honour,—though I tell it only for the sake of those, who, when coop'd in betwixt a natural and a positive law,[5] know not for their souls, which way in the world to turn themselves. [. . .]

[3]Facetious.
[4]Shrewd.
[5]Between moral feelings and moral laws.

Thou has left this matter short, said my uncle *Toby* to the corporal. [. . .]—In the first place, when though madest an offer of my services to *Le Fever*, [. . .] thou didst not make an offer of my purse; because, had he stood in need, thou knowest, *Trim*, he had been as welcome to it as myself.—Your honour knows, said the corporal, I had no orders;—True, quoth my uncle *Toby*,—thou didst very right, *Trim*, as a soldier,—but certainly very wrong as a man.

In the second place, for which, indeed, thou hast the same excuse, continued my uncle *Toby*,—when thou offeredst him whatever was in my house,—thou shouldst have offered him my house too: [. . .] Thou art an excellent nurse thyself, *Trim*,—and what with thy care of him, and the old woman's,[6] and his boy's, and mine together, we might recruit him again at once, and set him upon his legs.—

—In a fortnight or three weeks, added my uncle *Toby*, smiling,—he might march. [. . .]—An' please your honour, said the corporal, he will never march, but to his grave. [. . .] He'll drop at last, and what will become of his boy?—He shall not drop, said my uncle *Toby*, firmly.—A-well-o'day,—do what we can for him, said *Trim*, maintaining his point,—the poor soul will die:—He shall not die, by G—, cried my uncle *Toby*.

—The ACCUSING SPIRIT which flew up to heaven's chancery with the oath,[7] blush'd as he gave it in;—and the RECORDING ANGEL as he wrote it down, dropp'd a tear upon the word, and blotted it out[8] for ever. [. . .]

from Chapter X. *The story of* Le Fever *concluded.*

The sun looked bright the morning after, to every eye in the village but *Le Fever*'s and his afflicted son's; the hand of death press'd heavy upon his eye-lids. [. . .] My uncle Toby, who had rose up an hour before his wonted time, entered the lieutenant's room, and without preface or apology, sat himself down upon the chair by the bed-side. [. . .]

—You shall go home directly, *Le Fever*, said my uncle *Toby*, to my house,—and we'll send for a doctor to see what's the matter, [. . .]—and the corporal shall be your nurse;—and I'll be your servant, *Le Fever*.

[6]Toby's servant.
[7]With a record of Toby's "by G—"; taking God's name as a casual oath is a profanity.
[8]Erased it.

There was a frankness in my uncle *Toby*,—not the *effect* of familiarity,—but the *cause* of it,—which let you at once into his soul, and showed you the goodness of his nature; to this, there was something in his looks, and voice, and manner, superadded, which eternally beckoned to the unfortunate to come and take shelter under him; so that before my uncle *Toby* had half finished the kind offers he was making to the father, had the son insensibly pressed up close to his knees, and had taken hold of the breast of his coat, and was pulling it towards him.—The blood and spirits of *Le Fever*, which were waxing cold and slow within him, and were retreating to their last citadel, the heart,—rallied back,—the film forsook his eyes for a moment,—he looked up wishfully in my uncle *Toby*'s face,—then cast a look upon his boy,—and that *ligament*, fine as it was,—was never broken.—[. . .] My uncle *Toby*, with young *Le Fever* in his hand, attended the poor lieutenant, as chief mourners, to his grave.

What the Reviewer_d Said

The Ca_dtle of Otranto

The author named in the first edition, "Onuphrio Muralto," drew attention, and the name of "H. W." (clearly Horace Walpole) in the second edition increased interest. The reviewer (unsigned) suspicious of the original ruse is more positive in his second review than was noted poet and translator John Langhorne, who was duped, and whose second review reveals his anger over the deceit. The first reviewer also applauds Walpole's patriotism.

Critical Review 19 (January 1765): 50–51

The driving force behind The Critical Review, *a Tory and Church paper, was Tobias Smollett. Editor from 1756 to 1763, he intended to make it into "an Academy of the Belles Lettres," as he said in a letter to a friend. The following two reviews were published anonymously.*

The ingenious translator of this *very curious* performance informs that it was found in the library of an ancient catholic family in the north of England: that it was printed at Naples, in the black letter, in the year 1529; and that the stile is of the purest Italian: he also conjectures, that if the story was written near the time when it is supposed to have happened, it must have been between 1095, the aera of the first crusade, and 1243, the date of the last, or not long afterwards.

[*Reviewer quotes and paraphrases the opening paragraph of the first preface.*]

Such is the character of this work given us by its judicious translator; but whether he speaks seriously or ironically, we neither know nor care. The publication of any work, at this time, in England, composed of such rotten materials, is a phænomenon we cannot account for. That our readers may form some idea of the absurdity of its contents, we are to inform them that Manfred, prince of Otranto, had only one son, a youth about fifteen years of age, who on the day appointed for his marriage was "dashed to pieces, and almost buried under an enormous helmet, an hundred times more large than any casque ever made for human being, and shaded with a proportionable quantity of black feathers." This helmet, it seems, resembled that upon a statue of Alfonso the Good, one of the former princes of Otranto, whose dominions Manfred usurped; and therefore the helmet, or the resemblance of it, by way of poetical justice, dashed out his son's brains.

The above wonder is amongst the least of the wonderful things in this story. A picture comes out of its pannel, and stalks through the room, to dissuade Manfred from marrying the princess who had been betrothed to his son. It even utters deep sighs, and heaves its breasts. We cannot help thinking that this circumstance is some presumption that the castle of Otranto is a modern fabrick;[1] for we doubt much whether pictures were fixed in pannels before the year 1243. We shall not affront our reader's understanding so much as to describe the other monstrosities of this story; but, excepting those absurdities, the characters are well marked, and the narrative kept up with surprising spirit and propriety. The catastrophe[2] is most wretched. Manfred stabs his own daughter inadvertently, and she dies. The true heir of Alfonso's throne is discovered, whose name is Theodore. Manfred relents and repents, and at last the whole moral of the story turns out to be, "That the *sins* of the fathers are visited on their children to the third and fourth generation."[3]

[1]Construction.
[2]Plot climax.
[3]Cited in *Otranto* (p. 5).

Critical Review 19 (June 1765): 469

We have already reviewed the *Castle of Otranto* and we then spoke of it in terms pretty near the character given by the author. He solves, by his preface to this edition, the phænomenon for which we could not account, by his diffidence[1] as to his success; and he asks pardon of his readers, for having offered it to them under the borrowed personage of a translator. He says that it is an attempt to blend the two kinds of romance, the ancient and the modern; and besides many ingenious reasons to justify his undertaking, he brings the authority of Shakespear's practice, who, in his *Hamlet* and *Julius Caesar*, (he might have added many other of his plays) has blended humour and clumsy jests with dignity and solemnity.

Notwithstanding the high opinion we have of this writer's acquaintance with whatever relates to his subject, we cannot but think if Shakespear had possessed the critical knowledge of modern times, he would have kept these two kinds of writing distinct, if the prepossessions and habits of the age could have suffered[2] him.

We are pleased with the just freedom with which this writer has animadverted[3] on Voltaire, who, while he is apologizing for the ignorance of the French noblesse in Corneille's time, makes Robert Dudley and the earl of Leicester, queen Elizabeth's favourite, different persons. We applaud the noble warmth with which our author has expressed in defence of Shakepear against Voltaire, who, he says, is a genius, but not of Shakespear's magnitude. We are sorry this ingenious gentleman has put those two names in the same sentence. Voltaire is so far from being a genius, that he is not a poet of the first magnitude, even in his own country, the most fruitful in poetry, but the most barren in genius (if we except Germany) of any perhaps under the sun.

We have thought this tribute of praise due to the noble spirit which Mr. W. has shown in defence of the glory of this country, against a Frenchman, who, in poetry, never could arrive so high as even to rival the imperfections of that divine writer.

---

[1]Distrust.
[2]Allowed.
[3]Commented critically.

[John Langhorne], *The Monthly Review* 32 (February 1765): 97–98

> *Founded by the nonconformist Ralph Griffiths,* The Monthly Review *was sympathetic to progressive causes. Country rector, translator of Plutarch, and author in his own right, John Langhorne (1735–79) wrote over 300 reviews for* The Monthly *between 1761 and 1768. William Wordsworth deeply admired Langhorne's poem* The Country Justice *(1774–77).*

Those who can digest the absurdities of the Gothic fiction, and bear with the machinery of ghosts and goblins, may hope, at least, for considerable entertainment from the performance before us: for it is written with no common pen; the language is accurate and elegant; the characters are highly finished; and the disquisitions into human manners, passions, and pursuits, indicate the keenest penetration, and the most perfect knowledge of mankind. The Translator, in his Preface, informs us that the original 'was found [. . . .]

[*Langhorne quotes the first preface, from the beginning up to "the mind is kept up in a constant vicissitude of interesting passions."*]

The natural prejudice which a translator[1] entertains in favour of his original, has not carried this gentleman beyond the bounds of truth; and his criticisms on his Author bear equal marks of taste and candour. The principal defect of this performance does not remain unnoticed. That unchristian doctrine of visiting the sins of the fathers upon the children, is certainly, under our present system, not only a very useless, but a very insupportable moral, and yet it is almost the only one deducible from this story. Nor is it at all rendered more tolerable through the insinuation that such evils might be diverted by devotion to St. Nicholas; for there the good canon was evidently preaching in favour of his own houshold. However, as a work of genius, evincing great dramatic powers, and exhibiting fine views of nature, the *Castle of Otranto* may still be read with pleasure. To give the Reader an analysis of the story, would be to introduce him to a company of skeletons; to refer him to the book will be to recommend him to an assemblage of beautiful pictures.

---

[1]This is said on the supposition that the work really is a translation, as pretended [Langhorne's note].

[John Langhorne], *The Monthly Review* 32 (May 1765): 394

When this book was published as a translation from an old Italian romance, we had the pleasure of distinguishing in it the marks of genius, and many beautiful characteristic paintings; we were dubious, however, concerning the antiquity of the work upon several considerations, but being willing to find some excuse for the absurd and monstrous fictions it contained, we wished to acquiesce in the declaration of the title-page, that it was really a translation from an ancient writer. While we considered it as such, we could readily excuse its preposterous phenomena, and consider them as sacrifices to a gross and unenlightened age.—But when, as in this edition, the *Castle of Otranto* is declared to be a modern performance, that indulgence we afforded to the foibles of a supposed antiquity, we can by no means extend to the singularity of a false taste in a cultivated period of learning. It is, indeed, more than strange, that an Author,[1] of refined and polished genius, should be an advocate for re-establishing the barbarous superstitions of Gothic devilism! *Incredulus odi*[2] is, or ought to be a charm against all such infatuation. Under the same banner of singularity he attempts to defend all the *trash* of Shakespeare, and what that great genius evidently threw out as a necessary sacrifice to that idol the *cæcum vulgus*,[3] he would adopt in the worship of the true God of Poetry.

Horace Walpole, Letter in Reply to Mme. Du Deffand (March 1767)[1]

Mme. Du Deffand had told Walpole that the rage in Paris was Le Château d'Otrante, par Horace Walpole.

Someone has therefore translated my *Castle of Otranto*; it was done apparently to hold me up to ridicule; fine!—hold to your course of not

---

[1]From the initials, H. W. in this edition, and the beauty of the impression, there is no room to doubt that it is the production of Strawberry-Hill [Langhorne's note].

[2]"I disbelieve and hate" (Horace, *Ars Poetica* 188).

[3]Blind crowd.

[1]From *Letters of the Marquise du Deffand to the Hon. Horace Walpole*, ed. Mary Berry (London, 1810), 130–31, n. 2; my translation.

discussing it at all; let fall the criticisms; they do not make me angry; I didn't write it for this century, which wants only *cold reason*. I admit to you, *ma Petite*,[2] and you will find me more crazy than ever, that of all my works this is the only one that pleased me; I let run my imagination; visions and passions warmed me. I wrote it despite the rules, the criticisms, and the *philosophes*;[3] and it seems to me that nothing is worth more. I am even persuaded that some time from now, when the sense of taste takes back the place that philosophy now occupies, my poor *Castle* will find some admirers: it has some currently in England; I am just at the point of delivering a third edition. That which I have just said is not meant to instruct you to give it your approbation; I have always said that you would not like it; your visions are of an entirely different kind. I am not completely angry that they translated the second preface; however the first works better at generating the fiction; I had wanted it to pass for ancient, and almost everyone was fooled. I do not seek to quarrel with Voltaire, but I will maintain to the death that our Shakespear is a thousand times better.

Ann Yearsley, "To the Honourable H——E W——E, on Reading The Castle of Otranto" (December 1784)

The poetry of this "Milkwoman of Bristol"—the author named on the title page of Poems on Several Occasions *(1785)—was discovered and sponsored by Hannah More at a moment when the Yearsleys were near starvation (Ann's mother died). As a woman who milked cows and gathered waste from other kitchens to feed her pigs, Yearsley has a relation to the "domestics" or servants in the novel that differs from that of critics questioning the aesthetic propriety of such characters.*

To praise thee, WALPOLE, asks a pen divine,
    And common sense to me is hardly given,
BIANCA'S Pen now owns the daring line,[1]
    And who expects *her* muse should drop from Heaven.

---

[2]Walpole's pet name ("my little one") for his close friend.

[3]French encyclopedic philosophers dedicated to enlightenment through reason.

---

[1]Writing in the guise of Bianca, the foolish servant of Matilda in the novel, Yearsley proceeds to show this servant's capacity for insight and sympathy.

My fluttering tongue, light, ever veering round,   5
   On Wisdom's narrow point has never fix'd;
I dearly love to hear the ceaseless sound,
   Where Noise and Nonsense are completely mix'd.

The empty tattle, true to female rules,
   In which thy happier talents ne'er appear,   10
Is mine, nor mine alone, for mimic fools,
   Who boast *thy* sex, BIANCA's foibles wear.

Supreme in prate² shall woman ever sit,
   While Wisdom smiles to hear the senseless squall;
Nature, who gave me tongue, deny'd me wit,   15
   Folly I worship, and she claims me all.

The drowsy eye, half-closing to the lid,
   Stares on OTRANTO's walls; grim terrors rise,
The horrid helmet strikes my soul unbid,
   And with thy CONRAD, lo! BIANCA dies.   20

Funereal plumes now wave; ALPHONSO's ghost
   Frowns oe'r my shoulder; silence aids the scene,
The taper's flame, in fancy'd blueness lost,
   Pale spectres shows, to MANFRED only seen.

Ah! MANFRED! thine are bitter draughts³ of woe,   25
   Strong gusts of passion hurl thee on thy fate;
Tho' eager to elude, thou meet'st the blow,
   And for RICARDO⁴ MANFRED weeps in state.

By all the joys which treasur'd virtues yield,
   I feel thy agonies in WALPOLE's line;   30
Love, pride, revenge, by turns maintains the field,
   And hourly tortures rend my heart for thine.

Hail, magic pen, that strongly paint'st the soul,
   Where fell Ambition holds his wildest roar,
The whirlwind rages to the distant pole,   35
   And Virtue, stranded, pleads her cause no more.

²Chatter.

³Drafts, drinks.

⁴Recall that Manfred's grandfather Ricardo poisoned Alphonso and forged his will, so as to bequeath the land to Ricardo's line.

Where's MANFRED's refuge? WALPOLE, tell me where?
    Thy pen to great St. NICHOLAS points the eye,
E'en MANFRED calls to guard ALPHONSO's heir,
    Tho' conscious shame oft gives his tongue the lie.   40

MATILDA! ah, how soft thy yielding mind,
    When hard obedience cleaves thy timid heart!
How nobly strong, when love and virtue join'd
    To melt thy soul and take a lover's part!

Ah, rigid duties, which two souls divide!   45
    Whose iron talons rend the panting breast!
Pluck the dear image from the widow's side,
    Where Love had lull'd its every care to rest.

HYPOLITA! fond, passive to excess,
    Her low submission suits not souls like mine;   50
BIANCA might have lov'd her Manfred less,
    Not offer'd less at great Religion's shrine.

Implicit Faith, all hail! Imperial man
    Exacts submission; reason we resign;
Against our senses we adopt the plan   55
    Which Reverence, Fear, and Folly think divine.

But be it so, BIANCA ne'er shall prate,
    Nor ISABELLA's equal powers reveal;
You MANFREDS boast your power, and prize your state;
    We ladies our omnipotence conceal.   60

But, Oh! then strange-inventing WALPOLE guide,
    Ah! guide me thro' thy subterranean isles,[5]
Ope the trap-door where all thy powers reside,
    And mimic Fancy real woe beguiles.

The kind inventress dries the streaming tear,   65
    The deep-resounding groan shall faintly die,
The sigh shall sicken ere it meet the air,
    And Sorrow's dismal troop affrighted fly.

Thy jawless skeleton of JOPPA's wood
    Stares in my face, and frights my mental eye;   70

[5] Aisles.

Not stiffen'd worse the love-sick FREDERIC stood,
　When the dim spectre shriek'd the dismal cry.

But whilst the Hermit does my soul affright,
　Love dies — Lo! in yon corner down he kneels;
I shudder, see, the taper[6] sinks in night,　　　　　　　　　　75
　He rises, and his fleshless form reveals.

Hide me, thou parent Earth! see how I fall,
　My sins now meet me in the fainting hour;
Say, do thy Manes[7] for Heaven's sake vengeance call,
　Or can I free thee from an angry power?　　　　　　　　　　80

STELLA![8] if WALPOLE'S spectres thus can scare,
　Then near that great Magician's walls ne'er tread,
He'll surely conjure many a spirit there,
　Till, fear-struck, thou are number'd with the dead.

Oh! with this noble Sorcerer ne'er converse,　　　　　　　　　85
　Fly, STELLA, quickly from the magic storm;
Or, soon he'll close thee in some high-plum'd hearse,
　Then raise another Angel in thy form.

Trust not his art, for should he stop thy breath,
　And good ALPHONSO'S ghost unbidden rise;　　　　　　　　90
He'd vanish, leave thee in the jaws of death,
　And quite forget to close thy aching eyes.

But is BIANCA safe in this slow vale?
　For should his Goblins stretch their dusky wing,
Would they not bruise me for the saucy tale,　　　　　　　　95
　Would they not pinch me for the truths I sing?

Yet whisper not I've called him names, I fear
　His ARIEL would my hapless sprite[9] torment,

---

[6]Candle.

[7]In classical mythology, spirits of the dead.

[8]"Stella" is Yearsley's name for Hannah More (*First Feminists*, ed. Moira Ferguson [Bloomington, IN: Indiana Univ. Press, 1985], 384–85).

[9]In Shakespeare's *The Tempest* (1611), Prospero's servant-spirit Ariel often inflicts torments at his behest.

He'd cramp my bones, and all my sinews tear,
    Should STELLA blab the secret I'd prevent.[10]   100

But hush, ye winds, ye crickets chirp no more,
    I'll shrink to bed, nor these sad omens hear,
An hideous rustling shakes the lattic'd door,
    His spirits over in the sightless air.

Now, MORPHEUS,[11] shut each entrance of my mind,   105
    Sink, sink, OTRANTO, in this vacant hour;
To thee, Oh, balmy God! I'm all resign'd,
    To thee e'en WALPOLE'S wand resigns its power.

Anna Letitia Barbauld, "Walpole" (1810)[1]

Although neither The Castle of Otranto *nor* The Man of Feeling *was well reviewed, their inarguable popularity compelled both Anna Letitia Barbauld and Walter Scott to include them in their multivolume editions of British novels.*

The Castle of Otranto was written by The Honourable Horace Walpole, son of Sir Robert Walpole, who at the close of his life became Earl of Orford. It was printed at Strawberry Hill, and composed, the author tells us in one of his letters, in eight days or rather evenings.[2] Though a slight performance, it is calculated to make a great impression upon those who relish the fictions of the *Arabian Tales*, and similar performances. It was one of the modern productions founded on appearances of terror.

Since the author's time, from the perusal of Mrs. Radcliffe's productions and some of the German tales, we may be said to have "supped full with horrors,"[3] but none of the compositions have a

---

[10]Her identity.

[11]God of sleep.

---

[1]From *The British Novelists*, 1820, 22.i–ii.

[2]Barbauld is relying on hearsay more than accurate information. The letters are to William Cole (9 March 1765) and William Mason (17 April 1765).

[3]About to be vanquished, and hearing of the death of Lady Macbeth, Macbeth sighs, "I have supp'd full with horrors" (5.5.13).

livelier play of fancy than *The Castle of Otranto*. It is the sportive effusion of a man of genius, who throws the reins loose upon the neck of his imagination. The large limbs of the gigantic figure which inhabits the castle, and which are visible at intervals; the plumes of the helmet, which rise and wave with ominous meaning; and the various enchantments of the place, are imagined with the richness and wildness of poetic fancy. A sufficient degree of interest is thrown into the novel part of the story; but in the characters of some of the attendants there is an attempt at humour which has not succeeded.

The works of Horace Walpole are well known. He was a gentleman author, and wrote and printed for his own amusement, living in literary ease at his elegant seat of Strawberry Hill, in the architecture and furniture of which he has also shown a predilection for the romantic ideas connected with gothic and chivalrous times.

Walter Scott, "Prefatory Memoir to Walpole" (1823)[1]

As in his "Dedicatory Epistle" to Ivanhoe, *a romance set in Gothic England, Scott contends that creating a historical milieu is not a matter of linguistic archaisms but of portraying universal human feelings in a scene marked by accurate descriptions of ancient customs. Much of the Preface, beginning with "It is doing injustice" (p. 275), was used to introduce* The Castle of Otranto *in Bentley and Colburn's Standard Novels series (1834), 134–40. The publishers originally planned to put* The Castle of Otranto *in a volume bound with Mary Shelley's* Frankenstein *(1831).*

THE *Castle of Otranto* is remarkable, not only for the wild interest of the story, but as the first modern attempt to found a tale of amusing fiction upon the basis of the ancient romances of chivalry. [. . .] Under Charles II, the prevailing taste for French literature dictated the introduction of those dullest of dull folios, the romances of Calprenede and Scuderi,[2] works which hover

---

[1] From *Ballantyne's Novelist's Library*, 5.lx–lxi, lxiv–lxv, lxx–lxxviii.

[2] When Charles I was executed in the English Revolution of the 1640s, his son Charles fled to France, where he developed an affection for court culture that continued into his monarchy (1660–85). La Calprenède wrote sentimental pseudo-histories; the prolific Madeleine de Scudéry was a scholar as well as a writer of romances.

between the ancient tale of chivalry and the modern novel. The alliance was so ill conceived, that they retained all the insufferable length and breadth of the prose volumes of chivalry, the same detailed account of reiterated and unvaried combats, the same unnatural and extravagant turn of incident, without the rich and sublime strokes of genius, and vigour of imagination, which often distinguished the early romance; while they exhibited all the sentimental languor and flat love-intrigue of the novel, without being enlivened by its variety of character, just traits of feeling, or acute views of life. Such an ill-imagined species of composition retained its ground longer than might have been expected, only because these romances were called works of entertainment, and there was nothing better to supply their room. Even in the days of the *Spectator*, Clelia, Cleopatra, and the Grand Cyrus (as that precious folio is christened by the butcherly translator,) were the favourite companion of the fair sex.[3] But this unnatural taste began to give way early in the eighteenth century; and, about the middle of it, was entirely superseded by the works of Le Sage, Richardson, Fielding, and Smollett;[4] so that even the very name of romance, now so venerable in the ear of antiquaries and book-collectors, was almost forgotten at the time the *Castle of Otranto* made its first appearance.[5]

The peculiar situation of Horace Walpole, the ingenious author of this work, was such as gave him a decided predilection for what may be called the Gothic style, a term which he contributed not a little to rescue from the bad fame into which it had fallen, being currently used before his time to express whatever was in pointed and diametrical opposition to the rules of true taste. [. . .]

Mr. Walpole's domestic occupations, as well as his studies, bore evidence of a taste for English antiquities, which was then uncommon. He loved, as a satirist has expressed it, "to gaze on Gothic

---

[3]Joseph Addison and Richard Steele wrote *The Spectator* (1711–12); de Scudéry's *Clelia* was translated into English in 1655; *Artamenes, or, The Grand Cyrus* in 1653. The Cleopatra in Scudéry's *Les femmes illustres, or, Twenty heroick harangues of the most illustrious women of antiquity* (trans. 1693) is less willing to be Antony's concubine than the Cleopatra in Plutarch's *Parallel Lives*.

[4]All popular novelists of the day, of an anti-romantic bent.

[5]On romance vs. novel, see Clara Reeve's *Progress of Romance* (p. 218).

toys through Gothic glass,"[6] and the villa at Strawberry-Hill, which he chose for his abode, gradually swelled into a feudal castle, by the addition of turrets, towers, galleries, and corridors, whose fretted roofs, carved pannels, and illuminated windows, were garnished with the appropriate furniture of scutcheons; armorial bearings; shields, tilting lances, and all the panoply of chivalry. The Gothic order of architectures is now so generally, and, indeed, indiscriminately used, that we are rather surprised if the country-house of a tradesman retired from business, does not exhibit lanceolated windows, divided by stone shafts, and garnished by painted glass, a cup-board in the form of a cathedral-stall, and a pig-house with a front borrowed from the façade of an ancient chapel.[7] But, in the middle of the eighteenth century, when Mr Walpole began to exhibit specimens of the Gothic style, and to show how patterns, collected from cathedrals and monuments, might be applied to chimney-pieces, ceilings, windows, and balustrades, he did not comply with the dictates of a prevailing fashion, but pleased his own taste, and realized his own visions, in the romantic case of the mansion which he erected. [. . .]

As, in his model of a Gothic modern mansion, our author had studiously endeavoured to fit to the purposes of modern convenience, or luxury, the rich, varied, and complicated tracery and carving of the ancient cathedral, so, in *The Castle of Otranto*, it was his object to unite the marvellous turn of incident, and imposing tone of chivalry, exhibited in the ancient romance, with that accurate display of human character, and contrast of feelings and passions, which is, or ought to be, delineated in the modern novel. [. . .]

It is doing injustice to Mr Walpole's memory to allege, that all which he aimed at in *The Castle of Otranto*, was "the art of exciting surprise and horror"; or, in other words, the appeal to that secret and reserved feeling of love for the marvellous and supernat-

---

[6]T. J. Mathias, *The Pursuits of Literature: A Satirical Poem in Dialogue* (London, 1797): "Yet speak, the hour demands: Is Learning fled? / Spent all her vigour, all her spirit dead? / Have Gallic arms and unrelenting war / Borne all her trophies from Britannia far? / Shall nought but ghosts and trinkets be display'd, / Since Walpole ply'd the virtuoso's trade, / Bade sober truth revers'd for fiction pass, / And mus'd o'er Gothic toys through Gothic glass?" (77–78).

[7]Lanceolated: shaped like a lance. Newly rich merchants tried to emulate the aristocracy, sometimes laughably. Scott nearly bankrupted himself building his own gothic estate, Abbotsford, in imitation of Strawberry Hill.

ural, which occupies a hidden corner in almost everyone's bosom. Were this all which he had attempted, the means by which he sought to attain his purpose might, with justice, be termed both clumsy and puerile. But Mr Walpole's purpose was both more difficult of attainment, and more important when attained. It was his object to draw such a picture of domestic life and manners, during feudal times, as might actually have existed, and to paint it chequered and agitated by the action of supernatural machinery, such as the superstition of the period received as matter of devout credulity. The natural parts of the narrative are so contrived, that they associate themselves with the marvellous occurrences; and, by the force of that association, render those *speciosa miracula*[8] striking and impressive, though our cooler reason admits their impossibility. Indeed, to produce, in a well-cultivated mind, any portion of that surprise and fear which are founded on supernatural events, the frame and tenor of the whole story must be adjusted in perfect harmony with the main-spring of the interest. He who, in early youth, has happened to pass a solitary night in one of the few ancient mansions which the fashion of more modern times has left undespoiled of their original furniture, has probably experienced, that the gigantic and preposterous figures dimly visible in the defaced tapestry,—the remote clang of the distant doors which divide him from living society,—the deep darkness which involves the high and fretted roof of the apartment,—the dimly-seen pictures of ancient knights, renowned for their valour, and perhaps for their crimes,—the varied and indistinct sounds which disturb the silent desolation of a half-deserted mansion,—and, to crown all, the feeling that carries us back to ages of feudal power and papal superstition, join together to excite a corresponding sensation of supernatural awe, if not of terror. It is in such situations, when superstition becomes contagious, that we listen with respect, and even with dread, to the legends which are our sport in the garish light of sunshine, and amid the dissipating sights and sounds of every-day life. Now, it seems to have been Walpole's object to attain, by the minute accuracy of a fable, sketched with singular attention to the costume[9] of the period in which the scene was laid,

[8]Specious wonders, (im)plausible miracles.
[9]Custom as well as costume.

that same association which might prepare his reader's mind for the reception of prodigies congenial to the creed and feelings of the actors. His feudal tyrant, his distressed damsel, his resigned yet dignified churchman,—the Castle itself, with its feudal arrangements of dungeons, trap-doors, oratories, and galleries,—the incidents of the trial, the chivalrous procession, and the combat;—in short, the scene, the performers, and action, so far as it is natural, form the accompaniments of his spectres and his miracles, and have the same effect on the mind of the reader, that the appearance and drapery of such a chamber as we have described may produce upon that of a temporary inmate. This was a task which required no little learning, no ordinary degree of fancy, no common portion of genius to execute. The association of which we have spoken is of a nature peculiarly delicate, and subject to be broken and disarranged. It is, for instance, almost impossible to build such a modern Gothic structure as shall impress us with the feelings we have endeavoured to describe. It may be grand, or it may be gloomy; it may excite magnificent or melancholy ideas; but it must fail in bringing forth the sensation of supernatural awe, connected with halls that have echoed to the sounds of remote generations, and have been pressed by the footsteps of those who have long since passed away. Yet Horace Walpole has attained in composition, what, as an architect, he must have felt beyond the power of his art. The remote and superstitious period in which his scene is laid,—the art with which he has furnished forth his Gothic decorations,— the sustained, and, in general, the dignified tone of feudal manners,—prepare us gradually for the favourable reception of prodigies[10] which, though they could not really have happened at any period, were consistent with the belief of all mankind at that in which the action is placed. It was, therefore, the author's object, not merely to excite surprise and terror, by the introduction of supernatural agency, but to wind up the feelings of his reader till they became for a moment identified with those of a ruder age, which

Held each strange tale devoutly true.[11]

---

[10]Extraordinary or inexplicable events.

[11]What the fearful poet does in William Collins's *Ode to Fear* (1746), ll. 53–56.

The difficulty of attaining this nice accuracy of delineation may be best estimated by comparing *The Castle of Otranto* with the less successful efforts of later writers; where, amid all their attempts to assume the tone of antique chivalry, something occurs in every chapter so decidedly incongruous, as at once reminds us of an ill-sustained masquerade, in which ghosts, knights-errant, magicians, and damsels gent,[12] are all equipped in hired dresses from the same warehouse in Tavistock-street.

There is a remarkable particular in which Mr Walpole's steps have been departed from by the most distinguished of his followers.

Romantic narrative is of two kinds,—that which, being in itself possible, may be matter of belief at any period; and that which, though held impossible by more enlightened ages, was yet consonant with the faith of earlier times. The subject of *The Castle of Otranto* is of the latter class. Mrs Radcliffe[13] [. . .] has endeavoured to effect a compromise between those different styles of narrative, by referring her prodigies to an explanation founded on natural causes, in the latter chapters of her romances. To this improvement upon the Gothic romance there are so many objections, that we own ourselves inclined to prefer, as more simple and impressive, the narrative of Walpole, which details supernatural incidents as they would have been readily believed and received in the eleventh or twelfth century. In the first place, the reader feels indignant at discovering that he has been cheated into sympathy with terrors, which are finally explained as having proceeded from some very simple cause; and the interest of a second reading is entirely destroyed by his having been admitted behind the scenes at the conclusion of the first. Secondly, the precaution of relieving our spirits from the influence of supposed supernatural terror, seems as unnecessary in a work of professed fiction. [. . .] The reader, who is required to admit the belief of supernatural interference, understands precisely what is demanded of him; and, if he be a gentle reader, throws his mind into the attitude best adapted to humour the deceit which is presented for his entertainment, and grants, for the time of perusal, the premises on which the fable depends. [. . .]

---

[12]Pretty (archaic).

[13]Ann Radcliffe's wildly popular gothic novels are *The Mysteries of Udolpho* (1794) and *The Italian* (1797).

It cannot, however, be denied, that the character of the super-natural machinery in *The Castle of Otranto* is liable to objections. Its action and interference is rather too frequent, and presses too hard and constantly upon the same feelings in the reader's mind, to the hazard of the diminishing elasticity of the spring upon which it should operate. The fund of fearful sympathy which can be afforded by a modern reader to a tale of wonder, is much dimin-ished by the present habits of life and modes of education. Our ancestors could wonder and thrill through all the mazes of an inter-minable metrical romance of fairy land, and of an enchantment, the work perhaps of some

> Prevailing poet, whose undoubting mind
> Believed the magic wonders which he sung.[14]

But our habits and feelings and belief are now different, and a transient, though vivid, impression is all that can be excited by a tale of wonder even in the most fanciful mind of the present day. By the too frequent recurrence of his prodigies, Mr Walpole ran, per-haps, his greatest risk of awakening *la raison froide*, that "cold common sense," which he justly deemed the greatest enemy of the effect which he hoped to produce. It may be added also, that the supernatural occurrences of *The Castle of Otranto* are brought for-ward into too strong day-light, and marked by an over degree of distinctness and accuracy of outline. A mysterious obscurity seems congenial at least, if not essential, to our ideas of disembodied spir-its, and the gigantic limbs of the ghost of Alphonso, as described by the terrified domestics, are somewhat too distinct and corporeal to produce the feelings which their appearance is intended to excite. This fault, however, if it be one, is more than compensated by the high merit of many of the marvellous incidents in the romance. The descent of the picture of Manfred's ancestor, although it borders on extravagance, is finely introduced, and interrupts an interesting dia-logue with striking effect. [. . .] There are few who have not felt, at some period of their childhood, a sort of terror from the manner in which the eye of an ancient portrait appears to fix that of the spec-tator from every point of view. [. . .]

[14]William Collins, *An Ode on the Popular Superstitions of the Highlands of Scot-land, Considered as the Subject of Poetry* (1788), stanza 12, ll. 198–99.

That part of the romance which depends upon human feelings and agency, is conducted with the dramatic talent which afterwards was so conspicuous in [Walpole's play] *The Mysterious Mother*. The persons are indeed rather generic than individual; but this was in a degree necessary to a plan, calculated rather to exhibit a general view of society and manners during the times which the author's imagination loved to contemplate than the more minute shades and discriminating points of particular characters. But the actors in the romance are strikingly drawn, with bold outlines becoming the age and nature of the story. Feudal tyranny was, perhaps, never better exemplified, than in the character of Manfred. He has the courage, the art, the duplicity, the ambition of a barbarous chieftain of the dark ages, yet with touches of remorse and natural feeling, which preserve some sympathy for him when his pride is quelled, and his race extinguished. The pious Monk, and the patient Hippolita, are well contrasted with this selfish and tyrannical Prince. Theodore is the juvenile hero of a romantic tale, and Matilda has more interesting sweetness than usually belongs to its heroine. As the character of Isabella is studiously kept down, in order to relieve[15] that of the daughter of Manfred, few readers are pleased with the concluding insinuation, that she became at length the bride of Theodore. This is in some degree a departure from the rules of chivalry; and, however natural an occurrence in common life, rather injures the magic illusion of romance. In other respects, making allowance for the extraordinary incidents of a dark and tempestuous age, the story, so far as within the course of natural events, is happily detailed, its progress is uniform, its events interesting and well combined, and the conclusion grand, tragical, and affecting.

[. . .] It is for the dialogue that Walpole reserves his strength; and it is remarkable how, while conducting his mortal agents with all the art of a modern dramatist, he adheres to the sustained tone of chivalry, which marks the period of the action. This is not attained by patching his narrative or dialogue with glossarial terms, or antique phraseology, but by taking care to exclude all that can awaken modern associations. In the one case, his romance would have resembled a modern dress, preposterously decorated with antique ornaments; in its present shape, he has retained the form of the ancient armour, but not its rust and cobwebs. [. . .]

---

[15]Put into relief, feature.

If Horace Walpole, who led the way in this new species of literary composition, has been surpassed by some of his followers [. . .], more yet will remain with him than the single merit of originality and invention. The applause due to chastity and precision of style,—to a happy combination of supernatural agency with human interest,—to a tone of feudal manners and languages sustained by characters strongly drawn and well discriminated,—and to unity of action, producing scenes alternately of interest and of grandeur;— the applause, in fine, which cannot be denied to him who can excite the passions of fear and pity, must be awarded to the author of *The Castle of Otranto.*

The Man of Feeling

Would reviewers have been more generous had Mackenzie been English rather than Scottish? Like Scott, they might have drawn comparisons to Sterne, rather than simply declaring Sterne superior. Even so, these reviewers clearly saw the equation of strong sympathetic feeling with moral worth and so entered the culture of sympathy, or pretended to. The brevity of the reviews below is typical rather than disparaging to Mackenzie.

The Monthly Review 44 (May 1771): 418

This performance is written after the manner of Sterne; but it follows at a prodigious distance the steps of that ingenious and sentimental writer. It is not however totally destitute of merit; and the Reader, who weeps not over some of the scenes it describes, has no sensibility of mind. But it is to be observed, that the knowledge of men it contains, appears to be rather gathered from books than experience; and that, with regard to composition, it is careless, and abounds in provincial and Scottish idioms. It is probably a first work; and from the specimen it affords of the talents of its Author, we should not be disposed to think that he will ever attain to any great eminence in literature. He may amuse himself at the foot of Parnassus;[1] but to ascend the steeps of the mountain must be the task of those on whom their benignant stars have bestowed the rare gifts of true genius.

Critical Review 31 (June 1771): 482–83

By those who have feeling hearts, and a true relish for simplicity in writing, many pages in this miscellaneous volume will be read with satisfaction. There is not indeed fable enough in this volume to keep up the attention of the majority of novel readers; there is not business enough in it for the million: but there are several interesting situations, several striking incidents, several excellent reflections, which sufficiently discover the author's invention and judgment, delicacy and taste. The story of Old Edwards is exquisitely affecting: the whole thirty-fourth chapter, indeed, in which it is introduced, is written in a very masterly manner.

The London Magazine (August 1771)

> *Launched in 1732 by powerful booksellers to rival the* Gentleman's Magazine, The London Magazine *was roomy enough ideologically to publish conservative authors such as James Boswell (who co-owned it briefly) as well as contributors to the more progressive* Monthly Review. *Ceasing publication in 1787, it is not to be confused with the journal of the same name started by John Scott in 1820. The following review is anonymous.*

There is much good sense, but very little order, in this novel; the sentiments do honour to humanity, and the general propriety of the observations give such striking lessons upon life, that we cannot dismiss the article without laying an extract before our readers.

The Pupil. A Fragment.

being a narrative in the consequence of a discourse upon Education, between an old gentleman and the man of feeling, Mr. Harley. [*Reviewer quotes the fragment, pp. 196–201, above.*]

---

[1]Mountain home of the Muses.

Town and Country Magazine 3 (August 1771): 436

Often eighteenth-century magazines provided only one or two lines of notice about a work, as here.

There is considerable merit in this novel; which is both instructive and entertaining.

"M.," *Scots Magazine* 33 (August 1771): 427

Written after the manner of Stern. Not destitute of merit; and the reader who weeps not over some of the scenes it describes, has no sensibility.

Anna Letitia Barbauld, "Mackenzie" (1810)[1]

Anna Letitia Barbauld's hint that the interrupted plot line is due to ineptitude is answered by twentieth-century critic G. A. Starr's view that non-interruption would imply a progress antithetical to the novel's nostalgic mood (188–89).

With the readers of sentimental novels, those of Mr. Mackenzie have been great favourites. They exhibit real powers of pathos, though the judicious reader will probably be of the opinion that at the time they were published they were somewhat overrated. They imitate the manner of Sterne, who was then much in fashion, and whose light and delicate touches of nature had made so strong an impression that it raised a kind of school of writers in that walk.

The very title of *The Man of Feeling* sufficiently indicates that the writer means to take strong aim at the heart of the reader. It is difficult, however, to form a clear and consistent idea of the character of the hero of the piece. The author has given him extreme sensibility, but of that timid and melancholy cast which nearly incapacitates a man for the duties of life and energies of action. The general impression upon the reader is that of a man "sicklied o'er with the pale cast of thought,"[2] languid and delicate; yet he is also supposed to be animated

[1] From *The British Novelists*, 29.i–iii.
[2] Hamlet's self-diagnosed disease (*Hamlet* 3.1.84).

by that ardent and impetuous enthusiasm which acts by sudden and irresistible impulses, and disregards every maxim of prudence: in short, a temperament like that of Mr. Cumberland's *West-Indian*.[3]

When Harley is about to relieve the prostitute, to whom, by the way, he had given half-a-guinea the night before, and who could not therefore be in any immediate danger of perishing, he was in such a hurry that, "though two vibrations of a pendulum would have served him to lock his bureau, they could not be spared." Yet with these lively and ungovernable feelings, this man of sensibility, being deeply in love with a young lady, who seems all along to have had a very tender partiality for him, allows himself to languish and pine away without declaring his passion; and at length dies, whether of love or of a consumption is not very clear, without having made any effort to obtain her hand. We are not more active in serving others than in serving ourselves: such a one might be "a man of feeling," but his benevolence would be confined to mere sensations. Yet the last chapter, entitled, *The Man of Feeling made happy*, the reader will find, at least if he happen to be in a tender mood, pathetic. Harley, in the last stage of weakness, has an interview with his mistress, in which he receives an avowal of her regard for him, and then dies contented.

But by far the most interesting part of this novel is the story of Edwards, particularly the scene where he is taken by the press-gang. It would be a good subject for the painter. It deserves the pencil of Mr. Wilkie.[4] The whole harmless family are represented in high glee, playing at blind man's buff; young Edwards, with his eyes covered, is trying to guess which of them he has caught, when the ruffian's voice bursts upon him like thunder, and overwhelms them all with despair. Yet, in endeavouring to draw as many tears as he can from his readers, an author of this class is apt to represent the virtuous and industrious in low life as continually exposed to oppression and injustice, and it is hardly to be wished that even our virtuous feelings should be awakened at the expense of truth. There is no connected story in this work, except that of Edwards. The thread of the history is supposed to be broken by the imperfection of the manuscript. A convenient supposition.

[3]Richard Cumberland's *The West Indian: A Comedy* (1771) was reprinted as vol. 18 of Elizabeth Inchbald's *The British Theatre* (1808).

[4]Early 19th-c. artist Sir David Wilkie, known for genre and historical paintings.

Walter Scott, "Prefatory Memoir to Mackenzie" (1823)[1]

As an author, Mr Mackenzie has shown talents both for poetry and the drama [. . .] But it is as a Novelist that we are now called on to consider our author's powers; and the universal and permanent popularity of his writings entitles us to rank him among the most distinguished of his class. His works possess the rare and invaluable property of originality, to which all other qualities are as dust in the balance; and the sources to which he resorts to excite our interest, are rendered accessible by a path peculiarly his own. The reader's attention is not rivetted, as in Fielding's works, by strongly marked character, and the lucid evolution of a well-constructed fable; or as in Smollet's novels, by broad and strong humour, and a decisively superior knowledge of human life in all its varieties; nor, to mention the authors whom Mackenzie most resembles, does he attain the pathetic effect which is the object of all three, in the same manner as Richardson, or as Sterne. [. . .] Without depriving [Richardson] his due merit, it must be allowed that he has employed preparatory volumes in accomplishing what has cost Mackenzie and Sterne only a few pages, perhaps only a few sentences.[2]

On the other hand, although the two last named authors have, in particular passages, a more strong resemblance to each other than those formerly named, yet there remain such essential points of difference betwixt them, as must secure for Mackenzie the praise of originality, which we have claimed for him. It is needless to point out to the reader the difference between the general character of their writings, or how far the chaste, correct, almost studiously decorous manner and style of the works of the author of *The Man of Feeling*, differ from the wild wit, and intrepid contempt at once of decency, and regularity of composition, which distinguish *Tristram Shandy*. It is not in the general conduct or style of their works that they in the slightest degree approach; nay, no two authors in the British language can be more distinct. But even in the particular passages where both had in view to excite the reader's pathetic sympathy, the modes resorted to are different. The pathos of Sterne in some degree resembles his humour, and is seldom attained by simple means; a wild, fanciful, beautiful flight of thought and expression is

[1]From *Ballantyne's Novelist's Library*, 5.li–lv.
[2]*Pamela* commands two hefty volumes, *Clarissa* several more.

remarkable in the former, as an extravagant, burlesque, and ludicrous strain of thought and language characterizes the latter. [. . .] If the one claims the palm of superior brilliancy of imagination, that due to nature and accuracy of human feeling must abide with Scottish author. [. . .]

We are hence led to observe, that the principal object of Mackenzie, in all his novels, has been to reach and sustain a tone of moral pathos, by representing the effect of incidents, whether important or trifling, upon the human mind, and especially on those which were not only just, honourable, and intelligent, but so framed as to be responsive to those finer feelings, to which ordinary hearts are callous. This is the direct and professed object of Mackenzie's first work, which is in fact no narrative, but a series of successive incidents, each rendered interesting by the mode in which they operate on the feelings of Harley. The attempt had been perilous in a meaner hand; for, sketched by a pencil less nicely discriminating, Harley, instead of a being whom we love, respect, sympathize with, and admire, had become the mere Quixote of sentiment, an object of pity perhaps, but of ridicule at the same time. Against this the author has guarded with great skill; and while duped and swindled in London, Harley neither loses our consideration as a man of sense and spirit, nor is subjected to that degree of contempt with which readers in general regard the misadventures of a novice upon town, whilst they hug themselves in their own superior knowledge of the world. Harley's spirited conduct towards an impertinent passenger in the stage-coach, and his start of animated indignation on listening to Edwards's story, are skilfully thrown in, to satisfy the reader that his softness and gentleness of temper were not allied to effeminacy; and that he dared, on suitable occasions, do all that might become a man. [. . .]

The other novels of Mr Mackenzie, although assuming a more regular and narrative form, are, like *The Man of Feeling*, rather the history of effects produced upon the human mind by a series of events, than the narrative of those events themselves.

Further Reading

Editions, Biographies, and Other Primary Resources

The Works of Henry Mackenzie, Esq. 8 vols. Edinburgh: Constable, Creech, Manners and Miller; London: Cadell and Davies, 1808. The standard edition with notes by the author.

Henry Mackenzie: Letters to Elizabeth Rose of Kilravock. Ed. Horst W. Drescher. Münster, Germany: Aschendorff, 1967.

The Works of Horatio Walpole, Earl of Orford. 5 vols., ed. Mary Berry. London: G. G. and J. Robinson, and J. Edwards, 1798. The first two volumes are from a Works volume planned and corrected by the author in 1770.

The Yale Edition of Horace Walpole's Correspondence. 48 vols., ed. W. S. Lewis. New Haven: Yale University Press, 1937–83.

Barker, Gerard A. *Henry Mackenzie.* Twayne English Authors Series. Ed. Sylvia Bowman. Boston: G. K. Hall, 1975.

Brownell, Morris R. *The Prime Minister of Taste: A Portrait of Horace Walpole.* New Haven: Yale University Press, 2001.

Dobson, Austin. *Horace Walpole: A Memoir, with an Appendix of Books Printed at the Strawberry-Hill Press.* New York: Dodd, Mead, and Co., 1890.

Fothergill, Brian. *The Strawberry Hill Set: Horace Walpole and His Circle.* Boston: Faber and Faber, 1983.

Hazen, A. T. *A Bibliography of Horace Walpole.* New Haven: Yale University Press, 1948.

Horace Walpole: The Critical Heritage. Ed. Peter Sabor. New York: Routledge & Kegan Paul, 1987. A handy compendium of reviews of all Walpole's works, from 1757 to 1840.

Kallich, Martin. *Horace Walpole.* Twayne's English Author Series. New York: Twayne Publishers, 1971.

Lewis, W. S. *Rescuing Horace Walpole*. New Haven: Yale University Press, 1978.

Lewis, W. S. *Horace Walpole*. Bollingen Series, 35. A. W. Mellon Lectures in the Fine Arts, 9. New York: Pantheon Books, 1961.

The Lewis-Walpole Library. Yale University. Accessed July 17, 2005, at http://www.library.yale.edu/walpole/. A prime source for the study of Horace Walpole, Strawberry Hill, and eighteenth-century culture.

Mowl, Tim. *Horace Walpole: The Great Outsider*. London: Murray, 1996.

Sabor, Peter. *Horace Walpole: A Reference Guide*. Boston, MA: G. K. Hall, 1984.

Thompson, Harold William. *A Scottish Man of Feeling*. New York: Oxford University Press, 1931. The standard biography of Henry Mackenzie.

Critical Studies

Aldrich, Megan Brewster. *Gothic Revival*. London: Phaidon Press, 1994.

Barker-Benfield, G. J. *The Culture of Sensibility: Sex and Society in Eighteenth-Century Britain*. Chicago: University of Chicago Press, 1992.

Benedict, Barbara. *Framing Feeling: Sentiment and Style in English Prose Fiction, 1745–1800*. New York: AMS Press, 1994.

Botting, Fred. *Gothic*. New York: Routledge, 1996.

Brooks, Chris. *Gothic Revival*. London: Phaidon Press, 1999.

Brown, Marshall. *The Gothic Text*. Stanford, CA: Stanford University Press, 2005.

———. *Preromanticism*. Stanford, CA: Stanford University Press, 1991.

Byron, Glennis, and David Punter, eds. *Spectral Readings: Towards a Gothic Geography*. New York: St. Martin's Press, 1999.

Campbell, Jill. "'I am no Giant': Horace Walpole, Heterosexual Incest, and Love among Men." *Eighteenth-Century: Theory and Interpretation* 39.3 (Fall 1998): 238–60.

Castle, Terry. *The Female Thermometer: Eighteenth-Century Culture and the Invention of the Uncanny*. New York: Oxford University Press, 1995.

Clark, Kenneth. *The Gothic Revival: An Essay in the History of Taste*. 1928; 3rd ed. 1962; London: John Murray, 1995.

Clery, E. J. *The Rise of Supernatural Fiction, 1762–1800*. New York: Cambridge University Press, 1995.

Clery, E. J., and Robert Miles, eds. *Gothic Documents: A Sourcebook 1700–1820*. New York: Manchester University Press, 2000.

Crane, R. S. "Suggestions toward a Genealogy of the 'Man of Feeling.'" *ELH* 1 (1934): 205–30.

Crook, Joseph Mordaunt. *John Carter and the Mind of the Gothic Revival*. London: Society of Antiquaries, 1995.

Davis, Terence. *The Gothick Taste*. Rutherford, NJ: Farleigh Dickinson University Press, 1975.

Eastlake, C. L. *History of the Gothic Revival*. 1872; Deposit, NY: American Life Foundation, 1975.

Frank, Frederick S. *Guide to the Gothic: An Annotated Bibliography of Criticism*. Metuchen, NJ: Scarecrow Press, 1984. Criticism before 1983.

———. *Guide to the Gothic: An Annotated Bibliography of Criticism, 1983–1993*. Lanham, MD: Scarecrow Press, 1995. Criticism after 1983.

Frye, Northrop. "Towards Defining an Age of Sensibility." *ELH* 23.2 (1956): 144–52.

Gamer, Michael. *Romanticism and the Gothic: Genre, Reception, and Canon Formation*. New York: Cambridge University Press, 2000.

Goring, Paul. *Rhetoric of Sensibility in Eighteenth-Century Culture*. Cambridge, U.K.: Cambridge University Press, 2005.

Haggerty, George. *Gothic Fiction/Gothic Form*. University Park, PA: Pennsylvania State University Press, 1989.

———. "The Gothic Novel, 1764–1824." In Richetti, 220–46.

———. "Literature and Homosexuality in the Late Eighteenth Century: Walpole, Beckford, Lewis." In *Homosexual Themes in Literary Studies*. Ed. Wayne Dynes, Stephen Donaldson. New York: Garland, 1992, 167–78.

———. *Men in Love: Masculinity and Sexuality in the Eighteenth-Century*. New York: Columbia University Press, 1999.

———. "'What is this Secret Sin?' Sexuality and Secrecy in the Writings of Horace Walpole." In Novak and Mellor, 127–49.

Hagstrum, Jean H. *Sex and Sensibility: Ideal and Erotic Love from Milton to Mozart*. Chicago: Chicago University Press, 1980.

Harkin, Maureen. "Mackenzie's *Man of Feeling*: Embalming Sensibility." *ELH* 61.2 (Summer 1994): 317–40.

Hogle, Jerrold. "Frankenstein as Neo-Gothic: From the Ghost of the Counterfeit to the Monster of Abjection." In *Romanticism, History, and the Possibilities of Genre: Re-Forming Literature, 1789–1837.* Ed. Tilottama Rajan. New York: Cambridge University Press, 1998, 176–210.

———. "The Gothic Ghost of the Counterfeit and the Progress of Abjection." In Punter, 293–04.

———. Introduction. *The Cambridge Companion to Gothic Fiction.* Ed. Jerrold Hogle. New York: Cambridge University Press, 2002.

Hunter, J. Paul. *Before Novels: The Cultural Contexts of Eighteenth-Century English Fiction.* New York: Norton, 1990.

Jacobs, Edward H. *Accidental Migrations: An Archeology of Gothic Discourse.* Lewisburg, PA: Bucknell University Press, 2000.

Janowitz, Anne F. *England's Ruins: Poetic Purpose and National Landscape.* Cambridge, MA: Blackwell, 1990.

Lewis, Michael J. *The Gothic Revival.* New York: Thames & Hudson, 2002.

London, April. "Historiography, Pastoral, Novel: Genre in *The Man of Feeling*." *Eighteenth-Century Fiction* 10.1 (1997): 43–62.

Manning, Susan. "Enlightenment's Dark Dreams: Two Fictions of Henry Mackenzie and Charles Brockden Brown." *Eighteenth-Century Life* 21.3 (1997): 39–56.

McCarthy, Michael. *Origins of the Gothic Revival.* New Haven: Yale University Press, 1987.

McKeon, Michael. "Generic Transformation and Social Change: Rethinking the Rise of the Novel." *Cultural Critique* 1 (1985): 159–81.

———. *The Origins of the English Novel, 1600–1740.* Baltimore: Johns Hopkins University Press, 1987.

———, ed. *Theory of the Novel: A Historical Approach.* Baltimore: Johns Hopkins University Press, 2000.

Miles, Robert. *Gothic Writing 1750–1820: A Genealogy.* New York: Routledge, 1993.

Morrissey, Lee. *From the Temple to the Castle: An Architectural History of British Literature, 1660–1760.* Charlottesville, VA: University Press of Virginia, 1999.

Motooka, Wendy. *The Age of Reasons: Quixotism, Sentimentalism and Political Economy in Eighteenth-Century Britain.* New York: Routledge, 1998.

Mullan, John. *Sentiment and Sociability: The Language of Feeling in the Eighteenth Century.* Oxford: Clarendon Press, 1988.

Mulvey-Roberts, Marie, ed. *The Handbook to Gothic Literature.* New York: New York University Press, 1998.

Napier, Elizabeth. *The Failure of Gothic: Problems of Disjunction in an Eighteenth-Century Literary Form.* New York: Oxford University Press, 1986.

Norton, Rictor. *Gothic Readings: The First Wave, 1764–1860.* New York: Leicester University Press, 2000.

Novak, Maximillian E., and Anne Mellor, eds. *Passionate Encounters in a Time of Sensibility.* Newark: University of Delaware Press, 2000.

Pinch, Adela. *Strange Fits of Passion: Epistemologies of Emotion from Hume to Austen.* Stanford, CA: Stanford University Press, 1996.

Punter, David, ed. *A Companion to the Gothic.* Malden, MA: Blackwell, 2000.

Richetti, John, ed. *Columbia History of the British Novel.* New York: Columbia University Press, 1994.

Sedgwick, Eve Kosofsky. "The Character in the Veil: Imagery of the Surface in the Gothic Novel." *PMLA* 96.2 (1981): 255–70. Gathering together in a very condensed way ideas first presented in her book, this article marks a landmark in Gothic studies, clearly demonstrating the centrality of gothic literature to the realistic canon.

———. *The Coherence of Gothic Conventions.* 1976; New York: Arno Press, 1980.

Spector, Robert Donald. *The English Gothic: A Bibliographic Guide to Writers from Horace Walpole to Mary Shelley.* Westport, CT: Greenwood Press, 1984.

Spencer, David G. "Henry Mackenzie: A Practical Sentimentalist." *Papers on Language and Literature* 3 (1967): 314–26.

Starr, G. A. "Sentimental Novels of the Later Eighteenth Century." In Richetti, 181–98.

Tinkler-Villani, Valeria, and Peter Davidson, eds. *Exhibited by Candlelight: Sources and Developments in the Gothic Tradition.* Atlanta, GA: Rodopi, 1995.

Todd, Janet. *Sensibility: An Introduction.* London: Methuen, 1986.

Tompkins, J. M. S. *The Popular Novel in England, 1770–1800.* Lincoln, NE: University of Nebraska Press, 1961. Discusses Mackenzie's novels briefly.

Van Sant, Ann Jessie. *Eighteenth-Century Sensibility and the Novel: The Senses in Social Context.* New York: Cambridge University Press, 1993.

Watt, Ian. *The Rise of the Novel.* Berkeley: University of California Press, 1957.

Williams, Anne. *Art of Darkness: A Poetics of Gothic.* Chicago: University of Chicago Press, 1995.